Socialcide®

How America Is Loving Itself to Death

(A Psychospiritual Exploration)

By

Leo J. Battenhausen, *MA, MSW, LCSW, LCADC*

3255 Lawrenceville-Suwanee Rd. Suite P250
Suwanee, GA 30024
publishing@faithbooksandmore.com
faithbooksandmore.com

Ordering Information:
Quantity sales. Special discounts are available on quantity purchases by corporations, associations, and others. For details, contact the publisher at the address above.

Orders by U.S. trade bookstores and wholesalers. Please contact Ingram Book Company: Tel: (800) 937-8000; Email: orders@ingrambook.com or visit www.ingrambook.com.

Disclaimer The purpose of this book is to empower, educate, and offer hope. The author of the book achieved that through his own experiences, expertise, and research. Consequently, this book should only be used as a road map. This book is not intended to be nor is it represented as legal advice. The author is not liable or responsible, to any person, or entity, for any and all claims, demands, damages, causes of action, suits in equity of whatever kind or nature, caused or alleged to have been caused, directly or indirectly, by the information contained in this book or the author's past or future negligence or wrongful acts.

"Great civilizations are not murdered.
They commit suicide."
— Arnold Toynbee

Socialcide®

[soh-shuhl-sahyd] *noun.* The slow, insidious, self-perpetuating destruction of a society through the degradation and loss of basic values for human life, respect for self and others, and spirituality. The systematic killing of a society.

The author is donating a portion of the proceeds from this book to the Friends of Linden Animal Shelter, a dedicated, Federal IRS501(c)(3) non-profit group of volunteers that care for and find homes for lost and abandoned dogs and cats. They are a 100% no kill facility, and they do FANTASTIC WORK!

If you would like to help support their efforts, please send donations to:
FOLAS
P. O. Box 2151
Linden, New Jersey 07036

(732) 388-6300
www.folas.org

For Rudy

Acknowledgments

In the process of compiling *Socialcide: How America Is Loving Itself to Death*, I have needed and appreciated many, many people. It's been more than an emotional experience to leave my professional comfort zone to explore and expose what I believe to be a plague that has no medical or psychological foundation or basis. Sharing my *personal feelings*, sometimes void of scientific *fact* or *reason*, is not something I ever do or feel compelled to do in my daily work, but I believe strongly that it *had* to be done in the case of this work.

I struggled greatly in looking within my professional, clinical world for a common denominator, a root cause for all of what I was witnessing, experiencing, and hearing about from my clients and seeing in society around me, as well as in daily television news reports. I knew there had to be something behind the widespread decay in morals, values, behaviors, and attitudes, but it was eluding me. After many attempts to find a reasonable or believable foundation within the scope of my education and experience as a therapist, I had come up with nothing.

Then it came to me! In limiting my search for a cause to my professional set of beliefs and practices, I had not allowed myself to really explore or acknowledge the true cause of Socialcide: America has lost its connection with God, good, righteousness, and morality!

Spirituality, if I may, is lacking in our culture. After two-hundred-plus years of having it, we are now in a place where we are pushing it away. We have lost the basic ideals and building blocks of being the best people, communities, families, and country we had possessed, and are relying more and more on things and ideas that do not fill or feed our collective *souls*. So *Socialcide* was born in my mind, inspired first and foremost by God. And to Him, I am most thankful.

I must also say that this book would never have happened without the never-ending love and support of my wonderful wife, Cori. She pushes me, encourages me, and sacrifices much of our time without question to keep me on track. This book would never have become a reality without her love, and I am the luckiest husband in the world!

My friend and the world's best editor is Ruth H. Cohen. To her I am extremely thankful. Ruth cleaned up and clarified my work, adding her very purposeful insights into it. She has gone above and beyond grammatical errors and indentations to make this book what it is. I cannot imagine publishing any book without her on my side.

I must not forget my friend Sean Herriott and Relevant Radio for their long-standing support and regular radio shows, featuring me on the *Mind Mender* segment of their station. That organization is a wonderful bunch of people who have promoted me and this book since its inception. Truly a God-send!

Thanks to my colleague and friend John Kelly, who has always been there for me and has been a huge support in all my endeavors. Thanks to Shanna Hogan, *New York Times* bestselling author, who I have gotten to know personally. I greatly appreciate her work and her friendship. Thanks also to my clients. I learn as much from them as I hope they learn from me. And finally, thanks to all my friends, both "real-life" and from social media. You guys are fabulous! Thank you for all your support and encouragement.

Last, but certainly not least, a special *thank you* to Kip Ayers, who took my idea for a cover design and turned it into art. In finding Kip, I made a great friend, and will be working with him again, I am sure.

Table of Contents

Chapter Twenty-Two: Teach Them How to Think, Not What to Think

Foreword

I have known Leo Battenhausen for more than twenty years, both professionally and personally. I have seen, first-hand, his work as a therapist, social worker, addictions counselor, case manager, director and author grow more and more powerful and effective throughout his career. He never slows down or gives up when difficult cases or situations, or even personal or family situations, arise. He is a truly rare, creative, and intelligent professional, as well as an approachable, funny, down-to-earth person. Upon meeting him, even a stranger would feel as if he or she has known him forever. His dedication to the field of helping others is second to none. I am more than honored to provide this personal piece to him for *Socialcide: How America Is Loving Itself to Death*.

When I say Leo is rare, I must also say that the information he has gathered and put forth in this book is a rare risk for a clinician in the field of Psychology, especially today. Yet it is much-needed. Most clinically-trained professionals would never dare cross the proverbial line between science and religion, and perhaps that line is part of the problem feeding Socialcide and fooling Americans today.

My work as a psychotherapist and forensic criminal profiler has brought me face-to-face with some of the most evil, intelligent, sadistic, and sociopathic people America has ever known. To say they are extreme narcissists is an understatement.

Perhaps you have heard of Henry Lee Lucas. Once called "America's most prolific serial killer," Lucas was convicted of eleven murders, but was most likely responsible for countless others. Speaking to him was akin to addressing a void. He was a soulless, arrogant being that wanted me to write a letter for him to give to his warden, asking that he be allowed to continue smoking his six packs of cigarettes a day. Narcissists do not agree to interviews such as the one I was conducting for my profiling studies without a payoff of some sort. The trade-off was well worth it; the cigarette letter was his.

Understand, I was trying to discuss his murderous life's rampage and to find out more about his background, but nothing meant more to him than those cigarettes. Selfish, unremorseful, arrogant, and believing his appeal would get him off of death row, his demeanor was simply not human. There was not a word from him about his victims or their families; he simply did not care about anything except smoking and getting out of jail.

This particular type of narcissist is at the top of the narcissistic "food chain," if I may, but disregard for other people is what characterizes narcissists. Few narcissists are killers, but not one of them cares about who they hurt, use, manipulate, or abuse to fulfill their addictions to themselves.

Socialcide speaks to the country's current "self-addiction" plague across the board. How many times does a child need to see his or her picture posted on a social media site before he or she is satisfied?

This is a very real addiction today, and is most definitely keeping our children from doing the work they need to do as children in order to become responsible adults. Battenhausen's identification of this plague—this detrimental social crisis,—is timely, necessary, and extremely important, especially for parents.

I firmly believe that the family is the most essential guide and role model for every child. If children do not have to answer to their parents they will not answer to teachers, authorities, or others. Battenhausen's connection between the disappearing spirituality in America and the alarmingly fast-growing number of self-loving and entitled children makes excellent sense.

I remember going to the movies as a child and seeing one news flash that would pop up on the screen: "The Family that Worships Together, Stays Together." Can you imagine if that message appeared in movie trailers today? Or if the nightly television commercial, "It's 10:00 PM; do you know where your children are?" still aired? Broadcasting used to start its the day with a morning prayer by a rabbi, pastor, priest or deacon. Times have certainly changed. This is not the country we used to know, and it shows.

According to information compiled by *Mayors Against Illegal Guns* and *Moms Demand Action for Gun Sense in America*, there has been a school shooting every ten days since the tragedy that occurred at Sandy Hook Elementary School in New Town, Connecticut on December 14, 2012. When will America say and believe enough is enough? Taking away guns will not stop this evil. Restoration of family values will, but the government does not talk of such things.

Socialcide: How America Is Loving Itself to Death is an excellently written, frighteningly true call to action—action that will restore the family values that made this country great, and action that will reveal how the lack of these values is destroying us.

John Kelly
*John Kelly is a Forensic Social Worker, Criminal Profiler, Co-founder of S.T.A.L.K., Inc. (System to Apprehend Lethal Killers), Author, and Co-Star of Investigation Discovery Channel's show, "Dark Minds." He is also founder and Clinical Director of Extracare Health Services, L.L.C., with offices in New Jersey.

Introduction

Considering the idea of a well-functioning, healthy *society*, it is clear that America is becoming less and less so every day. It is safe to say that *"things ain't what they used to be"* anywhere anymore, and the ways of society have taken a tremendous nose-dive when it comes to kindness, morality, respect, and values. Some of us to wonder *what has happened to this world and all that was good,* while others wander aimlessly, taking what they believe to be theirs without question, caring less and less about anyone or anything except themselves and where to obtain the next big thrill to make them feel good.

Depression, marital problems, infidelity, drug addiction, stress, anxiety, sleep disorders, severe credit card debt, interpersonal issues, "drama," teenage suicide, school shootings, murder, child pornography, domestic abuse, children experiencing emotional instability; the list is almost endless. The presence of these issues today in our country is at an all-time high.

If you are a typical American, chances are extremely high that you have heard the terms *narcissist, psychopath,* and *sociopath* on used on televised news to describe individuals who have committed certain criminal acts. Maybe you have even been affected by one of these people in your personal life. The Narcissistic Nation, a generation called *Millennials* (or the *Me, Me, Me Generation*), has been making its presence known throughout this country at an ever-increasing rate.

These Millennials are Americans born between 1980 and 2000. There are roughly seventy-eight million of them in our country. Statistically, individuals of this generation have tested higher than any preceding generation in the area of narcissism. They demonstrate the highest levels of self-love and entitlement America has ever seen. My interest in this new generation and the associated high level of narcissism has been piqued over the past few years as I have been observing dramatic changes in the news, the world of crime, the culture of our country, and the new trend of issues people bring into therapy sessions with me.

I believe the rise of narcissism is, in part, due to lack of real interactions in people's lives today. Narcissists live in a "magical land" where they are above and beyond all others. The irony of that fact is that they are truly fragile, insecure, and hollow people, void of any true *self.*

We seemingly have become prisoners of our own demise, recluses at the hands of our own technology. Children spend their playtime in front of a screen of some sort, mesmerized for hour upon hour by video games, rarely venturing outdoors to play or enjoy fresh air. In fact, many parents are so terrified of *allowing* their children to go out to play that getting kids away from those screens is no easy feat. They *don't want to go out.* I believe this is also true of too many adults today; they don't want to go out. This cannot be healthy!

We have adopted an existence that depends on rapidly evolving technology, leading to less and less *need* for true socializing. Indeed, there is very little that cannot be accomplished from the confines of the home these days with the ease of a keystroke on the computer or a tap on a touch pad. This dark existence offers the individual less dependency on others. Primary communication is made through the media, music, movies, and television shows. We become frightened with tales of "bogeymen" on every corner of our neighborhoods, so we do not let our children play with other children. Children's need to socialize is satisfied by drawing their undivided attention into video games and "computer-grounds" as opposed to playgrounds.

What many fail to see (or choose to ignore) is that this dark existence is crippling souls, relationships, childhoods, marriages, families, love, empathy love, empathy, faith in a God of one's choice, and human compassion and kindness.

When technology becomes a factor in human development, there can be no worthy outcome. If we live as robots, so will we become—and so will our children. And that's a problem, a problem that is showing itself more and more frequently in the form of personality disorders.

Many younger people have become self-absorbed, lacking in social skills such as common courtesy, respect, and fear of consequences. We are left to wonder how this has happened. Our schools have become war zones, social media has become the new playground for bullying and destruction of character, and the number of childhood "disorders" has seen an increase like never before in history.

A report by MacKenzie Yang (*Time Newsfeed:* May 2013) stated that seventy-three percent of nine- and ten-year-olds and eighty percent of thirteen- and fourteen-year-olds suffer severe sleep deprivation, and their school performance reflects this loss. This is startling information. Yet sleep is the least of children's problems these days, considering the epidemic levels of Attention Deficit Hyperactivity Disorder (ADHD), Attention Deficit Disorder (ADD), Asperger's Syndrome, Autism, and Major Depression diagnoses, and treatment with this drug or that. If our country's children are so affected and emotionally "out-of- order," what does that suggest about our adults?

Much has changed during the past thirty or so years in how we raise our children, how they are socialized, how they are taught, and what parents are willing to tolerate. I have watched the societal changes, trends, news, crimes, and factors in an attempt to identify a true cause for such a drastic difference in how people are today—emotionally, socially and personally—from what they used to be. The common denominator appears to be an extreme loss of conscience.

Without conscience, there is nothing to guide us to do what is right, and to steer us away from danger. Indeed, when healthy persons people make mistakes the their conscience nudges them to make a wrong a right, with true remorse. The conscienceless have no regrets, no matter how wrong or damaging their actions. This characteristic is evident in many youth today, as well as in many young adults.

There is a new generation amongst us. They are not Pilgrims; they are not warriors. They pursue no cause other than their own needs, desires, and instant gratification. They walk among us more now than at any other time in human history; they know no other love than self-love, though they can be extremely convincing otherwise until one becomes trapped in their web of deception and manipulation.

This generation has been lured, courted, and groomed very well. This has happened right under our noses—in our schools, in our own homes. It happened while we were watching, and while we were busy looking the other direction at all the things we have to take care of, manage, and control. It happened through well-packaged media that made its way into our lives under beneficent or neutral cover. We didn't see it coming; we didn't know to look for it, and we did not know from whence it came, until now.

In considering narcissists, much research and numerous reports of them include the description "evil." This makes sense. An individual void of a conscience is bound to be evil. Think of history's most evil, despicable, and cruel people: the psychopathic cult-leaders, serial killers, and murderers who have made history. Not one of them has ever shown a shred of remorse for the atrocities they have committed, or empathy for those they have wronged.

More currently, and on a lesser scale, consider today's entertainers and celebrities—the Justin Biebers, Miley Cyruses, Kanye Wests of the world. Their self-indulgent behaviors are appalling to many because of the blatant disrespect they demonstrate and their adamant "I do what I want to do" attitudes. But for many others, they are role models, justification for "I can do that, too." So if narcissists have no conscience, they are highly likely to be evil. Without goodness or empathy, all that remains is evil.

America is being manipulated and duped into "loving itself to death" in the spiritual sense. Socialcide speaks to America's neglect of the forces of *good* in the world. My belief is that our conscience is our soul, and that soul that we are born with is our earthly connection to our God, our spirituality. That connection is our barometer to guide us to do what is right and to correct or warn us when we are wrong. Narcissists do not have that connection anymore. Somewhere along the line it was destroyed. Sadly, once it is gone, it is gone forever.

There is no cure for narcissism.

The disappearance of *good* or God in our families, country, and lives has everything to do with our growing disbelief in God's existence. Some folks intentionally push God out of their consciences, because in doing so they can also push out their belief in *evil* or Satan. The problem is that Satan does not need "believers" in him; he needs only disbelievers in God.

Evil does not creep around looking like a madman, with shifty eyes, wearing a dirty trench coat, dagger in hand, gurgling obscenities from a dark, rainy street corner. It has no obvious horns on its head, or cloven hooves on which it dances around a pentagram of flames, but it certainly would want you to believe it did! Because when you believe that's what evil looks like, it can sneak in without being recognized. And so it has.

In fact, as a society, we have welcomed evil into our homes and lives with open arms! We have nurtured it, cradled it all along, with its controlling, conniving, and so very insidious growth. While we held it, it manipulated us. You see, it wants people to love it more than they can possibly love anything else! More than children, more than spouses, more than dignity, more than God, and definitely more than life itself! In fact, it only survives on adoration from others and itself. Complete submission is required.

Herein lies my basic concept of Socialcide. *Socialcide* is happening as you read. Until now, though, it has been silent, incredibly luring, and magnificent. That it took control over most of the previous generation's understanding of what it takes to *be* human, and replaced it with what it takes to *feel* human. Now a new generation is being raised with the same intention. Those of us who preceded the birth of this darkness helplessly sit back and watch as all that was valued and all that was good in people and society vanishes like a toothpick in a bonfire. We are not innocent.

We, too, were overtaken by the allure of this evil. Those of us born in earlier generations toyed with it, invited it in, and maybe even made good use of it, but it does not have ultimate power over most of us because we were not raised with it. This darkness has gotten what it needed from us, however. And as those generations dwindle away, no one will ever remember the "good old days." That is, until the final battle of good versus evil is complete.

When the long-heard bell strikes one final time at the first hour of a new day, the battle will be over. The darkness that had lain still, comforting, will crouch no longer. Socialcide will be complete and America will have *loved itself to death.*

SECTION I
The Good Old Days

Chapter One

The Way We Were

"When a nation goes down, or a society perishes,
one condition may always be found; they forgot where they came from.
They lost sight of what had brought them along."
— Carl Sandburg

I recently came across a very inspiring study by John Tierny, published in the *New York Times: Science Section* on July 8, 2013, about the benefits of *reminiscing* and *nostalgia*. In it, Tierny discovered that when people take a stroll down the proverbial memory lane they feel less sad, more romantic with their partners, less lonely, bored, and anxious, and are far more tolerant of strangers than those who do not. In fact, being nostalgic literally makes a person feel warmer. In following the study subjects' lives for ten years and observing their moods and frequency of engagement in nostalgia, the news and the information were good.

Initially, when the word was coined by Swiss doctor Johannes Hoffer in 1688, "nostalgia"was believed to be a demonic neurological disease. Since then, most people avoid "living in the past," exclaiming how "depressing"that is, and telling those who are more apt to reminisce, "You are just going to upset yourself with that. The past belongs in the past!" Indeed, the practice of reminiscing or of being nostalgic is a bittersweet experience, but memories of who we were, where we were, what we did, and who we did it with validate our sense of place, and the impact we have had. Memories are precious. They exist for many reasons. But today there is a slow erasing of what many of us used to know as life and how it was lived back then.

Before the world began running on twenty-four-hour clocks, Saturdays used to be such special days. As a child, back in the 1950s and 1960s, I noticed it was magically easier to jump out of bed in the morning knowing there was no school that day. You could just sense a state of calm in the world, especially in warm weather. The breeze blew slower and more gently. There were fewer cars driving by, allowing for more silence, making it possible to hear the birds singing. And there was a particular time of day when everyone was normally home—the morning. A big breakfast, chores around the house, the wonderful Saturday morning cartoons. The noon air-raid drill siren blew, then for the young it was out to play until supper time. "Be home by five!" our mothers called.

Out to play could have been a two-on-two baseball or basketball game, wandering through the woods, stick ball, or simply being outside. We had no cellphones. We practiced caution, but we did not fear other people. Everyone knew the locals and the strangers. The neighbors knew all of us kids. We would exchange hellos and sometimes were told, "Tell your mother to call me," as we walked by. Yes, neighbors knew us and our parents, and even knew our phone numbers. That was a double-edged sword. If we were doing something wrong they would tell our parents. But they also looked out for us, providing a safety net of comfort in knowing we could go to them in a time of need, and be helped. This sense of community is not something we see much today, if at all. Most "neighbors" left long ago, and only a "hood" remains.

We *earned* our money as well. If we were lucky and behaved as expected, we were given an allowance. Other times we could do extra work, such as raking leaves for neighbors, helping people carry grocery bags to their cars, or shoveling snow after a storm. In those days the value of hard work to earn money was instilled in us at an early age.

This type of childhood not only taught us a valuable work ethic, but also was extremely beneficial to our emotional growth. It fostered socialization, manners, respect, and knowing right from wrong. If we did wrong, we were punished. We learned through discipline that it was best to listen to mom and dad, or else! That is not to say we always did, but when we didn't, we felt it.

When Did the Neighbors Leave the 'Hood?'

So how and when were the seeds of Socialcide planted?

The significant year in the birth of Socialcide was 1978. Some very interesting beginnings took place then, and have grown like weeds ever since. The "appetizers" America was fed have morphed into multi-course meals for the self-serving lust of the masses, and ever since we have been devouring the rations and demanding more. But before we review the "menu," let's set the table and take a look at how society lived back in 1978.

Most homes had only one telephone. More affluent families had two lines. Generally, though, the phone was shared by the family. There was no Caller ID, so to know who was calling someone had to actually answer the phone when it rang. This resulted in more *talking* to whoever was calling This phone system allowed parents, at times, to speak to their children's friends, boyfriends, girlfriends, etc., providing them with the benefit of being kept in the proverbial "loop"as to whom their kids were speaking to, and when.

In school, when a teacher or professor assigned a research paper, a student actually had to go into a library and use what was known as a *card catalogue* to look up the subject, author, or titles of books they needed for their research.

When working on a research project in the library, a student could be seen carrying a huge stack of books to a table to look through them, or carrying them to a machine to make Xerox copies of pages they needed so they could take them home to take home. Yes, this was cumbersome and time consuming. And when it came to writing the paper, there was no "cut and paste" option. Once the project was done, however, a good grade earned through planning, effort, time, and thinking was a true accomplishment.

Playtime back then was very different too. Children would normally play outside with their friends. They would go to playgrounds, parks, the empty lot at the end of the street, or to each other's backyards and find things to do. Stickball, hide-and-seek, hopscotch, jump rope, climbing trees, building forts, or simply making up games were common activities. Kids back then had to be creative. But that was part of the fun, and kids came up with lots of things to do to fill and enjoy the hours after homework or on days off and weekends. When the dinner bell rang or the street lights came on everyone knew it was time to go home.

Most people in a neighborhood knew, or knew of, each other. That helped keep kids out of trouble. If a child was seen by a neighbor doing something they shouldn't, there was a good possibility the neighbor would either reprimand the child on the spot or call his or her parents. Children, of course, could try to sneak around nosy neighbors, but they knew there were watchful eyes everywhere. Back then, the thought of getting caught was an effective deterrent.

Shopping areas consisted of independently-owned businesses. Merchants were familiar with most of their customers, and vice-versa. Downtown areas were extensions of the neighborhoods surrounding them, and stores offered personalized services and products for local patrons.

When children got old enough to work they rushed to get their "working papers" (official documents obtained from school that allowed minors of at least age 16 to be legally employed) so they could get a job and earn money, not because their parents made them or needed them to (although that was sometimes the case), but because they *wanted* to. By the time they were old enough to work, they were also old enough to go downtown and spend their earnings on what they wanted.

At home, children did at least a fair share of chores, and if they were lucky, they received an allowance for doing these chores.

Children also were to taught to hold doors open for others; to say thank you, excuse me, and please; to respect their elders; and to show appreciation for what they were given. Did all children in 1978 do these things? Of course not. But a far greater number of children did, compared with today's children. It was the societal standard. Children were *in the community and in the neighborhood.* They communicated with relatives, neighbors, business owners, and others every day. They learned on a daily basis how to interact with people

30

of different ages and positions.

In school, teachers were respected, and sometimes even feared, much more than they are today. Most authority figures were. Children had something to lose if their grades were poor, their behavior was deviant, or their actions were out of line.

Autism, Attention Deficit Hyperactivity Disorder, Attention Deficit Disorder, Asperger's Syndrome, and Depression in children were not seen or diagnosed in anywhere near the record numbers they are today. In fact, most of those disorders were unheard-of then. Childhood obesity was also virtually nonexistent. Today it is an epidemic.

In 1978, adults were not afflicted with major depression in such extreme numbers; and stress, panic, and sleep disorders were rarely heard of. Children with excessive energy were considered hyperactive, and prescription drugs for it were not handed out like candy on Halloween. Instead, parents and teachers worked together to remedy such situations.

Speaking of prescription drugs, in 1978, commercials for medications you should "ask your doctor"about were not shown on the four or five television channels available. Thought, planning, and being actively involved in each other's lives socially was the norm of the day. Frankly, none of this over-diagnosing, over- prescribing nonsense was present *at all.*

Which leads me (and many of you, I am sure) to wonder: What is going wrong with society today, that parents are seeking and giving pills to their kids by the millions, instead of putting time, thought, energy, and love into actual parenting? Why don't families and neighborhoods exist anymore? Why and when did the *neighbors leave the "hood"*?

To many young people today those rules, expectations, and ways of living seem overly restrictive, primitive, or simply old fashioned. Perhaps they were in some ways, but they were also very liberating and beneficial in other ways. Today what young children are allowed to play outside? When do parents feel comfortable enough to let their kids go out at all? Do kids even play outdoors anymore?

**CASE STUDY
"I Don't Like Mondays"**

Deep in the recesses of the California Institution for Women in Chino, California lives Brenda Ann Spencer. Now 51 years old, she has existed there since the age of 16. Brenda inspired a very famous and profitable song for the Irish band, *The Boomtown Rats,* in 1979, and is also credited for a scene in the very popular movie *The Breakfast Club* where the expression, *"I Don't Like Mondays"* is written on a wall. Neither of these claims to fame made her a penny, but certainly her quote made money for the Boomtown Rats and The Breakfast Club, although not due to the graffiti on the wall.

No, Brenda Ann Spencer is not concerned today about any possible royalties she may be owed, but she is concerned that she may have inspired the epidemic of school shootings in America. She didn't recall ever saying "I don't like Mondays"when she spoke of her motive after killing two and wounding nine in America's first high-profile multiple random-victim school shooting at Grover Cleveland Elementary School in San Diego, California.

Brenda currently watches the news and reads about the all-too- frequent school shootings, and expresses concern and remorse for possibly being the role model or predecessor for each and every one of them. What is unusually interesting about Spencer's rampage is that she planned to kill herself, like many other murderers have done, but she claims she "got scared," and laid down her twenty-two caliber rifle purchased for her by her father for Christmas. Brenda had wanted a radio, but instead her dad bought her a rifle. She didn't know why.

Her survival and subsequent remorse and regret lead others to wonder how many of the other killers might have felt regret for what they did at a later time in their lives, had they survived. We will never know. Suicide is always a permanent solution to a temporary problem, and Spencer certainly did not lead a charmed life. Her rage and thoughts of suicide were likely fueled by big problems in her life.

During the interrogation after her arrest she was asked if any adult had noticed any signs of her being dangerous to herself and others. She said her high school counselor had, and took her to see a psychiatrist. The psychiatrist recommended Spencer be hospitalized as a danger to both herself and others. This may have been the perfect intervention for her well-being and the salvation for those she eventually killed and wounded, but her father claimed she was fine and asked that they be left alone.

Her father had divorced his wife and been awarded custody of their three children, of which Brenda was the youngest. After the divorce, Brenda became sullen, withdrawn, and strange. Neighborhood friends and acquaintances reported she would use drugs, cut school, steal, and was cruel to animals. They also reported she developed a fascination with guns. According to Brenda's account, her emotionally-distant father began molesting her when she was nine, sleeping in the same bed with her and sexually assaulting her virtually every night. This information has never been validated, nor has her father ever been convicted, so this remains hearsay on her account. Incidentally, when Brenda was incarcerated, her father began a new relationship with a woman who remarkably resembled her but was younger—a woman he later married.

She sought peace in drug use. She likely abused animals to feel some sort of control in her life and to relieve her anguish, harming other living creatures because she was at a loss for what to do to make herself feel better, much like every other serial killer has done before crossing over to human victims.

So here was a sixteen-year-old girl who had lost contact with her mother at the age of nine, and had allegedly been sexually abused daily by her father ever since. Prior to the divorce, she appeared to be a normal, growing girl with no indications of emotional, social, or family problems. And in the midst of all this, her father bought her a gun instead of a radio for Christmas, and told the school counselor and psychiatrist, "She is fine; please leave us alone."

Spencer claimed that at the time of the shootings she was under the influence of alcohol, marijuana, and benzodiazepines (downers). Urinalysis allegedly contradicted her claim.

The case of Brenda Ann Spencer is a tragedy on many levels. It speaks to the horrors some children face on a day-to-day basis. It speaks to the injustice and meaninglessness of murder. It speaks to the failing systems we believe are in place and working to keep us safe and secure. And it speaks to just how fragile some individuals can be, and how evil can infiltrate many lives when least expected. When authorities—parents or caretakers— are "asleep at the wheel," evil will gladly take it for us.

So why am I telling you this now? Because on January 29, 1979, Brenda Ann Spencer became America's first high-profile school shooter and murderer.

Chapter Two

Normalizing Evil

"Information should be used as food for thought,
not poison to the soul."
—Shellie R. Warren

Much of the news we hear today consists of nothing short of examples of the pure evil that exists in some people. This may sound severe, but there is simply no other frank and direct way to describe these acts, which are some of the most atrocious, violent, despicable acts one person can commit against another. Horrendous acts of murder, slaughter, kidnapping, child sexual abuse by predators, school killings, and every other evil act reported on the evening news leave us horrified and thinking it can get no worse—until the next horrific act is reported.

I imagine the news of three hundred years ago—theft of livestock or even a bank robbery—would have caused people to shake their heads in fear. Today that kind of news would hardly even make the broadcast. Society is inundated with the most gruesome reports of serial killers and truly sick individuals who recklessly and casually cause evil for no reason or purpose whatsoever other than to satisfy their demented fetishes, drives, obsessions, and ghoulish lusts.

Is this a sickness? Is it the criminal mind? Label it whatever helps you sleep at night, or makes it more comfortable to talk or think about, but it is evil, plain and simple. And as time goes by, the intensity of such grows while, in some very strange way, society becomes more desensitized to it. With every new *"murder du jour"* served up by the media on the evening crime news we become more engrossed in the grossness. Perhaps we love to hate the criminals;

perhaps we are supporting the victims as best we can; or perhaps we are simply fascinated by the enormity of it all. Whatever the cause of fascination and the associated desensitization, millions of Americans are absorbing evil every day.

Many of the news, legal, and crime shows are hosted by venomous personalities who, in my opinion, are as self-serving as their guest experts who argue points of the crime and the criminals' minds. All these experts are quick to label the criminals *psychopaths, sociopaths,* and *narcissists,* while at the same time they suck up as much airtime as they can to satisfy their own need to feed their narcissism and self-gratification. In fact, these crime shows are a microcosm of our society today. On them, you can see reports on the very worst the criminal narcissist has to offer (murder, rape, etc.), delivered by the more harmless form of narcissist—the egomaniac who needs constant adoration and exposure.

More than ever before, society includes various levels of the self-serving. Statistics show that people born between 1978 and 2000 are more narcissistic than people born into every other generation in history. That means they are less apt to care about other people, to have less-to-no ability to love or empathize, and are less likely to have a conscience, or experience guilt than any other age group alive today. There is no real treatment or cure for narcissism. Why then does the diagnosis exist at all? It is my professional opinion that narcissism is not a "mental disorder" but the presence of raw evil in a person outwardly displayed by committing acts of savagery against a fellow human beings.

Who or what is a narcissist anyway? The word comes from the name of the mythological Greek figure Narcissus, who saw his reflection in a pond and fell so in love with his own image that he could not break away from staring at it, and died. It is not difficult to relate such self-inflation and grandiosity to much of today's society. In fact, such behaviors and feelings are now encouraged and supported in just about all that consumes people's time and minds.

This epidemic of self-love or narcissism is not happening due solely to some psychological phenomenon that any field of science can figure out.

Psychology will always look closely at the family background and history of a narcissist—whether they are a serial killer or simply an obnoxious pathological liar—to determine the possibility of negative influences that may have caused the narcissistic behavior to occur. However, the discovery of possible "causative influences" for one particular person does not mean that if those influences exist in someone else's life that person will exhibit the same narcissistic behaviors.

For example, Charles Manson's mother sold him for a pitcher of beer, due to her chronic alcoholism (and perhaps being a narcissist herself). This fact does not determine or define the reason Charles became a psychopathic murderer. Why not? Because there are millions of other people who grew up with similar life experiences or worse conditions of neglect who became caring, normal people. It is true that many of the serial killers that have been caught and studied came from abusive homes, having been raised by abusive parents. But again, that influence in a person's life does not cause serial-killer behavior. If it did the world would be filled with serial-killers and serial-killer sibling groups.

In the field of psychological research there is a lot of talk about a "narcissistic gene." To date, there is no proof of such a gene. Have you ever heard or read about a serial killer who has a child or grandchild who is also a serial killer? Why don't the children of serial killers become serial killers? Because there is no gene to blame.

Years ago mental disorders were believed to be of a spiritual or demonic nature. Prayer and exorcisms were used as the first line of treatment before confinement, if that became necessary. I am *in no way* suggesting we can simply "pray away"depression, schizophrenia, or any other mental disorder. However, in a science so subjective, I am hard-pressed to find any harm in prayer, provided the client is open to it.

We are seeing more and more mental, social, and emotional disorders on the rise today, which has to make us speculate that something is not working about the way we are currently attempting to help people suffering with them, and the way we are trying to eliminate them ([the disorders, not the people afflicted with them)]. Whereas modern medicine has grown and flourished with new treatments and care for diseases once considered incurable, the frequency and severity of mental illnesses continue to get worse, and those afflicted and diagnosed are younger and younger.

There is something going on in society today that is causing this rise in frequency, intensity and failure of treatment.

The Personality Disorders, as they are known, are of significant interest and importance to the understanding of Socialcide. Most of them are incurable through medication or therapy, and many are quite suspect as to their origins and whether or not they should even be considered "mental illnesses" included in the *Diagnostic and Statistical Manual of Mental Disorders,* or *DSM.*

There has been much controversy concerning how to define and categorize some of the Personality Disorders, especially the Narcissistic Personality Disorder, formerly known as Psychopathic and Sociopathic Personality Disorder.

Narcissists are people who are incapable of feeling empathy, love for others, guilt, compassion, remorse, understanding, or any other of the best traits and emotions a human can experience—the emotions that *make us human.* Narcissists have an exaggerated sense of self. They desperately crave the undivided admiration of others and, in their grandiosity, have absolutely no regard for the feelings of others; only for their own personal gain.

Narcissists are master manipulators. Initially, they can impress people and gain their admiration and trust. However, their true nature of perpetual deception and insatiable need for self-gratification eventually makes itself known, usually once they feel their "prey" is well-entangled in their web of lies. The narcissist population includes many of the world's rapists, murderers, pedophiles, cheaters, thieves, and various other demented connivers that exist in our society today. The word "narcissist" has recently become one of the most commonly Googled words, because more and more people (usually women) are becoming romantically involved with narcissists and are struggling terribly with the emotional roller coaster ride they find themselves powerless to get off of.

Today narcissists come in many forms. They are not necessarily criminally-minded, but they are all indeed self-minded, and know nothing of "The Golden Rule"—nor do they care to. The number of cases of narcissism in children, teens, and college students is frightening. This generation has come to be known as the "Me, Me, Me Generation" or "Millennials."

Popular media chuckles at this epidemic; Psychology tries to understand it. Narcissistic Personality Disorder was almost eliminated from the latest edition of the DSM, the *standard* and only official diagnostic tool used by Psychology and Psychiatry. This caused quite a stir. Why?

Many in the fields of Psychology and Psychiatry believe that Narcissistic Personality Disorder is *too common in society today to be considered a mental disorder!* In other words, so many people born in 1978 or later have become so emotionless, so self-serving, so manipulative, so cold and calculating, living solely for their own gain and pleasure, that society and those at the top of the professional fields of Psychology and Psychiatry believe these behaviors to be "just how people are"—healthy and normal in the evolution of human beings. Narcissism has become *normalized!*

To help you understand the potential impact this could have on public consciousness, I offer an example of a disorder that has finally been removed from the DSM: homosexuality. Let me preface this example by stating that *I am in no way, shape or form* judging lifestyles, or anyone's choice in that regard. Not long ago, homosexuality was considered sexual deviancy and was a "diagnosis" categorized in the DSM. As more and more people "came out" and society began to accept the choices people make to freely and openly state and live their lives as who they are, this diagnosis was removed from the DSM completely (in 1986). This made good sense, and helped contribute to society's acceptance of individuals. (Not completely yet, but much more than previously).

My point in this example is that removing a diagnosis from the DSM means that people exhibiting characteristics of that particular state of being are no longer considered ill or needing treatment, but are considered "normal." To connect the dots, if Narcissistic Personality Disorder is removed from the DSM, narcissism will be seen as normal and acceptable human behavior. It is *not!*

Homosexuality was removed from the DSM because it did not belong there. The number of people currently self-identifying as homosexual is growing, yet it is not a diagnosable condition. Similarly, the number of people identifiable as narcissistic is growing; however, it is a diagnosable and far-from-normal condition.

Fortunately for society at large, the verdict as to whether or not to include Narcissistic Personality Disorder in the current DSM was to leave it in. However, the criteria necessary for a diagnosis of Narcissism is now much stricter. These new criteria were a compromise made to appease both sides of the argument. However, with its diagnostic criteria more difficult to meet, fewer people will be diagnosed with the disorder, making it likely that the disorder will be excluded from the next publication of the manual.

This *by no means* indicates that narcissism does not exist or that narcissists are healthy, normal people who just make bad behavioral choices, so we should accept their behavior. It simply means that more people will have many of its traits, but not enough to be diagnosed, and fewer people will receive a diagnosis. In other words, there will be many more undiagnosed narcissists in our world.

This reflects a significant move toward acceptance of narcissism as common in America. Now a person must be a "super narcissist" to receive the diagnosis.

Sadly, this is a moot point. There is no cure or treatment for this personality disorder, which then begs the question, "Why bother with diagnosis?" The answer is simple: To help professionals and society recognize and know who we are dealing with, so we can avoid personal interaction.

Another reason that a diagnosis of Narcissistic Personality Disorder may be considered pointless is that a person must *acknowledge* they even have a problem before anything can be done to treat it, and a narcissist will never admit to any such thing.

With all that said, it seems to me that all this haggling about where to draw the defining line between a diagnosable and an un-diagnosable narcissist should be viewed like a diagnosis of, say, pregnancy. You can't be "a little pregnant;" you either are, or you aren't.

Narcissism is actually in a category by itself. When people who cannot love, empathize, feel compassion, feel guilt, have a conscience, or contribute to anything good in society grow in number and become *accepted and normalized by society* will not much longer exist. Those who are not of a narcissistic mind must always be on guard because narcissists are cunning and believable. Narcissists can (and do) say the right things at just the right times; they can charm the pants off a motorcycle gang if they must. In romantic relationships or in the employment hiring process, narcissists appear "too good to be true"—and we know what *that* means. There *is no such thing*. This is how evil works as well.

In my practice, clients are coming to me at an alarming rate because they are struggling with narcissistic abuse or entanglement. This trend is growing, and it is frightening. Where is it coming from? Why is it happening now? What can we do about it?

Socialcide is not about serial killers; and it's not about genetics that cannot be proven. Socialcide is about how America has been losing control of itself by producing people who are more obsessed with themselves than with others, or with fulfilling the mutual need to love and be loved. That basic human need or gift is what we were created to do and be. It is obvious that the obsession with self-gratification and self-adoration is spreading. We need to understand why and by whom *before* society ceases to exist. Because if nothing is done, it will.

Chapter Three

The Haves and Have Nots

"To love our neighbors as ourselves is such a truth for regulating human society, by that alone one might determine all the cases of social morality."
— John Locke

Every society throughout history has had its "Haves" and "Have Nots." Generally, those groups are defined based on real or perceived income levels and physical possessions. Socialcide concerns itself not with the external, material type of Haves and Have Nots, but specifically with the internal, conscious/personality type of Haves and Have Nots.

In terms of Socialcide, the Haves are those people who have a strong sense of right and wrong, and who feel badly if they don't do right; those who have a healthy soul filled with spirituality and hope and love for mankind; those who have a conscience, understand right and wrong, and attempt to do what's right even when it is difficult. The Have Nots are those, in contrast, who have lost their consciences, and do not seem to care about doing what's right; who don't seem to even know there is a difference between right and wrong; and who seem to have no soul.

The Haves are potentially understanding and compassionate about and toward the people around them, and show humanity and empathy. Their conscience guides them to lean toward goodness. Haves can recognize when they are wrong, and will do what they can to repair the resulting damage. Have Nots don't care about much, other than themselves.

Haves act with emotion, compassion, understanding, consciousness,

43

awareness, mindfulness, and goodness. Have Nots do not. Have Nots do not struggle with why bad things happen to good people. They just don't care. The Haves, however, do struggle with such things.

In addition to the Haves and Have Nots, there is a third category of people—the Blessed. The *Blessed* are those Haves who are beyond wondering why they struggle, why life is unfair. They have made the emotional and spiritual connection with knowing why they suffer. They know their own spirituality is fine, and they are okay with who they are. They know suffering is part of life, and they don't question it anymore. They also see Have Nots for who they truly are: conscienceless, narcissistic individuals who are beyond repair. And they know to avoid relationships with them whenever possible.

Today, Haves suffer—sometimes silently, sometimes verbally—with extreme discomfort over what people do and "get away" with, suffering made even more frustrating when they remember what *life used to be like.* Younger Haves (those in their teens or early twenties) suffer more with the issue of why they "do all the right things, but never get a break in life." They also struggle with ideas of "why should I try so hard when I can look at my parents and their generation and see that their hard work just doesn't seem to have paid off." These younger Haves don't come from a context of years of life experiences from which to compare society today with how it "used to be." They also don't have the benefit of having lived in a society where people cared about one other, and spoke to each other in person, not via social media. So while they do not lament what has been lost, their lives are lived without the benefit of experiencing the value of that which has been lost.

As you can imagine, there is a huge gap between the Blessed and the Have Nots, and this is becoming all too common, obvious, and familiar. In looking at these two groups it's not difficult to draw the conclusion that they symbolize the major difference between Good and Evil, Narcissistic and Not, right and wrong, and every other variation of what humans were *meant to be versus what someone or something is creating.*

There is no gene involved in creating these distinctions. There are influences. Yet those influences (technology and the media, for example) affect and sway only the Have Nots.

Though it may seem, in extreme cases, that intelligence level plays a role here, that is not necessarily the case. There are highly intelligent Haves and Have Nots, and there are less intelligent Haves and Have Nots. It should be noted that the highest functioning narcissists (all narcissists fall intothe Have Not category), such as serial killers, can be as intelligent as Wall Street executives with narcissistic personalities. The Self-Loving are often of extremely high intellect. They can achieve, mesmerize, amaze, manipulate, and make even the strongest, most intelligent person believe their lies. They have developed their craft so well that when they fall, they bring down with them all those with whom they are involved.

Conversely, there are people with hearts a million times larger than their minds will ever be. These individuals may be unable to balance a checkbook, but they understand human need. They can identify suffering when they see it, and if needed, will be the first to give the proverbial shirt off their backs to keep someone warm. And they will do this expecting nothing in return. These people with limited intellect rarely become narcissistic or self-serving individuals with only their own needs to fill.

So while it's possible for Haves and Have Nots to possess varying degrees of intelligence, it is also reasonable to deduce that any "force" *seeking* a candidate for *its* own needs is seeking someone with a level of at least average intelligence to do *its* dirty work. Evil needs people who need and have some clout, the ability to manipulate, and who have something that will help its cause. People with low intellect just don't make enough of a splash in life, command enough authority, or wield enough perceived power for evil to find them useful.

For the Haves, life is a struggle every day. They seek love, happiness, relationships, understanding, and the need to be needed. These individuals want to be successful, liked, and accepted, and they "do the right thing" to get it. Circumstances in life, especially those involving Have Nots, cause them great confusion, hurt, and anger. These negative feelings lead them to believe there is something wrong with them when, in reality, they are fighting a battle against the truly uncaring and evil.

In my practice as a therapist, I see many more Haves than Have Nots seeking help—by an extremely high percentage. My belief is that for every single client I see there is someone in their life who should be sitting on that therapy couch instead. But, of course, Have Nots never believe there is anything wrong with them—exactly like a narcissist. This is why narcissists will never seek help with their disorder. They are "fine,"and their only "need" for other people is to gain something from them.

Returning to the Haves, these people possess every human feeling needed to be a good person, but have a difficult time understanding the Have Nots and what makes them tick. Sometimes the Haves will engage in relationships with Have Nots as friends, lovers, co-workers, or by default via family connections and relations. Often Haves will feel a sense that something is not right with the relationship, but can't quite place what it is. Unfortunately, they often believe there must be something wrong within themselves.

Have Nots often bumble through life, following the crowds as to what to wear, what movies to see, what music to listen to, etc. They demonstrate very little, if any, creativity, originality, or uniqueness. They can be your "Regular Joe"—harmless but aloof, and simply disconnected from or disinterested in the depth of human issues. Or they can be self-centered and engrossed in caring only for themselves, unable to demonstrate tact, compassion, or even a shred of care for how they are affecting those around them—especially those who love them.

Currently, there are numerous books and reports out that speak of the "dumbing down of America," describing how education, media, and culture are depleting and eroding the intelligence of the American people. This theory supports the idea of Socialcide in that the more *Regular Joes* or *followers* ["dumbed-down"folks] there are in the world the less *thinking* and *feeling* we have going on. And the less thinking and feeling going on, the less compassion and caring exists. Without compassion and caring, the more self-serving people are subject to the influences of the media, technology, and other forces on the prowl for souls.

Let's face it: Over the past thirty-five years or so, America has thrown away the better part of its humanity and decency. We see it in fashion, children's clothing styles, music, movies, television, and all over the news. More and more people commit more and more horrendous crimes as time goes on. Teenagers are committing suicide in record numbers; childhood disorder diagnoses are out of control; terrorism and shootings are feared in every level of schools, movie theaters, military bases, work places, shopping   malls, supermarkets, and just about anywhere people publicly gather.

Things have never been this horrific in the history of America. This leaves many to think, "Maybe there is no God." It certainly appears that God, too, has thrown in the towel on this mess of a society we have created and now live in. And that is exactly what the extreme narcissist of the universe wants people to believe! No God? Be your own god!

I say, "Beware!" Narcissists often have a fantastic sales pitch, one that uses our doubts and fears to convince us to believe them—at least initially.

So you see, if America is being "dumbed down," more of us are feeling less connected with—or have faith in or need for—any spiritual guidance or belief. We live in social chaos because there is no good guiding our souls. We stop thinking and feeling. We stop listening to our hearts telling us to do what's right. We become robotic and begin to think we can do whatever we want because, "who cares?" While this may sound freeing and enticing, and therefore positive, it is a false positive that can lead to madness, mental disorders, evil hearts, and, of course, narcissism.

Folks, this is *already* happening. Have Nots and "dumbed down" Americans are increasing in frightening numbers every day.

Chapter Four

The End of the World as We Know It

"Technological society has succeeded in multiplying the
opportunities for pleasure, but it has great
difficulty in generating joy."
— Pope Paul VI

Now let's look at the birth of this beast I call Socialcide. In 1978 society still appeared strong, and values were respectable and respected. There was not enough evil present in the world—*yet*. The forces behind Socialcide had a vision, a mission, a plan, and a method, but it would take time to bring those to fruition and to gather more souls to its purpose. You see, to get people to commit Socialcide willingly, Socialcide would have to seem *normal* and "how Americans are supposed to be." The process of quietly shifting society's values had to be a slow one, because each step of gradual change required time to *normalize* itself. The past thirty-five years have allowed for lots of normalization, and have produced great success in spreading this sick evil. As you read, the process is nearing completion.

In 1978, under the guise of convenience and progress in technology, several inventions eerily came to life that would turn out to be instrumental in facilitating the progress of Socialcide. These inventions would eventually become "necessities" for most Americans. The ultimately dangerous power they held was hidden behind the face of the "miracles" they offered. What a crafty source of social destruction!

The Illinois Bell Company introduced the first ever cellular mobile phone system in 1978. Far from what we know today as iPhones or Smartphones, this concept was revolutionary and contributed greatly to the decline of the spoken word, and eventually to the demise of face-to-face communication, letter writing, and even spelling, grammar, and basic proper use of language. It is interesting to note that today's mobile phones are called "i"and "Smart," and Socialcide is ultimately about how narcissistic and self-engrossed individuals have become. The pure potential for evil and harm cell phones can cause was never even a thought in Americans' minds as this device hit the market in 1978 and began to firmly implant itself in lives. Evolving from a "neat thing to have" to "I cannot get through the day without it," this technology has facilitated the degradation of our spoken and written language. It has made it possible for people to have relationships without actually having to speak face-to-face, and to communicate things they possibly would not have expressed if they'd had to witness the person's reactions.

One of the most insidious problems this amazing invention created was that it led people to start believing they were so important in the world that they actually needed to be able to be reached twenty-four hours a day, seven days a week. When the cell phone was first available on the mass market it was a benefit to professionals who had legitimate needs or reasons to be reached when they were out of the office. For the most part, though, Americans just did not need to be reachable every minute of every day. But the technology was there, so we used it. And its roots took hold and allowed us to feel good about ourselves because "now I can be reached at any time. I must be important!" And while feeling good about yourself is not a bad thing, allowing an object to define your perceived level of value and to bring you to a place where you believe *you really are that important* is a bad thing.

The cell phone also removed boundaries between public and private spaces. Prior to cell phones business took place for the most part outside the home, during work hours. Home was non-work time reserved for family, and for personal use. Once the cell phone became widely used it became yet another source of resentment and disconnection within the family. The more we use cell phones, the more we lose our ability to draw the line between work and family, and keep some time and space in our lives from being intruded upon by work. This furthers the decline of familial relationships and the opportunity for true downtime.

Another huge technological advancement that occurred in 1978 was the commercial availability of home video games. Intruders from outer space could now be destroyed in the comfort of people's living rooms, instead of only at arcade centers. The slow rise of widespread obsession with these new and exciting "must have one of my own"objects is not news to anyone, but their content and level of intensity has changed drastically over the years. It is the same path of degeneration movies, music, and television have taken between 1978 and now. Yes, games at the arcade centers cost money each time you played them, but arcades provided opportunities for in-person socialization between players. The home versions have the dangerous effect of keeping our little ones mesmerized for countless hours, never seeing the light of day at times, and choosing to forgo time with friends or playing outside in favor of staying in to "invade space." Another irony is that "invading space" has come to mean something completely different from its original meaning.

Again, no one saw what was coming with video games. We comfortably call games "virtual reality" and "fun." While most people — especially adults — recognize that games represent very little, if any, of the general population of true reality, the young, impressionable minds playing these games are not capable of drawing a clear and stable distinction between reality and fantasy, especially when the settings and characters look so real. So as they sit killing former humans with clubs, running over pregnant women to escape the police, role playing with characters that are idealized versions of real humans, or slaughtering opposition forces with reckless abandon, "reality"and "fun"are the words that are being indelibly tied to these behaviors. This evil content— like that in music, movies, and television — has been a slow, steady evolution over time. This is *exactly* how Socialcide works. Slow, destructive mind control behind the guise of *innocence, fun, normalcy,* and *convenience.*

The final invention I want to focus on in this chapter is not related to a device, but to a person. Louise Brown was born on July 25,1978, in England. Most people don't recognize her name, or know why she is famous. Through no fault of her own, her birth has changed the course of history and the lives of countless souls over the past thirty-five years. Not only did her birth potentially redefine the possibilities and characteristics of *family* as we knew it, but her "miracle birth"after conception in a test tube proved that Medical Science could now "play God" when it came to conception and fetal development. Babies could now be created for couples that God and Nature had determined could not conceive. Babies could also now be created for individuals.

Part-Time Parents

Today, many women and couples put off having children to fulfill their career or educational goals, or simply to have them later in life. It is not uncommon for women in their late forties to have children, but most of them are assisted with conception and pregnancy by modern medicine, not the will of God, or even of Nature.

Perhaps this is not such a bad thing. People have the right to choose to have children according to their own schedules. The hope is that because these mothers (and couples) are, theoretically, more mature, they will be more prepared emotionally, financially, and socially to take on the task of one of the most important and challenging jobs in the world:— raising a child.

Unfortunately, both young and later-in-life parents find themselves in employment, financial, or personal situations where they are not able to fully care for their own children, so they must hand over some or most of the childrearing responsibilities to hired help and become part-time parents. There are daycare centers and nannies available in abundance to aid the busiest of parents, neither of which seem fair to the true needs. Using either or both of these services also causes conscious and unconscious feelings of guilt to occur within the parents over not spending adequate time with their kids. This new way of childrearing is a breeding ground for budding narcissists to learn their craft.

Before I go on I want to make it clear there are many part-time parents who put tremendous and successful effort into raising their children during the time they do get to spend with them, and who compensate in healthy ways for the time they are not able to spend with them. These are not the people or situations to which I am referring here.

Part-time parents often overcompensate for their absence by doing much more for their children than necessary. Overcompensation can come in many different forms, purchasing more than the child needs without the child earning such gifts; over- praising the child; and bailing the child out of any trouble at school, with peers, neighbors, or police, and by minimizing or denying the child's responsibility.

Common sense dictates children who always get what they want, when they want it, who are constantly being told by parents how wonderful, unique, and special they are, and who never have to face responsibility or be held accountable for their wrongdoings or inappropriate behavior, will grow into adults expecting the same type of treatment from society, employers, mates, and life.

Children of overcompensating parents learn to manipulate through guilt. "Love" becomes defined in the child's mind as gifts, getting away with things, disappointment, and manipulation. When adults find themselves unable to love, it is often a direct result of the false love (through overcompensation) provided to them as children due to part-time or absent parents.

True full-time parents are certainly capable of raising narcissistic children, and part-time parents can raise wonderful, compassionate children. Full-time parents can overcompensate in many ways and protect children from experiencing the consequences of their actions.

Since Socialcide speaks more to the rise in narcissism since 1978, we must consider the new parenting methods and circumstances that have come into existence since then. Something is causing the spike in cases of narcissism, and the overcompensating, busy, later-in-life parent—those who may have resorted to artificial means to conceive—cannot be left off the list of possible contributing factors.

Thinning the Herd

In my last book, *Defeating Depression: The Calm and Sense Way to Find Happiness and Satisfaction*, I presented timeless remedies to help people feel better and enjoy living, all based upon the traits of empathy and compassion for others. For thousands of years, scientists and philosophers have found that helping others is a powerful way of helping ourselves. This was how we developed in tribes, groups, communities, neighborhoods, and eventually, *society*. These traits provided people with an evolutionary advantage, and assisted us in raising our children with the same beliefs as those who came before us.

As compassion and empathy diminish over time, so will human reproduction. We are falling into a dangerous area of not *needing* or *wanting* other people around us unless we can somehow benefit from them, or the benefit we derive from having them in our lives outweighs the cost. The age and institution of altruism has begun to turn in reverse. Now it's not the altruistic "What can I do for you?" as much as it is the narcissistic "What can you do for me?"

With relationships like this becoming more and more the norm, the human carnage created by narcissists ranges from the destruction of others' finances and self-esteem to their ultimate death and dismemberment, depending on the level of narcissist the into which person has come in contact.

The very popular AMC show *The Walking Dead* has millions of viewers. The show is about a group of survivors struggling to find safety and maintain their humanity after a zombie apocalypse has left their world mostly empty of healthy humans, but filled with "walkers" and "biters" that eat humans. Healthy humans who were attacked by the zombies, but who didn't die are infected with the zombie plague. These infected humans then join the ranks of the walking zombies. The zombies have no goal other than to kill and eat the remaining living humans. Structure has completely collapsed, and the primary surviving human characters rely solely on each other to remain alive and safe. They must repopulate the world, but can only do so by destroying the zombies and keeping enough uninfected humans alive. To destroy the zombies, they must either shoot them or cut off their heads and destroy their brain stems. The show is *very* graphic, yet very popular. In fact, the whole concept of an actual Zombie Apocalypse on the horizon has become quite popular in general. (The CDC is even using the idea to teach the importance of emergency preparedness.)

I see this show as a metaphor for what we are actually seeing and experiencing in society today, and Socialcide is the "zombie plague" of our reality. Every day there are people trying to survive by helping each other and warding off zombies [narcissists/evil ones]. In the show, within the living group, if one—just one personality—has intentions of going his or her own way, or in any way trying to go against the goals of the group as a whole, *huge interpersonal problems arise, and the success of the group suffers tremendously.* Isn't that what happens in families—in organizations, in communities—when members don't respect each other, follow the rules, or choose to engage in unhealthy activities?

In my mind, the final days of the world as we know it will somehow resemble this show, but demons will be the zombies, and those with God in their hearts will be those trying to survive until God ends the battle. Socialcide is creating a world of zombies now by creating more and more narcissistic ways and trends that make it so much easier for the total transformation of society in the future to occur. In other words, the more desensitized people become to self-satisfaction at the expense of others— conning, lying, stealing, manipulating, and even more horrific behaviors such as slaughtering, mutilating, and dismembering others—the easier the "transformation" will be.

This Millennial Generation is only the beginning. Their children will come, and then the children of their children, and so on, all along the way thinning down all that is good and cohesive among people until only a handful of the "uninfected" survive. And, you see, the devil is such the coward that he will want as few of God's living people to conquer as possible, so he will continually thin them out until he believes few enough are left and victory for him is guaranteed.

Chapter Five

Changing Times, Changing Minds

"There is so much potential out there in young people and they aren't getting the right
information or being encouraged in the right ways.
This is our duty as a society."
—Benjamin Carson

Years ago, families seemed to remain closer than today's families. New parents then had more resources for childcare or babysitting by family members. There is much more benefit to both child and parent in this situation versus daycare or non-family-member caregivers. In the family scenario there is a blood- or familial-connection between child and caregiver, so fewer feelings of guilt in parents are likely to arise. Also, with family caregivers the child is being cared for either one-on-one by a relative, or along with other young relatives, such as cousins, with whom the child is already familiar and comfortable. Children in this scenario more often feel truly loved, and even though they are spending time away from their parents, they are still "in the family," and are usually at a location that is familiar, and in which they also spend time with their parents. Everyone benefits from not having to send the child out of the extended family space for care.

The daycare scenario is the exact opposite situation. It has a "warehousing" effect. Children can easily get lost emotionally and socially in situations where people are watching large numbers of non-relatives and who, even one-on-one, do not have a familiar shared-experience relationship. That is not to say non-family childcare providers cannot form healthy emotional relationships with children in their care, or that children in non-family situations cannot feel cared for or respected. However, the situation is and feels different, for children and their young, fragile, tender personalities are left to be influenced

57

and molded by hired help. Children in hired care situations, regardless of how safe and loved they feel there, often feel "you keep sending me away from you, and I want and need you to be with me."

So while it is clear that the family-based scenarios are the better choice, that option has become both less available or practical, and less opted for when available these days. The reasons behind parents making these choices are varied (some absolutely necessary and noble, some not so much), but when looking at the *effect* of early life experiences upon children the reason parents made one choice or another is not the point. The result of the choice is. Non-family early childhood care cannot be how God planned for children to grow up, nor can it be the most beneficial way to raise a child. Yet it is standard procedure today.

Could this shuffling around of children, and the over compensating parenting I spoke about in the previous chapter also be contributing to the record numbers of childhood behavioral and emotional disorders we see today? These are major factors in the early developmental stages of children's lives, so we must consider them along with all other factors that have changed so drastically in the lives of children during the past thirty-five years. We must look at who is raising America's children, how they are doing it, and how this has changed from the way things were thirty-five years ago.

Spare Us the Children

The rise of childhood depression and other psychological disorders along with the increase in teenage suicide is proof, I believe, of the *suffocating factor.* And it's not just affecting children. Many adults are also trying their best to *breathe what good air is left* in the world. And these people are living among the evil; they struggle daily, trying to continue to do the right things, and find balance and peace in a world where they have quickly become the minority and are more and more in competition (not by choice) with the *infected ones.*

The *suffocating children* are those who are being parented fully and patiently, given rules and guidelines, held to standards, expected to be respectful of others, who make the effort and often get good grades, and are well- engaged in some form of spirituality or religion. These kids have an extremely hard time competing in a world so filled with "infected"children, who are left to their own devices and, in most cases, are lacking true love and parenting at home.

When a child feels no true love and safety at home, he or she will gravitate toward *something else* that will provide that sense of feeling safe and loved. This is where involvement in a religious community, faith, healthy family, and positive community are most important. But in the absence of these things children (and adults) must look elsewhere. This is *never* a good idea, but is occurring today with alarming frequency. The infection is spreading.

Suffocating children are the most susceptible to becoming depressed. That is not to say that the children without guidelines and full parenting do become depressed. They sometimes do. But the kids who do not attempt to cure their depression by turning to destructive behaviors or self-absorption are more often the ones being prescribed antidepressants, which can *add* to their depression, because they then feel even more out of place, confused, or inferior to their peers who are engaging in drug use, sex, bullying, and doing whatever they want at home or in school. These suffocating children are normally the ones who are *bullied* because they are different: they follow the rules and most likely do not partake in the wrong activities they see around them. If they *do,* and that information somehow *leaks out* through email, text messages, or even cell phone video, that child is in extreme danger of being the brunt of constant bullying and emotional brutality by his or her evil, infected peers.

Because of these potential dangers, and the challenging peer environment these days, children need nothing *less* than very strong parenting, guidance, and support. Actually, they also need no *more* than strong parenting, guidance, and support. They need an adult they can go to in times of need, one they are able to truly *trust.* It is extremely difficult to be an adolescent, and always has been. The explosion of hormones, body changes, emotional growing spurts, and social confusion are all standard events for teens. But as much as teenagers—and children, for that matter— will fight tooth and nail with parents over enforced rules and expectations, they absolutely must be told *no* at times.

I see many teachers in my practice. Most of them are early childhood or first- to-fourth grade educators. They can attest to the horrific changes they have seen over the years in children and their parents. They see children failing, uncaring, disrespectful, and detached from learning and following school rules. And these are five- to- ten-year- olds. The most oppositional children are the ones whose parents are unreachable, unavailable, and uninterested. When their child gets in some form of trouble they are quick to blame the school, the teacher, or the other child involved. You have to wonder what type of home life these children experience. Such situations both saddens and frustrates teachers, to say the least.

Those of us older than thirty-five may remember one or two troubled kids in our classrooms. There were just a few, but everyone in the school knew who they were, because their behavior was so different from everyone else's. Today it's the kids who are respectful, who behave appropriately and follow school rules that stand out, because there are so many troubled kids. Sadly, these good kids are losing out on a full education because of constant classroom disruptions the teacher deals with on a daily basis.

We "Old Timers" may also recall our parents' involvement with our grades, homework, and teachers. If we misbehaved at school, a note from the teacher was sent home with us, and we knew we were also in trouble at home! Even so, we delivered that note. Today, kids fail to deliver notes, report cards, and detention slips. So, to ensure that parents receive notifications, most schools send emails directly to parents. This practice increases the chances that parents receive information, but it only works if they have email addresses on file with the school, and if they bother to read their messages and respond. Sadly, there are many intentionally unavailable and unreachable parents. It is almost impossible for a school the kids who are respectful, who behave appropriately and follow school rules that stand out, because there are so many troubled kids. Sadly, these good kids are losing out on a full education because of constant classroom disruptions the teacher deals with on a daily basis to nurture and educate children appropriately without the support of parents or guardians. When parents are absent from the education equation, so are the children.

Children with behavioral issues, statistically, are found in disproportionately higher numbers in urban schools than in suburban, higher-income communities. This does not mean children from higher-income families are not demonstrating increased levels of self-absorbed behaviors, just different behaviors. Urban children act out more verbally and physically in the classroom, whereas suburban children do so more at home, or in the community. Statistically, it is in suburbia that more dangerous, experimental drug and alcohol abuse is present among younger children. It is also in suburbia where children exhibit more sexual acting out, and more defiance of restrictions that mom or dad attempt to enforce.

In urban areas children are less likely to have rules and guidance at home. Suburban parents attempt to enforce rules and regulations, but are quickly disregarded by children. In either case, it seems that if and when parents or any authority figures attempt to correct bad behaviors it is simply too little, too late. Psychologically speaking, the formative years from birth to age four are crucial, and serve as the springboard to future personality traits. If full-time, caring, connected, and concerned parenting is not present during those years the odds of unhealthy emotional, behavioral, or social issues is greatly increased. This is clearly a factor in why we are seeing so many children with these disorders today.

Socialcide also concerns itself with what children take in to their young minds today via media, movies, video games, and music, and how much.

Their young, impressionable minds get overloaded with images and scenarios of sex, violence, infidelity, drug use, excesses, death, and other issues that they are in no way equipped to adequately process or understand. They are unable to effectively—if at all—distinguish fantasy from reality.

I also work with many police officers in my practice. One particular client was recently discussing a terrible car crash to which he'd responded. The driver of one car, a woman, was hanging halfway out of her car, bleeding profusely. The other car was upside-down. A group of high school students was walking past the scene. Every one of them was filming the incident with their iPhones. Not one offered assistance, and not one listened to the officer's instructions to move away from the scene. My guess is that each one of those kids wanted to be the first to post this horror on their YouTube account—real life tragedy as entertainment. Wow! Nothing seems to shock, scare, or even trigger a compassionate response from the majority of the youth of today.

More recently, *The New York Daily News* (April 2, 2014) reported an incident involving fifty-two-year-old Jose Robles. Robles was walking to his job at a popular New York City delicatessen where he had been manager for more than twenty-five years. At 5:34 a.m., in front of the busy Port Authority Bus Terminal, he was attacked and mercilessly pummeled to the point of requiring hospitalization for two black and bloody eyes, and for reconstruction of his left arm, that had been broken in three places (including his elbow). His shoes were taken from him and thrown into the street. He yelled for help, but according to Robles, onlookers were too busy "watching, and they were having a good time filming."

Not one single, solitary soul tried to help this man. The attacker was not armed. Still no one tried to help. Robles had to call 911 on his own phone, *while being beaten.* So one must wonder, why? Why was filming this man's tragedy with a cell phone more important than physically trying to subdue the attacker, or at the very least simply dialing 911? This is a situation where not one, not two, but a large group of New Yorkers did absolutely nothing to aid a fellow human being. They could have, but they chose instead to film it. Who benefits here?

Fortunately, the attacker was caught. However, Robles was not as disgusted with him as he was with those who stood by and did nothing to help him. He explained, "I want people to have a little more conscience." Not only could I not agree more with that desire, I also firmly believe that Socialcide has been eroding compassion and empathy to the point of pure evil.

These specific situations are just examples of many sad but real signs of our younger *generation's* significant inability to sympathize over a potential life-and-death situation. Instead of exhibiting concern for another human being, the concern was for getting the video to post online.

Where is this lack of care and concern for others coming from? Compassion and empathy are learned—or not learned—at home, from our primary caregivers. In parenting, it's often just as much what we do as it is what we don't do. In other words, if you want your child to be compassionate, be compassionate yourself. If you are not, you cannot expect your child to be, and you certainly cannot be surprised or upset when he or she is not. And when children spend countless hours playing violent video games and watching violent movies and videos it really is unreasonable to expect them to be able to see an injured human being as something that's not going to just disappear or be fine when they turn away from the scene. After all, a young person might say, "All that blood and death—it's not real. The lady I just ran over and whose arm I severed—she's in the scene again once I turn the corner. There's not even blood on her dress anymore. It's not gross. It's not upsetting. It's just the way things go."

Socialcide is a well-greased machine, slowly but surely deteriorating love, value, and goodness from society, and no one is stopping it. When we don't monitor what our children are taking in, and we don't help them understand and properly process it all in a healthy way, we are essentially allowing evil to raise our children. Evil is everywhere, and comes in all forms, shapes, and sizes. "The devil doesn't come dressed in a red cape and pointy horns. He comes as everything you've ever wished for." (Tucker Max, an American author and public speaker who chronicles his drinking and sexual encounters on his website).

SECTION II

Taking Responsibility

Chapter Six

Is Virtual Reality?

"The new freedom of expression brought by the Internet goes far beyond politics. People relate to each other in new ways, posing questions about how we should respond to people when all that we know about them is what we have learned through a medium that permits all kinds of anonymity and deception."
—Peter Singer

When children don't receive the parental training they need to adequately socialize, and their brains fill up with violence—evil and sexual images they are not equipped to understand—and they live in fantasy worlds of video games and computer games for hours on end, and then they are placed in real-life social environments, they act out. Why? Because of a fear of, or inability to properly relate to, other real-life people!

Many of today's children are more comfortable in their own worlds or minds than they are in the real world, and they have no idea how to handle real-world situations. Other people are "not real" enough to children today because today's children have so little much less contact with peers and adults compared to children in the past.

It has practically become a daily occurrence to hear of another horrific slaying or rape—high school shootings, college shootings, teenagers killing their teachers, parents, or each other, or brutally gang-raping an intoxicated peer and then "advertising" their brutality on some form of social media forum. Crimes like these are being reported with alarming frequency. We can only wonder what goes through the minds of such disturbed personalities. Many—if not most—of this *new breed* of criminals are teenagers.

The media is quick to stream these tragic stories into our homes via television, websites, and newspapers; and then, *bang!*— all of a sudden there is instant celebrity for the perpetrator. It has often been said, "Bad publicity is better than no publicity," and these beasts get it in full. Could that be a part of the driving force behind their madness?

If you consider how we now live in a society where anyone can become famous overnight for positive achievements, as well as heinous crimes, some room must be left to consider the "fame factor" as at least partial motivation for bloody, sociopathic acts, especially since we are a society currently suffering an epidemic of social sickness and disease.

When we allow machines (computers, video games, and television)to raise our children, what can we reasonably expect them to behave more like, people, or machines? Can we reasonably expect them to care about others, or reach out and help them?

From what I've explained so far, it isn't difficult to conclude that the answer to those questions is that they are much more likely to behave like machines, and it's not reasonable to expect them to care about or reach out to help others. To illustrate the reality of these conclusions, let's look at a case of mass murder which took place in Farmville, Virginia. (It is ironic that it occurred in Farmville, the name of a very popular on-line video game.)

In 2009, Richard McCroskey was a twenty-year-old who lived in California. He was isolative, and a huge fan of what is called horror core, a fairly new type of hip-hop music that focuses on themes such as suicide, murder, Satanism, self-harm, rape, torture, cannibalism, and the supernatural. This music that attracts the self-proclaimed "rejects from the rejected." Sharing a love of this genre of music was teenager Emma Niederbrock, from of Farmville, Virginia. McCroskey (who went by the online name *Syko Sam*) met and Emma (whose online name was *Rag Doll*) met online through a social network called Myspace, and the pair discovered their mutual love of *horrorcore* music.

After almost a year of professing their "love" for each other on Myspace, the two made plans to attend a horror core concert together in Michigan.

Emma's divorced parents (Dr. Debra S. Kelley and pastor Mark Niederbrock) had reservations about their sixteen year-old daughter going to a concert with a twenty-year-old boy they had never met, especially so far away from their home in Virginia. After consideration, an arrangement was made that they could attend the concert, but Emma's mother and father would drive them there and chaperone the date.

Online, McCroskey came across as a stable, confident, sociable, and normal guy. When he arrived at the Virginia airport to meet Emma in person for the first time, after all their online communicating, both Emma and her eighteen-year-old friend Melanie Wells, were there to greet him. Both girls were unimpressed, especially Melanie. Melanie's initial impression of McCroskey was that he was strange, weird, and not right. McCroskey was in Virginia to ride to the concert with Emma, Melanie, two other friends, and Emma's parents Debra and Mark, then to spend a week with the two young girls at Debra's home.

According to reports, the ride to Michigan should have raised red flags about McCroskey for everyone. He was non-communicative, disconnected, unsociable, and extremely uncomfortable to be with. At the concert, his behavior became even worse. He did not talk to others there, seemed aloof, uncomfortable, and stood at the perimeter of the crowd while Emma and Melanie were enjoying the whole show right in front of the stage. Where had "Mr. Wonderful Online"gone?

Things did not go right for anyone involved. Emma was obviously uninterested in McCroskey and he was obviously beyond deficient in real social skills. Online he could be the *big man,* say the right things, and make himself appear so super, but when it came down to reality (meaning *real people, real places, real conversation, and socialization*), he couldn't do it. That comfort and confidence he had in the virtual world just did not exist in the real world. And now he had another week to deal with! How was he going to get through *that?*

Not well at all. To make this horrific story short, McCroskey was convicted of brutally murdering Emma, Melanie, Debra, and Mark. McCroskey was actually living with the four dead people for a few days before he headed to the airport to go back to California. In route, he wrecked the car he'd stolen from the murdered Mr. Niederbrock, was issued a summons for driving without a license, and was taken the rest of the way to the airport by a truck driver who said McCroskey "smelled like death."

The police finally apprehended McCroskey at the airport baggage claim area where he was sleeping and waiting for a flight back to California. He pleaded guilty to the four murders, and beat avoided the death penalty by offering up exactly how he bludgeoned these four victims to death—three of them while they slept—with an eight-pound wood-splitting axe. He received a sentence of life in prison with no chance of parole.

You see, Socialcide thrives on creating false confidence and identities online for individuals who have not learned or developed the real skills needed to actually be a person in the real world. This monster, McCroskey, took a huge risk by actually flying from California to Virginia to meet his love, but when push came to shove and reality set in, he just couldn't handle it, because it was simply *too real* for him to deal with.

Is this an excuse for him? Absolutely not! Four innocent people died because this monster took a risk, leaving his comfort zone of online, virtual living, to try life in the real world. In his mind, his reality did not include real people; he was not a "real person," but an online entity who never built learned real-world social skills, and most likely had very little, if any, ability to socialize. My belief is that upon stepping into the real world it was impossible for him to connect, converse, and be *real*, so he lost it. He knew he had a week of time to be with *real people*, which meant talking, relating, and communicating, but he simply broke down, because his emotions could not handle it.

I do not think he went to Farmville intending to kill, but he did so because, for him, it killing the four was easier than being a real person. This psychopath bit off far more than he could chew by flying three thousand miles, and instead of figuring out a way to cut the trip short and get back home, killing those he was staying with became the easier option than having to actually communicate.

This tragedy is exactly why we should be making sure our children socialize "actually" and not "virtually" via text messaging, instant messaging, using social media websites, and emailing. They are not reality! Nothing can replace physical contact and in-person communication with other people. That is why and how we were made, and electronics cannot, and will never, replace that.

We cannot hide behind computers and hope to be successful in the world. When your reality is shaped and created in isolation by typing words, emotions, and ideas into a computer, instead of in real-life situations, there is nothing real about us.

We were not created to develop in cyberspace, but in *true space*. When McCroskey flew out of his comfort zone to actually meet *live and in person* the *love of his life*, his abilities to cope, communicate, interact, and be in a real social situation did not exist. He crumbled into a million broken megabytes of nothingness. His sister Sarah has described him as a "meek and kind person who never fought back when picked on and wouldn't do anything unless provoked" (quoted in NBCBayArea.com, September 22,2009). The authorities who went to the home where McCroskey killed four people also described him as "calm and never acting strange or suspicious in manner"(NBCBayArea.com, September 22, 2009). The authorities who went to the home where McCroskey killed four people also described him as "calm and never acting strange or suspicious in manner"(NBCBayArea.com, September 22, 2009).

Chances are he did not give any indication of being the "Syko Sam" he purported to be online. That, perhaps, is the scariest fact about individuals who harbor such broken and defective socialization and empathy skills, due to a deprived history of developing real-life relationships. McCroskey claimed to be a rapper, and did indeed rap about killing people. Further investigation found him to be a devout Satan worshiper. His website showed him laughing at a Marine's grave site, turning a cross upside down, then rapping about this event of defiling a hero's grave.

Where were McCroskey's parents? Did they look for a source to blame for his "different" behavior? We don't know. However, many children today are tragically left to create their own realties when parents do not parent, do not intervene, encourage, support, and simply get involved in the lives of their children.

As the culture and institution of family continues to crumble, with parents who are less and less available to their children emotionally, socially, and morally, children are simply not gaining the necessary skills and guidance they need to be fully-developed, healthy individuals. With their parents nowhere to be found in many ways, they will seek someone, something, or somewhere to fit in and to give them some sort of love and acceptance, and help them feel they have a purpose of some sort.

These lost children, void of any moral foundation at home, are prime targets for gang-inclusion, childhood prostitution, drug addiction, and even isolative self-deprivation as they seek belonging in the darkest recesses of Internet enticement. The places they end up in their search include pedophilia, murderous intentions, and any kind of "how to" information you can imagine that fosters sickness, evil, hatred, and destruction in their seeking minds; all the while patting them on the back as if to say, *"There, there! We understand you! We are just like you!"* These are words and reassurances that are extremely important to adolescents in their need to truly be *understood.*

Teenagers are vulnerable; we all know that. This fact adds even more weight to the reason we are seeing such increases in teenage pregnancies and suicides today. With people becoming parents when they themselves did not receive adequate parenting, the fortification of morality and what is *right versus what is wrong* weakens more and more with each new generation.

Have we become a society that finds parenting as laborious as stopping our vehicles to pay a toll, or getting off the couch to change a channel on the television set? "Isn't there an App for that somewhere?" It appears that way. Then, when we see how sick these children can be or become as young adults, we wonder how this can be happening. In my field, or at least in my knowledge of human behavior and psychology, the first question that comes to mind is always: "Where were the parents?"

Chapter Seven

Pills Do Not Parent

"Attention-deficit disorders seem to abound in modern society,
and we don't know the cause."
—Marilyn vos Savant

The drastic increase in what we commonly call Attention Deficit Disorder (ADD), Attention Deficit Hyperactivity Disorder (ADHD), Asperger's Syndrome, Autism, and Depression should be a call to attention regarding the welfare of children today. Unlike any other time in history, these disorders are plaguing them in record numbers, and have been on the rise since 1978. Surprised? Statistics don't lie.

So what has been America's response to this growing tragedy? Medications. I remember a professor in one of my college classes speaking about headaches. He made the point that aspirin fools the brain into believing the pain is gone when it really isn't. The same is true for any of the pain pills millions are addicted to today, such as OxyContin and Percocet. They do not cure, solve, or even address the problem. They *only cover it up*. The solution of choice to any problem today is often a quick-fix in the form of a pill that Americans have come to rely on and believe in rather than identifying and treating the true issue. We see this same quick-fix thought process in part-time parents who overcompensate for their absence from parenting. To illustrate, we see parents who are not around the child because they are busy—working, traveling, or otherwise preoccupied. The child misses the parents. The parents return with gifts, praise, and over-dramatized attention. The child feels happy again. Then off go the parents once more. Quick fix, problem repeats. Each time it repeats, the long-term damage increases. After a few years of this cycle, the child has learned that love is superficial and material, that promises are not something you can believe in, trust is shaky at best, and there really isn't anything stable in life. Quick-fix, overcompensating parenting fools a child's brain and doesn't allow it the chance to develop in a healthy and positive way.

Let's take this a step further. When children behave in a way we don't like and can't control, instead of spending time with them and working with them to address the real issues, we look for a doctor who will prescribe them a drug to slow them down, calm them, dull their senses, and ultimately send them deeper into their own minds. We look for something to cover up the problem, instead of addressing it.

Sometimes, though, before demanding before a prescription, parents, push for a diagnosis. With a diagnosis, not only can parents get medications to address the issues;, they can also get a label to hide behind. They can clear their consciences of any responsibility for their child's bad behavior, and can blame a disorder. In the process, they are teaching their children that they have no responsibility in this either. Insidious, isn't it?

Most children diagnosed with ADD or ADHD are extremely difficult to teach. Their attention spans are nearly nonexistent in a classroom. They often cannot focus long enough to read a chapter in a book. However, most of these children can sit fixated on a video game for hours on end. Something is wrong with this picture!

Asperger's-afflicted children demonstrate social malfunctioning with other people. So do children who spend far too much time in virtual realities. They lack candor and couth in relationships, and are prone to make inappropriate responses to others without regard to proper etiquette. So do children who have not been taught proper social behaviors and skills, or have not spent much time practicing them. In the case of true Asperger's diagnoses Asperger's diagnoses, this is not due to any lack of intelligence or intent, but lack of socialization skills and know-how because of an *internal dysfunction*. These people live lonely lives because others are turned off by their comments and communications. They lack that filter needed to express a need or thought to another person without sounding weird or inappropriate. So do children who have not been properly socialized.

Asperger's Syndrome is a bizarre disorder, and relatively new. It was officially made a diagnosis in Europe in 1992, then in the United States in 1994. Originally termed "Autistic Psychopathy" by Hans Asperger in 1942, it received little attention for many years, for two reasons. First, all of Dr. Asperger's research on Autistic Psychopathy was written in German and never translated. Second, the disorder did not become as prevalent until the late 1980s. Again, we can presume it was becoming more present in children born from 1978 and on. This is no coincidence, an is further proof of Socialcide.

As this book was being written, a new report was released by the Centers for Disease Control and Prevention (March 2014) indicating that one in sixty- eight children has an Autism Spectrum Disorder, up thirty percent 30% from 2012. That is a thirty percent 30% increase in just two years! We have to question why and where these numbers are coming from. As if parents were not concerned enough about their children being afflicted with Autism or Asperger's Syndrome, these rapidly increasing odds for such a diagnosis would lead any parent who is worried about this to worry even more.

Several reasons for this staggering increase have been put forth by both experts in the field and doctors who study and treat Autism Spectrum Disorders (ASD). One speaks of the increased awareness of ASD, and with increased awareness comes an increase in diagnoses. We know that many people who are truly afflicted with an ASD suffer from self-injurious behaviors, limited language skills, intellectual disabilities, and are non-verbal. Since there are no accepted medical tests to clearly identify ASD, and the criteria for diagnosis have become far more encompassing (now including more children with only behavioral symptoms and no intellectual disabilities), there are children being diagnosed with ASD today who may have been diagnosed with a different disorder in the past, or with no disorder at all. So why such diagnoses now? What is causing this epidemic? Is it real?

Autism Spectrum Disorders are real. There is validity in many ASD diagnoses. There are many truly good, full-time parents who have children afflicted with ASD. It is *not* these families that to which I which I refer to with regard to Socialcide. However, in broadening the criteria, ASD is becoming a most unfortunate catch-all diagnosis for many children who do not truly have the disorders, but who exhibit social and behavioral issues that appear similar to those associated with ASD.

With a handy diagnosis available, instead of looking at social factors as cause for a child's issues, and looking to parents to be responsible for helping to resolve them, the child's behaviors can now be blamed on ASD, and the parents can tell themselves they didn't cause it, and they can't help to fix it. This is bad detrimental, not only for those children who are misdiagnosed with an ASD, and who will now not be helped in a way that can truly give them assistance, but also for those families who are dealing with true ASD diagnoses, in that it drains already sparse resources, and complicates much-needed research. It also creates a situation where society begins to doubt *all* ASD diagnoses, and creates an environment where families experience backward progress in recognition, acceptance, and respect from society for what they are experiencing. It is unfair in many ways to clump problematic children and adults into an emotionally ill category when their behaviors are not the result of any disorders, but exist simply because they are badly behaving people.

So as Socialcide progresses, diagnoses of mental health disorders across the board—not just those of ASD—are skyrocketing. The new criteria for diagnosing ASD broaden the scope to include children not actually suffering from those specific problems, but simply from social and behavioral abnormalities. It is the latter to whom I refer with regard to parenting and resulting behaviors. In no way do I mean to discredit or diminish true cases of ASD, or to lay blame on parents of children suffering with true Autism Spectrum Disorders. My intention is solely to point out another source of blame or excuses for radically changing behaviors in presumably normal children. To use a legitimate diagnosis as an excuse for bad behavior, regardless of the reason, is criminal. To give a faulty diagnosis, or write a prescription for drugs in lieu of actually putting time and energy into working with our children, is too.

And Socialcide continues to widen its path of devastation as Americans turn to drugs and diagnoses to cover up their problems.

Chapter Eight
Mental Manipulation

"Believe only half of what you see, and nothing of what you hear."
—Benjamin Franklin

The method to any narcissist's madness lies in his or her ability to manipulate other people's thinking. The first stages of mind control or manipulation rely on the "sale." Hitler sold the Germans and most of the world on his Nazi Party as the greatest savior to the German people ever to come along. In fact, *Time* Magazine honored him as "Man of the Year" in 1938, due to the success he had in turning around the German economy and morale after Germany's defeat in World War I. In the beginning, the German people fell in love with their Führer and, once infatuated, believed he could do no wrong.

James Warren "Jim" Jones buoyed himself to a similar position. Jones was an acclaimed preacher in the United States for many years, serving the poorer, less fortunate minorities at a time when few white men did such a thing. Once he captivated his targets with promises of salvation, protection, and a better, more peaceful world, the mesmerized flock willingly followed their leader to Guyana on the northern coast of South America, where he created a settlement and named it Jonestown. This place was unfamiliar to many of them, yet they followed him far away from family and friends into a jungle of uncertainty, and they fully trusted Jones would keep them safe and lead the way to peace and happiness.

Following the typical narcissistic pattern, once Hitler and Jones had their prey exactly where they wanted them, the next step was to strip away from them all sense of self, and any means of defending themselves. The narcissist's goal is to make victims so completely dependent upon him or her that no matter what the narcissist says, does, or wants, the victims will either comply, or they will suffer and quite possibly die.

It did not take long for some Germans and some of the Jonestown flock to realize what was truly going on in their individual situations. Narcissists' true colors eventually come through; however, by that time they have usually stripped away so much of their victims' ability to defect that defection is impossible. Fear of punishment was instilled deeply in them, and perhaps examples were made of those who tried to break away.

When victims are completely under control, the narcissist is free to use them for whatever self-serving sickness comes to mind: power, sex, slave labor, war, money, or any other form of personal gain you can imagine. The purposes are never for anyone's needs other than their own. If and when the narcissist is through with what a victim can provide to them, the relationship ends, either by death or abandonment. We all know how Hitler's Third Reich ended.

The Jonestown mass suicide (in 1978), by cyanide-laced Kool-Aid poisoning, was the largest, intentional, single-event loss of American life until the September 11, 2001 attacks. Both "saviors" died a coward's death, and thousands of innocent people died because of them.

I present these extreme examples of narcissists because I often wonder if they were somehow "test runs" for Socialcide. Hitler, Napoleon, and Nero were among many who were thought to be representations of the Antichrist we read of in the Bible's Book of Revelation. I believe Jones to be characteristic of such evil masked in salvation as well. With this knowledge of history, it's easy to lull ourselves into a false sense of security, based on a belief that society would recognize and put a stop to anyone who would try such things again. However, it's not necessarily the big monsters that are the most dangerous. Among us today are many, many little Neros, Joneses, and the like. Perhaps not all are murderers, but all are killers of individuals' freedoms and sense of self-worth.

These are the narcissists many people are affected by in daily life and relationships. Their brand of evil may not be lethal, but they effortlessly have the ability to destroy the lives of the many innocent victims who drink their proverbial Kool-Aid. There are thousands of them, and they are working their way through society as we speak, leaving trails of victims everywhere.

Propaganda

The Millennials (the Me, Me, Me Generation) are the first generation to have instant access to news from around the world, twenty-four hours a day, seven days a week. As such, there is a constantly available stream of graphic videos of wars, executions, mass slayings, and destruction via the Internet and television. The more exposed we become to such horrific sights, the more desensitized to them we become (even if it horrifies us as we watch it), and the less it affects us over time. Of all the sources of evil manipulation, the media is most likely the largest, since it can get to everyone any time of the day or night.

In fact, Americans are hungry for bad news. Murders, rapes, kidnappings, child abuse, and big crime stories are big moneymakers. Television channels have been created solely to report it all, every step of the way. We love to hear just how sick some people are, and the words "narcissist," "sociopath," and "psychopath" are as common on these shows as the word "is" is! Still, nothing is being done *socially* to address these tragedies, or remedy the problem. These days it seems we prefer to watch, and blame, and theorize, and gossip.

Consider North Korea today. North Koreans are constantly shown news of how evil America and Americans are, of how America continues to attack them, and of how they are winning by conquering us all the time. None of this is true. It is all propaganda; however, the government of North Korea pumps this into the minds of its people regularly, and they believe it to be true. Propaganda is a form of brainwashing that works very well.

In relationships, narcissists create their own propaganda, in order to win over their victims by promising many things over and over again, or degrading their loved one consistently, until the victims begin to wonder if the perpetrator is right. Anything we experience through our senses repeatedly will eventually become what we believe to be true. Perfect propaganda, if I may, satisfies three primary human senses: sight, sound, and emotion. It gets into our brains through the things we hear, see, and feel, whether we realize it or not. The media caters to all three of these twenty-four hours a day, seven days a week.

Consider this new media coverage and availability when looking at the Me, Me, Me Generation and their narcissistic trends and behaviors. The ultra-graphic, violent video games that are being played by children are simply precursors to what they will see and experience on the news. When a young brain (or any brain, for that matter) is "programmed" properly, nothing comes as a shock or surprise. The violence children experience (through sight, sound, and emotion), and are often the perpetrators of in the virtual reality of these video games, is similar to the *real* violence they experience through the news. Seeing the same types of violence in both virtual reality and actual reality makes it difficult to distinguish between the two. The lines are blurred, and which makes it so much easier for violent behavior against real humans to be thought and felt to be as harmless as violent behavior in video games. As a result, these children will most likely be the devil's elite warriors.

Mass killers have been *glamorized* to some extent via the media. Additionally, many people are fascinated by serial killers and serial rapists. Some evil-minded people find them to be heroic, and idolize them for what they have done. Evil breeds more evil. The more the media provides us with the names and deeds of criminals, the more those criminals feed off their stardom. The more they become household names, the more their evil continues to permeate the minds and hearts of the public. Is the media making heroes out of evil-minded killers?

I personally know of a few authors and criminal profilers who, specifically to *reduce* the glamorization of evil, will not appear on any news shows to comment on a criminal if that criminal's name is mentioned on the show. I believe that mass killings would at least be reduced if media ceased the publicizing of such evil behavior. If potential killers knew they would not be identified to the public, or known for what they did—and therefore, would not become instant celebrities—part of the allure of committing the crime would be gone, and maybe—just maybe—the crime would not be committed.

Historically, the media has advertised names of killers ad nauseam, making them household names.

With *every* name associated with evil deeds there is a certain presence of narcissism, psychopathic, or sociopathic behavior. None of these criminals have shown a shred of remorse, regret, or any sign of feeling about those they have destroyed because they "wanted to," or even more frightening, because they "had to." Even when they do *fake it,* in an attempt to show some compassion and understanding, they come across as insincere. Their words do not match their emotions or facial expressions.

Narcissists lack the ability to create and maintain interpersonal relationships. The ability to do this is a human trait that cannot be *taught, fixed, or gained* with any amount of psychotherapy, psychotropic medications, or medical technology. Much like pedophilia, where no cure exists, there is no fix for narcissism. This is, perhaps, what makes narcissists so dangerous, toxic, and destructive to others. From the most evil (serial killers, pedophiles, kidnappers, and rapists) to the most annoying (some celebrities, politicians, con artists, and adulterers), all narcissists leave a trail of torment, tragedy, broken hearts, and miserable despair in their tracks, and will never think twice about it.

Get Off the Couch!

Children today have little fear of any consequences for bad, defiant, or oppositional behaviors, and the variety and severity of what children are getting themselves into these days doesn't seem to show any signs of slowing down. Bullying, sexual antics, drug use, disrespect for authority, self-indulgence, and plain old meanness are quickly becoming the norm, and little, if anything, is being done to correct it.

The *grooming* of children early in life to be bad, or to love only themselves, has been in progress since 1978. The Evil that is behind this diabolical plan has learned well that the way to create and sustain a corrupted mind is to begin training it beginning in childhood. Much like the Hitler Youth program that instilled Hitler's evil and narcissistic ways into the youngest of boys and girls in Nazi Germany, Evil is instilling its ways into the youth of America when they are very young.

During the *Me Generation* (those born between roughly 1946 and 1964— the Baby Boomers) and part of *Generation X* (those born between roughly 1965 and 1979) which preceded the current *Me, Me, Me Generation* (those born between roughly 1980 and 2000), a strong emphasis was placed on literature, music, movies, therapy, and various grass-roots organizations, in an effort to help people begin to be self-aware and to "love themselves" more. It was a time of self-exploration, and openness to new ideas and societal changes that were meant to make people and the world around them a better place. The goal of the Me Generation was to build character, and reduce stuffy conservatism layered in guilt over wanting to be different and unique in a world that was stagnating in old ways that needed sprucing up.

The Me Generation tended to (and still does) unite into like-minded movements and for causes they believed were worth protesting for or against, such as ending the Vietnam War, free love, and peaceful co- existence. In contrast, the Me, Me, Me Generation stands for no social or like-minded movements other than their own self-gratification. Yes, there are some in this generation who do not fit the "Me, Me, Me"label. Sadly, though, they are the minority of this generation, and do not attract nearly the amount of attention as those who do fit the label.

The result is that Americans are more and more stagnant, uncaring, and unwilling to really get up and do something, when it comes to anything the governments of the world are up to these days. We have become so self-consumed and comfortable behind the latest technology that common bonds of even *friendships,* let alone social movements, are getting harder and harder to find. We just do not seem to care about much except ourselves. It's all about, "Me, Me, Me."

How convenient it is, then, for the evil forces of Socialcide to slip into our filled with an ever-increasing number of brain-dead, self-medicating, inactive citizens country, and infiltrate and brainwash the masses into believing—and eventually acting on—the idea that nothing matters more than what they want for themselves.

The good news, though, is there are still many of us left. We are the ones who remember how things used to be—how *people* used to be, —who see this destruction every day and simply cannot believe our eyes, who see the evil taking over our country, our society, our loved ones. And we are the ones who can and must take action—get off the couch, as it were— because Evil is winning, and complete Socialcide appears inevitable, unless drastic changes are made.

So what must be done to derail this narcissistic, evil plan? What can we do? How can we stop the climbing percentage from reaching one hundred?

Chapter Nine

It's Only a Game

"The saddest aspect of life right now is that science
gathers knowledge faster than society gathers wisdom."
—Isaac Asimov

At the time of this writing, there are more and more studies coming out that support the reality of Socialcide's presence and damaging power. Working as a psychotherapist, I have the opportunity to actually see this first-hand, and to deal directly with children, adolescents, and their parents on many of the issues pointed out in the aforementioned studies. The rise in frequency and necessity of adolescent treatment is astonishing to me; throughout the twenty or so years of my career, I have never seen anything like it. The frequency and intensity of children's defiance against their parents, schools, and society is truly chilling, and sometimes there is no amount or type of therapy that can make enough difference to break through the psyche behind the disturbing behavior. These are the children I worry about most, because they have the potential to become very dangerous to others.

When exploring causes of teenage isolation, defiance, and, in some cases, acts of murder, one factor that keeps coming up, and seems to be a clear common denominator, is a significant amount of time spent playing violent video games.

Without advertising its name, the newest edition of one of the most popular of these demonic games recently came out. Not one week after its release, the news reported the shooting of a grandmother by her eight-year-old grandson following his extended playing of this particular game. When this child was brought to court, the judge said he was"too young to understand the law and what he had done." Why in the world then was he allowed to play a game that has an M (Mature) rating, a game in which players kill policemen and prostitutes in order to get the victory the player wants? Besides being extremely heinous and violent, the objective of the game sounds very narcissistic to me.

Acts of bullying, sexual coercion, murder, and various other forms of deviant behavior *by children* are continually increasing in frequency. This is not because children   are   missing breakfast!   It is because they are being brainwashed by the media, video games, computers, and technology, and are being raised by parents who, if they are approximately thirty-five years old or younger, are also affected by Socialcide. As much as I dislike the term "perfect storm,"it is the best way to describe how Satan has coordinated all the *toys and necessities* we have today to be used in his effort to corrupt *goodness and Godliness* in society. Younger generations of parents have been desensitized to all the negative and damaging effects of these modern inventions, because they grew up with their scaled-down versions. Now, these toys have grown into their full-fledged *monster sizes,* and are quietly slipping by parents and infecting their children.

The role of the breakdown of the family cannot be overstated in these and *all* cases of Socialcide. Parenting is being replaced by artificial and technological means. I am not saying parents are aware that this is even happening. I am saying parents are faced more and more with extremely challenging children, who care for little, do less, expect more, and form more of their relationships via technological means instead of in person. When we communicate through technology, we are *not* engaged in *real life,* period. When we find difficulty in distinguishing *fact* from *fantasy,* we live only in our own minds, and not in the real world. This *is exactly* what we are facing today, and it is suffocating society and jeopardizing its existence.

So there is no misunderstanding, let me assure you, my readers, that not *all* children are going to rape or murder people, and not *all* children who play violent video games, are exposed to pornography, and who live in a less than ideal home are going to become sexual predators or serial killers. The ones who do are those who are Satan's easiest prey, and are the weakest spiritually and emotionally. Those narcissists are more visible, and are not the most skilled in the area of social graces. Perhaps that is exactly what makes them such easy targets for evil to gain a foothold in them so early in life, and perhaps that only adds to their demented, reasonless rage against others as time goes on.

These children are the emotionally and spiritually struggling (wholly different from the suffocating children who are struggling in other ways). These are the children who feel so left out, *so* different, and so misunderstood by their peers and society that they turn their anger into justified (in their minds) reasons for what they do to innocent people. The truth is, their intensely negative, self-induced beliefs about themselves do not reflect their actual reality. The problem is that their inability to find their place in the world, and their perception of such, is distorted, due to a lack of role models and strong parenting, and Satan's influence assuring them they are right and "no one wants them." Before the naysayers begin their ranting about how violent video games have nothing to do with psychopathic, sociopathic, and violent behaviors such as mass murders, consider this: *Before the inception of these brain-washing devices there were no reports of children going on murderous rampages.* It is far more than just a cause-and-effect problem though. Addiction to video games is an essential component of Socialcide's goal to manipulate youngsters into becoming self-absorbed monsters. It works insidiously, by blurring all lines between fact and fantasy, which is easy to do with children. Why? Because they have young, impressionable minds not yet fortified with a solid structure of what's right and what's wrong, compassion, and the true sanctity of human life, and they have brains that are not yet physically fully developed.

Sure, when we Baby Boomers were children we watched Wile E. Coyote's constant attempts to blow up the Road Runner end in not only failure, but in violent and unplanned self-destruction. We watched Heckle and Jeckle, Tom and Jerry, and Popeye and Bluto (or Brutus, depending on which year the episode was made) pulverize each other. But at the end of the cartoons all was back in place. We were not doing the killing, the characters did not look human, and we were not rewarded with extra points or privileges, other than a laugh or two at the end of the show

We also did not spend countless hours at a time consuming the cartoons. First, cartoons were not available at just any hour on a number of channels every day. We also had parents who set limits. We had lives, and we had other interests (such as playing outside) away from the screen. Over time, however, the   content   of cartoons and, of course, the   sickness of video games, intensified and began to steal children's brains away from reality. During this same time, parents began relying on electronic entertainment more and more to "parent" for them under the guise of keeping their kids "safe at home" from the media's increased propaganda of Boogey Men around every corner, and also to keep the kids busy so they wouldn't get bored.

I am sure those folks who are pro-violent-video-games are still unconvinced of the games' manipulative, destructive intentions. For those who doubt, I offer some supporting evidence from cases and people you may or may not have heard about.

Evan Ramsey was arrested in 1997 after he snuck a twelve-gauge shotgun into his high school in Bethel, Alaska and gunned down a fellow student and the principal. He also wounded two others in his sociopathic rage. In a 2007 interview from Spring Creek Correctional Center with Anderson Cooper, Ramsey stated that video games had warped his sense of reality. He further said, "I did not understand that if I pull out a gun and shoot you, there's a good chance you're not getting back up." Ramsey was addicted to a game called *Doom,* and also said, "You shoot a guy in *Doom* and he gets back up. You have got to shoot the things in *Doom* eight or nine times before it dies [sic]." Ramsey was a high school student, an adolescent who should have known better, and should have understood that *real guns kill real people,* but all the time he spent saturating his mind with the violent action of the video game replaced that knowledge with a fatal false reality.

Since Ramsey's rampage of violence, there have been many other killers, including Columbine psychopaths Eric Harris and Dylan Klebold, and

Norwegian mass killer Anders Breivik, who obsessed over violent video games prior to committing their horrific crimes. Socialcide has made certain that video games get only more violent and more realistic, as does their power to blur the lines of reality and fantasy in the minds of isolated, obsessed players.

Bruce Bartholow, an associate professor of psychology at the University of Missouri, studied this issue and said, "More than any other mode of media, these video games encourage active participation in violence. From a psychological perspective, video games are excellent teaching tools, because they reward players for engaging in certain types of behavior. Unfortunately, in many popular video games, the behavior is violence." It makes me wonder if parents even bother to see *for themselves* what their children are doing "safe and sound" from the Boogey Man in the park. Folks, the Boogey Man is in *your home!*

Still unconvinced? There is more; much more. In 1999, twelve students and a teacher were slain, and another twenty-four were injured, by Eric Harris and Dylan Klebold during the infamous Columbine, Colorado massacre. Harris and Klebold were reportedly obsessed with *Doom* as well. Then, there was twenty-three-year-old Seung-Hui Cho, who killed thirty-two people and wounded seventeen others at Virginia Tech University in 2007. According to the Washington Post, Cho was a big player of violent video games, especially one called *Counterstrike*.

Here are three more young psychopaths who, according to a report by Fox News (September 9, 2013), were all active players obsessed with violent video games: James Eagan Holmes, who killed twelve people in an Aurora, Colorado movie theater in 2012; Jared Lee Loughner, who killed six and injured thirteen, including U.S. Congressional Representative Gabby Giffords, in a 2011 Arizona shooting; and Breivik, who killed seventy-seven people in Oslo and Utøya, Norway, also in 2011. This report further stated that Breivik said he "actually used his video game, *'Call of Duty'* to train for mass murder," according to Dr. Paul Weigle, a child and adolescent psychiatrist at the Joshua Center in Enfield, Connecticut. Weigle reported that Breivik "called it training simulation." Weigle also pointed out that there were reports that Adam Lanza, the twenty-year-old responsible for the massacre of twenty children and six adults at Sandy Hook Elementary School in Newtown, Connecticut in 2012, "saw Breivik as a rival, and was also engaged in shooting games, and even the same one."

We can only imagine what is going on inside teenagers' minds as they sit isolated in their cold, dark rooms, obsessing over the destruction they can realistically cause by pushing buttons, hearing explosions and the sound of ripping flesh with each pull of the virtual trigger.

With the terrifying screams from their virtual victims, what power must they mistakenly believe—in the recesses of their impressionable, —that they have? At what point does the false power and fantasy of control take over any sense of reality and consequence? Do they even care about being caught once the deed is carried out? Socialcide does not care at all, and does not foster any form of empathetic thinking or compassion toward others. This is the devil's work at play. Psychology can dissect this current phenomenon for the rest of time, but it will always come down to the truth that the effect of these games, and whatever messages may be planted in them, are indeed fostering Socialcide in its sickest form.

When we imagine the isolative, socially "off" teen who spends countless hours allowing the brainwashing to fully take its toll, we must also understand that he (rarely she) is functioning on the lower side of the narcissistic behavior scale, but is perhaps the most dangerous type of narcissist. These kids are not "out there" in the sense that they are enticing the world to adore them in order to reap any rewards. They are "out there"in the sense that they come across as socially off the beaten path of normal. They may dress darkly or even in military fashion. Like all narcissists, however, they are noticeably friendless, unless they are conspiring with another low-functioning, socially isolative narcissist about their plan of attack.

That said, they are in no way low-functioning on an intellectual level and will manage to keep their grades up at least high enough to remain under the radar of suspicion. What they lack in social graces they make up for in intelligence. However, their full intellectual capacity is far from utilized. As their obsession grows, all efforts and thinking go into how they will destroy who or what they believe to be against them. Again, this is a common narcissistic trait, but in the lowest functioning narcissist, murder and human destruction is their way of feeling powerful; higher functioning self-lovers will satisfy their evil needs by manipulating people, conning them, causing confusing, lying, and basically destroying lives and personalities by deception.

I am often asked by parents if there are any specific warning signs to look for that may indicate their child could be in danger when it comes to violent video games. I am also asked why some children play these games and appear unaffected by them. My immediate response is always, "Why are you allowing your children to play violent video games in the first place?" The response to that is usually a universal, "Because all their friends are." Would that reasoning also work for you if your child wanted to shoot heroin?

Being a parent means setting the rules. Period. Learn to say no, and stick with it. According to Neil Young, a very favorite song writer and guitarist of mine, "The devil fools with the best made plans," so toughen up!

To further address the initial question, there are some signs that there may be trouble with your teen: apathetic demeanors, loss of friends, obsessive video game playing, and isolation from family and others. The best and most important thing you can do is to keep these games of death and destruction out of their reach.

Teens who isolate and dress strangely can may simply be being teens, so that is not always cause for panic. Teens are prone to moodiness, and can be defiant, so that behavior also is not necessarily cause for panic. However, if they are involved in isolative behaviors most of the time, parents need to know what they are up to, and why. Get into their space a little. Ask questions. Observe. *Talk with them.* Get—and *stay*—involved.

Dr. Weigle discussed another case in his report to Fox News. This was the case of eighteen-year-old Alabama teen Devin Moore, who had no history of any violent behavior. In June of 2003, in Fayette, Alabama, Moore was arrested for a minor traffic violation. While being booked inside the police station, Moore stole grabbed a gun from a police officer and used it to kill him, another officer, and the dispatcher. Then he stole a police cruiser to escape. The violence came seemingly out of nowhere and was completely out of character—or so his family believed.

Moore was caught and arrested before he could do any further damage. He had an explanation for his rage. A frequent player of *Grand Theft Auto,* he told police he was inspired by the game. Moore said, "Life is a video game. Everybody's got to die sometime." This is yet another horrific example of senseless slaughter that is directly attributable to the playing of violent video games, because of the false sense of power and control they give, and the underhanded way they shape and define how players *see and feel* about reality. These games give players a good feeling—of being in control and successful— which all humans need in order to have a positive self-image. But it is a *false* sense of ultimate control, power, and invincibility. And maybe scariest of all, it gives them a sense that they have the *right* to take the violent action. In reality, these games are actually controlling the players, right down to the way they think, and the way they make decisions.

The debate goes on and on among the living victims of these murderers, the game manufacturers, psychologists, and psychiatrists, the legal system, and the public as to the influence these violent games have over people, especially young children.

How many connections to mass slayings or single murders by children will it take before someone, somewhere takes responsibility? The common denominator in these tragedies continues to be the presence of violent video games. When it comes to children, the responsibility lies at home, but good parenting is also falling prey to self-adoration and standards of expectation that are far too lax. This can be due to parents' busy schedules, lack of attention, apathy, immaturity, or their own narcissistic ways. Don't forget, most younger parents were also raised on or with video games. Perhaps those games were not nearly as violent and corruptive as today's versions, but their own experiences with video games can cause parents to be desensitized to the fact that games can be *that bad*. The devil dances over the controversy and America's inability to take responsibility, while children fall prey to his seething greed for their souls.

Chapter Ten

Who's to Blame?

"Although issues of perfection in people's personal lives can cause people's unhappiness, images of perfect societies—utopian images—can cause monstrous evil. In fact, forcefully changing society to conform to societal images was the greatest cause greatest cause of evil in the twentieth century."
—Dennis Prager

Parenting is a talent, an art, a skill, and the most difficult job anyone can ever take on. Even so, there exists no book of rules or set of guidelines to rely upon when it comes to raising children. Historically, parents learned at least some techniques by observing their parents and relatives. In most families, the children were the priority, and life revolved around protecting them, guiding them, nurturing them, encouraging them, and disciplining them when necessary.

Parenting is on-the-job training. That means one must actually must actually be on-the-job to learn it properly. This will not happen, though, when parenting is "fit squeezed-in" to parents' existing schedules. Kids can easily and unwittingly get in the way of adults who expect things to run smoothly and according to how it is supposed to be. And when children become problems, parents cannot "reboot" them, pay someone to fix them, or trade them in. So what happens next?

There has been a huge increase in teen pregnancies during the past thirty years. One of the main reasons many teenage females *want* to have a baby is to have someone who provides them with unconditional love, something they should be (but are not) getting at home. As truly sad as that is, it reflects a large piece of why children intentionally get themselves into unhealthy situations. Feelings of acceptance, belonging, and purpose are normally provided by the family, and especially by the parents, but Socialcide is doing a great job of breaking down that formula and eating away at the institution of the family. The more children do not feel valued at home, the more they will seek that feeling elsewhere, and in ways that are not good. Seeking it in academic or athletic achievement can be positive.

Membership in gangs is at an all-time high today. They, like cults, lure children in with the promise of protection, belonging, family, and purpose. Gangs kill, steal, rape, and destroy. They are extremely narcissistic in nature, as they program members to feel no remorse, empathy, or love for those they murder or hurt. Society is doing very little, if anything at all, to counter-attack the gang banger lifestyle. Sending a policeman into a classroom to educate kids about the dangers of gangs is probably as effective as dropping a pebble into the Grand Canyon and hoping it will fill the hole.

Speaking of classrooms, Jacques Barzun (quoted in *The Guardian* (U.K.) said, "Teaching is not a lost art, but the regard for it is a lost tradition." I work with many teachers in my practice, who attest to the fact that the majority of their students (beginning as early as first graders) are failing terribly, and that this trend directly reflects parents' *non-involvement with their children's education.* It has become the teacher's job to discipline, guide, and guarantee successful grades, without any active support or participation from their students' parents. This is simply an impossible task. Yet states (at least New Jersey) continue to develop and design more and more expectations and requirements for *teachers.* This not only increases the overwhelming burden on them, but it also sends a clear message to already uninvolved parents that they do not have to do anything to help their kids when it comes to schoolwork. Further, it implies to parents who are partly involved or struggling with their involvement in their children's educations that they, too, can disconnect from the responsibility, and leave it all to the teachers.

This plays out in various ways as students' progress through their educations and careers. Many studies show that recent college graduates expect to be at the top in their jobs, without having put any effort into proper training, instruction, or experience along the way. The concepts of "paying your dues" and earning "sweat equity" have little or no value or meaning for these grads, and these concepts are a lost reality as Americans are quickly sliding down the international scale that measures viable business skills.

Richard Perez-Peña reported in *The New York Times* (October 8, 2013) that American adults fall far behind their counterparts in most developed countries when it comes to having the technical skills needed to compete in the modern workforce. Skills such as math, technology, and literacy are showing a well-documented pattern of decline in the United States. So in other words, Americans are becoming less competent and less intelligent. Lovely news.

The *Times* report also noted that these same middle-aged Americans appear "on paper" to be among the "best-educated people of their generation anywhere in the world," yet "are barely better than middle-of-the-pack in skills." Why would this be so? One would assume that if a person attended a top institution of higher learning and graduated with at least *good* grades, they would be prepared to take on their field of choice, and be successful in today's world of high tech businesses. However, clearly they are not. In fact, in a total of twenty-three countries studied, Japan ranked first, Finland second, with the U.S. somewhere near the middle in literacy, and toward the bottom in technology skills.

The media spin on this issue, as usual, takes any blame away from the students and places it on the schools. These findings "show our education system hasn't done enough to help Americans compete—or position our country to lead—in a global economy that demands increasingly higher skills," according to Arne Duncan, U.S. Secretary of Education education secretary. Can Duncan be for real? Kids are not being held responsible enough for their performance in grammar, middle, and high schools. If these kids then make it through college and cannot read, write, or compete mathematically with their international counterparts, it's the colleges' faults? It is only when this type of blaming and finger-pointing nonsense ceases (in this matter and in a thousand others), that we may be able again to take responsibility seriously, produce like we used to, and reduce the narcissistic Me, Me, Me society of uncaring, self-absorbed people the United States has created.

For doubters and blamers, consider this information reported in the same study which, I should add, was perhaps the most detailed of its kind: Among fifty-five- to sixty-five-year-olds, the United States fared better overall than those from other developed countries. Not so in the forty-five to fifty-four age group. In this group, American performance was average. Even worse, among younger people, *it was behind.* We can clearly see the regression of abilities and skills over the years as Socialcide spreads its "Why should I care?" attitude over America, while high-level, highly-paid executives in the field of education—from public schools to Ivy League universities—continue to focus on teachers' and schools' responsibilities, rather than on the responsibilities of the students and their parents

A parent's involvement used to be taken very seriously, and the child who did poorly in class was the *exception,* not the rule, as it has become today.

And if parents are showing no concern or care for their child's grades and education, why should the child?

So if parents are slacking off in the fundamental area of education, it's reasonable to expect they are also slacking off in love, nurturing, discipline, and other areas as well. Today's children are getting the message that "I don't matter" more and more, from their preoccupied, narcissistic parents. Children pick up on this message—directly and indirectly—through words, actions, and non-action. And the message is getting louder and louder. As a result, we see more and more horrific behaviors occurring with America's children and teens today. This is not a psychological problem as much as it is a social one, and the implications are not being addressed properly, if at all.

The reality is that a child who gets his or her way all or most of the time will not trust that parent, and will unconsciously feel uncared for. Giving in to what your child wants is doing him or her no favor in preparation for life. Parents who are often told, "I hate you," by their kids are probably doing their job correctly. And to these parents I say, "Deal with it." It is far easier to deal with than the alternative! Your job is to be their parent, not their friend, and to prepare them for life as productive, healthy, educated, contributing members of society. The friendship part will come later, when they are the adults you have prepared them to be. Unfortunately, today's younger parents are not even *in the ballpark,* let alone *stepping up to the plate,* when it comes to doing their job as parents

This disintegration of the family is also part of the evil master plan. Most often, lax parenting correlates with an absence of religion in the home. If a family is not being guided by some form of spiritual influence, then who or what is influencing them? Goodness in the world today is increasingly disappearing, as people more and more are morphing into being their own gods, and making their own rules as to what is right and what is wrong. And in the distance we can hear Satan laughing out loud over such influence, or lack thereof.

Who Are the Role Models?

When I meet a new adolescent client, I ask a lot of questions. One very interesting one is, "Who are your heroes?" Nine times out of ten, the client cannot answer me. Sometimes, though, I get an answer. Negative role models, like a rapper who "speaks his mind" about committing crimes against other, weaker humans (to put it gently); or a character in a movie who is a drug dealer and who successfully manipulates others, outsmarts the law, is rich beyond belief, and has no remorse for the kids who have died, or whose lives have been destroyed by the illegal drugs he manufactures and distributes. (This guy is a hero because he is "sick rich and doesn't have to work at all.")

How can this be? Are our children really without any positive role models? Do they not look up to *anyone* as a source of inspiration anymore? I am certain this hero question could have been answered easily years ago. And perhaps adolescents back then would have had a number of heroes, and they would have been personalities many of us would also have respected and admired. Today, though, I get blank stares. Should this concern parents? I am not sure, but I am sure that it should cause us all to think about what our society's children are doing, and what *does* influence and intrigue them.

Millennials have had the benefit of Reality TV shows, social networking websites, and every other "become famous for nothing"vessel ever known to man. This constant barrage of what's new and exciting is nothing more than a camera following around drug-addicted celebrities, low-income families, Barbie and Ken doll look-alikes trying to hook-up or find marriage, crystal methamphetamine-makers, and pregnant teenagers. To young minds, if it's on TV it's either glamorous or worthy of admiration or it's stupid and deserving of ridicule. Either way, these shows are more often than not teaching our youth to emulate negative, unhealthy behaviors, or giving them practice degrading others.

Who are today's *real* heroes and role models? Perhaps there are no real heroes today. At least none to whom this Me, Me, Me Generation can relate. Who is out there doing wonderful, brave things that will benefit the world, and leave a huge, positive influence on the generations to come? Will the generations to come even care? Perhaps *that* is the larger, more pressing question.

Real heroes and positive role models are an extremely important component in adolescent development. They inspire and demonstrate what accomplishments can be achieved with hard work and dedication to a passion or cause. Without them, it's no wonder how under-motivated youth are today. A frightening fact was reported by the Central Intelligence Agency after they interviewed and profiled many of the adolescent and young adult school shooters we sadly continue to hear about. Each one of these criminal youth reported that they did not have even one adult in their lives they could trust or talk to. *Not one.* Where were the parents? Where were the relatives? Where was anyone who *might have saved so many innocent lives?*

I am *not* implying that the blame for any of those murders falls on anyone other than the shooters. What I *am* saying is that the absence of any adult to trust or talk to speaks to something in society that needs to change. Why are these killers *admiring* other killers, instead of admiring teachers, parents, relatives, God, or someone who is trustworthy in their eyes? I am convinced these evil deeds are carried out in an attempt to "be someone" and gain attention in society. In this type of narcissist, there was certainly not enough parental nurturing at home, and the consequences were catastrophic and unnecessary, ending innocent lives, because of years of pent-up anger, neglect, and the influence of violence through video games and other media.

With these types of catastrophes occurring much too regularly, what does our nation do? We attempt to control guns. Parents rush their children away from in-person socialization and education at public and private schools and into home or Internet schooling. And we all shake our heads in disbelief and sadness as we barricade our lives into semi-isolation from one another while the root of the problem— Evil—continues to win.

Evil is in fact winning the race, leaving morality far behind, and America appears to be ignoring the fact. Those who do see what's going on and who fear it the most are those of us who grew up or were born before 1978, the year the beast and creator of Socialcide signed his plan to seduce people into killing themselves emotionally, and destroying all that is good and loving in the world.

The plan? Stop real communication, and replace it with technology. The more we become reliant upon machines, the more machine-like we become machines. The more machine-like we become machines, the closer Socialcide comes to completion.

God did not ever intend for us to become machines. He gave us the ability to think for ourselves, and also gave us freedom of choice, so we would not be machines, and so that we could freely choose to listen to

Him and decide to follow His plan for us. Evil would want nothing more than a world full of emotionally dead robots that choose to follow their own plans to do what they want, when they want, to whom they want. After all, "Who cares?" Apathy and ignorance allow evil to lead the way, and with all the "advancements" America has made during the past thirty-five years, it has lost all its *goodness* three-fold or more.

Chapter Eleven

The Great Pretenders

"Be careful who you trust. After all, the devil was once an angel."
—Unknown

I am not a preacher or a prophet. I am a psychologist with an unquenchable thirst for information, knowledge, and truth, especially when it comes to what makes people do what they do. Why are some people so evil and self-absorbed, and some so kind, open, and appealing to be with, speak with, and spend time with? How do we decide which people to interact with?

These days we tend to judge people, and assess their value to us, based solely on first impressions. Sometimes these impressions are accurate, and sometimes they are not. For example, people who have a "weirdness" about them, a chilling creepy feeling that makes us for some reason want to avoid them, are always labeled in our minds as "the enemy," or potentially dangerous. Then there are some absolutely charismatic people, who immediately win us over with their wit, humor, smiles, and seemingly genuine interest in us. We tend to gravitate more toward these people, because they seem good. Sounds reasonable, right? We should avoid the weird guy and be comfortable with the charismatic one. But it is often the "win-you-over" people that really should be feared more than those outright strange individuals. Perhaps "feared" is too strong a word.

Let's just say we should be at least be suspicious of their intentions. After all, narcissists hide well. Even the devil would not win over people's souls by breathing fire at them and sticking them with a pitchfork!

Then what causes so many Americans to fall prey to self-love, and focus their lives on the drive to fill their *Me, Me, Me* status? We were not created to be self-reliant centered, uncaring, or dismissive of other people's needs or assistance. Humans were created to need and be needed by other humans—to exist with others in symbiotic unions—not to live isolated lives peppered with parasitic relationships. Despite this, the younger generation of today seems to have no interest in any type of guidance or constructive criticism, especially regarding what they do or where they work. Unfortunately, that doesn't really seem to be working out all that well for them.

What Do You Mean, Work?

A *Time Magazine* article by Dan Schawbel (March 29, 2012) covered a poll that explained how Millennials differ from their Baby Boomer ancestors predecessors in the workplace. According to "Millennials vs. Baby Boomers: Who Would You Rather Hire?" even though folks in their twenties and early thirties are less likely to be in the workforce, they have very strong opinions about what their workplace experience should be. They are so Me-driven that they expect "more *me time* on the job, and nearly nonstop feedback and career advice from managers." They want to be able to set their own hours, and decide whether to go in to the office or to work remotely. They also admit they believe *they* can teach a thing or two to their bosses. And, last but not least, they want to wear jeans to work.

It is no wonder that I hear from numerous business owners, personnel staff, and bosses that they regularly have to fire new, young employees. Why? Because these new, young employees want a big title, but show up late for work, cannot get along with supervisors and co-workers, and are resistant to instruction or constructive criticism. There is no *work ethic* instilled in them whatsoever. Again, why? Because parents have been raising their children with what the children want, not what they need. Young adults have been so pumped up with *how wonderful, special, privileged, and entitled* they are that they have absolutely no understanding of how to obtain *knowledge and* wisdom, and how to use it them successfully.

In my practice, as I have stated before, it's quite the rarity to work with a child who has responsibilities at home, because so many parents think they are doing their kids a favor by not making them work too hard. Well, guess what? They take that lesson to their jobs. They show little to no *care* when they tell their bosses how to do their jobs, demand "me time on the job" and want free career advice. Why? Are they planning on looking for another job? Why not let the boss help them out with moving on?

Statistics clearly show how poorly recent college graduates perform in new positions. How can they do otherwise, though, when they never *felt like* mowing the lawn, never knew *how* to make a phone call to someone, never learned how to ask for help, and never learned how to actually *find* a job? This is the reality of today's generation. They are clueless when it comes to social graces, yet extremely full of belief that they are *above work, above training, above working their way to anything, and above advice or guidance from anyone.* There exists no respect. Period. "I want what I want, and I have always gotten what I want. Don't tell me no!"

Further, we see a so-called *Boomerang* phenomenon where young adults are returning home after college (or never leaving home to begin with). Sure, we can blame the economy that has been bottoming out since about 2007, but is it more due to Millennials' sheer laziness or unwillingness to work harder to find a way to start a life of their own? If you can't afford a McMansion right now, is living in an apartment not acceptable? Providing your own means to survive with food, utility bills, car insurance, and the like has become unnecessary when you can simply slip back into your childhood bedroom and continue to let mom and dad foot your bills. Schawbel's article reported that half of the Millennials interviewed admitted they "would rather have no job than a job they hate." That attitude can explain a lot about that *Boomerang* effect.

This lack of care, over-blown sense of entitlement, and apparent unwillingness or inability to start somewhere and work your one's way up seems to define the attitude of this generation. They want answers and attention, and they want it NOW! Being raised with cell phones and text messaging, Internet access and emails, they are perpetually connected to who and what they want and when they want it.

Millennials tend to be arrogant, ignorant, and narcissistic. Consider this finding from the a Pew Research Center's survey, in which where individuals from different generations were asked what made them unique. Baby Boomers responded with qualities, such as "work ethic." Millennials offered, "clothes." You cannot make up these findings up! Reality is reality, and parents, media, video games, and technology are all to blame for inviting and allowing Socialcide to erode all that is good, respectful, and *right,* and to ensure that it all be taken from our culture. What will be left of socialization and society fifty years from now?

The members of the Me, Me, Me Generation truly believes they should be loved and adored simply because they are, not because they have *earned* it. While these types may not become murderers, they do become manipulators, and are very good at convincing employers, potential love partners, and acquaintances to give them what they want. However, when the going gets rough, and the narcissists don't get what they need, they are quick to become "not as advertised," and trouble begins.

Many of these Millennials were raised with the belief that they have nothing to lose and everything to gain—*for themselves.* This is how Socialcide thinks; this is how evil thinks; and this is quickly becoming how America thinks. Religion and family work perfectly together when both are intact. In harmony, they teach right from wrong, selflessness from selfishness, giving from greed, and every other human characteristic that balances evil. But now there is disharmony. Consciousness of conscience is quickly becoming a thing of the past.

Chapter Twelve
Sex, Drugs, and Children

"In our society,daily experience teaches the individual to want and need
a never-ending supply of new toys and drugs."
—Christopher Lasch

Childhood obesity is currently at an all-time high, and kids don't "go out to play"anymore. This is due in part to parental restrictions, or media-induced fears, video games, and parents' taxiing services. Also, many children are being raised on a diet of junk food, perhaps due to the parents' busy schedules, or perhaps just laziness. Whatever the reasons, too many children these days do not move off the couch and engage in enough physical activity to maintain healthy weights.

With that said, more teens these days attend gyms not for *health* reasons, but for vanity. Competition to be the hottest and sexiest is extremely high among both boys and girls. And while they are washing down illegal prescription painkillers with a mixture of energy drinks and vodka, they are also posting pictures of themselves partially dressed on social networking websites, and sexting nude pictures of themselves to friends and "hook-up"partners.

Now, I do not buy for a minute that any teen who is smoking pot or "blunts" (cigars mixed with marijuana), is drinking excessive amounts of alcohol, or is taking club drugs (including "Mollies," Ecstasy, GHB, and "Special K") or any of the variety of the epidemically popular painkillers (including OxyContin, RoxyContin, Percocet, or Vicodin), is then going to a gym to work out for *health reasons*. The obsessive workouts they engage in are solely to make themselves more desirable or envied by their peers. And with the media's constant barrage of computer-altered images and pictures of the nearly impossible bodies of today's celebrities and "beautiful people," the pressure on teens to become what they see—and what they believe others see—as that "perfect picture" is tremendous.

Socialcide wants the focus of what makes a person *worthy, likeable, lovable, desirable, popular, and successful*—both in that person's own mind and in the perceptions of others—to be based solely on appearance and material worth. And with the assistance of technology—specifically the Internet, social media, and cell phones— less-than-perfect teens can suffer electronic humiliation and bullying wherever they go, *especially* at home. In this age of technology, home is no longer the safe haven it used to be. Through desktop computers, portable and hand-held devices, and cell phones, our homes and "personal spaces" are now open to predators and harassment—perhaps even more so than school is.

With the extreme amount of personal information teenagers are willing to post online (including nude pictures of themselves), any teen can become a target for bullying and abuse. These days many teens spend their free time at home, by themselves, in front of one screen or another, engaged with others only through technology and maybe a "Don't forget to do your homework!" shouted by Mom from somewhere else in the house. Isolated like this, and being harassed, bullied, and humiliated while in the space that is supposed to be safe, can be devastating—even lethal. Even for those with enough sense to not "sext"their pictures, bullying can lead the vulnerable adolescent mind to thoughts of suicide. Comments like, "You're pretty, but fat," have been posted enough so much to some young girls that they were driven to killing themselves! The media has labeled this abusive use of technology "cyber bullying." I call it cyber *murder.*

And let's not forget that we have the ability to create anonymous or fictitious online accounts, so we can say horrible things to others without having to identify who we are, or to take responsibility for what we say. It's so much easier to mistreat someone from behind a screen, anonymously. And, as with the desensitization to violence that comes with hours of violent video game- playing, once a person gets used to bullying and abusing anonymously via technology it becomes so much easier to feel comfortable enough and guilt-free enough to do it in person.

Are children becoming so cruel, so numb, so guiltless, so self-absorbed that they don't think twice about pushing their peers to the point of suicide *intentionally?* And what about the victims? Are they feeling that unloved, that worthless in the world, that disconnected from life, that they allow predators to steal their reason for living? Unfortunately, the answer is yes. Again, in the lives of both predators and victims, where are the parents? Who are the role models? Where is knowledge of right from wrong?

Take, for example, a very recent report concerning a group of seventeen-to-eighteen-year-old boys from a European country. These boys were not ashamed of what they were doing and how they were doing it. According to a report by Karen Rutherford from *3 News* dated November 3, 2013, this group of boys used social networking websites to publicly recruit other boys to join them in group sex sessions with girls, many of whom were underage. After the sex, the boys used social media to publicly name the girls and openly humiliate them online.

As if it were not enough to name names, they began using the same social media networks to post videos of the often drunk, underage girls they claimed to have violated. One of the boys was quoted in the report as saying, "You try and get with the amount of girls we do, this is a job; we don't do this shit for pleasure." What type of thinking is this, exactly, from a seventeen-or eighteen-year-old boy? Another boy recorded himself on another post stating, "We take what we do seriously. Some of you think this is a joke. It's not." I think he has that much correct, but for all the wrong reasons.

In true narcissistic style, the boys blame the victims, and excuse their own demonic actions, by saying the girls choose them knowing fully "What we are like, and they know what they're in for." Those are extremely chilling words. And even if the girls *do somehow know* they are going to engage in illicit behavior with these monsters, I do not believe they agree to the public humiliation and ridicule they face at the hands of these "innocent" demons, or understand the depth of pain and trouble it can cause.

These boys are continuing to recruit more boys to join them in their evil deeds. Police have no idea exactly how many girls have been led into this trap. At least one underage victim told police, "I just kept blacking out, 'cause I had drunken too much. You could say I got raped. I had sex with three guys at one time." While police and authorities have been aware of this group since 2011, none of the victims have been brave enough to make any formal complaints. The police do say they are "clearly traumatized by what has happened."

This trend is growing. More young men are starting their own groups of sexual predators, and the impact of the damage they will cause fits perfectly into today's Socialcide epidemic. Thanks to technology and social media, the "job" keeps getting easier. Let's not forget that parents who are "just not comfortable" talking with their children about sex and physical and physical abuse, and even what constitutes rape, are helping predators make easy prey of their children. A lasting statement from another boy of the group reflects what the school killers and other public slayers we have heard about all too often over the past years have expressed: "My first actual romp for the Group was bad. It was fun, I felt like a man." He concluded by saying, "I thought, this is going to go big, everyone is going to know about the Group." Indeed they will, but for all the wrong reasons.

This behavior "made him feel like a man?" Herein lies a huge part of what makes the heart of Socialcide beat. Adolescent boys do not have the true values and morals they need to *really feel like men*. These values and morals are not being taught to them by parents, movies, heroes, role models, or God. In Freudian language, the *ID* is running their lives. The *ID* is the symbolic part of the human psyche that wants what it wants, and when it wants it— now! Babies and toddlers are very ID-driven, but they are too young to know better. Teenagers, while believing they are invincible, are not fully-developed mentally, but do and should understand right from wrong.

In cases such as these, there is no excuse, except that evil has entered their lives, and is conveniently laughed at as fun or amusement. The *ID* feels no shame or guilt. *The Ego* and *Super Ego* (the other two parts of Freud's definition of what makes up our psychic apparatus) regulate those judgments, and so does God—if we let Him.

Those who are opposed the concept of Socialcide, or to the need for God in our collective consciousness, may most likely argue that crime has not increased any more than narcissism has, but rather we just hear more about these things because media and technology have made such news more available. Indeed, we have become a nation well-informed about every lurid, sickening, and evil deed people are capable of committing these days. Many even hunger for the thrill of such news. But one cannot argue against the fact that the *types* of criminal activity we are served up every day are far from the crimes of yesteryear. The sickness, selfishness, depravity, and lack of regard for humankind has never been as evil and prevalent as it is today. And it's only getting worse.

The culprit of evil destruction has placed its seeds in America's youth. People thirty-five years old and younger are far less shocked by the types of crimes and criminals we see today than their elders, because, as it has been planned, they have grown up with these news reports, and are much more desensitized to their horrific details than those of us of an older age. And in being such, they are far more easily influenced by Socialcide's grip and lure.

In fact, there are websites today specifically created for married people who want to cheat on their spouses. Married men and married women can pay to post themselves on these sites where there is an initial understanding that the user is going to stay married, but also wants sex on the side. One of these particular sites is making millions upon millions of dollars per year. Isn't that convenient?

My professional opinion of cheating spouses is that they are, of course, narcissistic at best. How one can be married (especially with children), go out and sleep with other individuals (married or single), and then come home and act as if nothing is going on, boggles my mind. Speaking of having no conscience, morality, or sense of right and wrong, cheating spouses are a prime example.

Now consider children today. They are much more sexualized than ever before, and are engaging in sex—either willingly or unwillingly—with each other in far greater numbers than did previous generations. In other words, our kids are (what they call) "hooking-up" with each other, void of any type of emotional connection. "Why buy the cow when the milk is free?" It is foolish to believe children get the idea that "giving away" sex as a favor or "because I can" came from anywhere other than their parents or adults in society and in the media cheating on their spouses like Roman emperors did. We reap what we sow, especially when it comes to our children.

It also does not help when today's role models are *twerking, tweeting, undressing, and cheating* on each other. Even many sports stars today are engaging in extra-marital affairs, so Socialcide has literally covered all bases in its exposure. Illicit sex has forever been the devil's most tempting poison, and Sigmund Freud would agree—sort of. Freud believed *everything* man does is motivated by sex. The media knows and exploits that well, as does every advertising company known to man. *Sex sells,* and certainly can also do much damage when it comes to children and narcissistic married individuals.

My ultimate point here is that if children are not being guided by parents, positive, trustworthy role models, and God, they will follow what they see and experience as acceptable to others, which is what they see out there prominently online, in the movies, on stage, on television, or even in the home. And if the very most intimate form of expressing love and connection becomes cheap, disposable, and bastardized in their minds at such a young age, what will they value in their lives? And do not think Satan desires anything more than young minds that couldn't care less about what they do and to whom they do it, as long as it is for themselves. *Me, Me, Me!*

A multi-year study was conducted by the Centers for Disease Control and Prevention (CDC) that was designed to look for the roots of adult sexual violence. The study found that one in ten high school and college-aged people have forced someone into sexual activity against his or her will. Again, in true narcissistic style, most of the respondents who have done so believe their victim was at least partially to blame.

It is no secret anymore how sexualized today's youth are. But now we are also seeing that even as teenagers they are developing the skills of a sexual predators, manipulating, and forcefully guilting partners, lust objects, or just random victims into satisfying their demands. Even more chilling is that, by far, the coercion is completed by psychological means, sometimes paired with intoxication. Physical force—either actually used or only threatened—is the least used form of this coercion.

If our *children* are perfecting these manipulative, narcissistic, and cunning skills of guilt-inflicting influence to force another child to provide him or her with the ultimate act of what was once reserved for relationships of true love and intimacy (but has now become a "favor" or a "hook-up" in today's terminology), what will they be capable of as adults? Certainly far worse, and far more coercing of evil deeds, if that can even be imagined. Frighteningly, though, today's news reports make that which many of us can't even imagine much more of a reality.

This CDC study also found that most perpetrators first forced sex either physically or psychologically at the age of sixteen, and the majority of these perpetrators were boys. But it was found that by the age of eighteen, girls had become much more involved in preying upon others, and were nearly as likely to become perpetrators as boys.

So was there a common denominator influencing this evil behavior among teens? The study looked at media use and found that most of the manipulators or perpetrators were likely to watch violent, X-rated materials.

Here again, we see the influence of the vivid distortion of reality versus fantasy. We also see the sense of entitlement and attitude of "what I want, I will get" shining through. Further, while most predators at least partially blamed their victims, they also admitted that "never getting caught," and the lack of consequences for their acts just further fueled their behaviors. Where are the parents?

Perhaps it was former President Bill Clinton's insistence that "oral sex is not sex" that has lingered in society's thinking enough to influence young people to provide "favors" such as oral sex to their friends, further blurring the boundaries and lessening the importance of what is right and what is wrong in terms of sexual behavior. In my practice, I hear all too often how young clients do not give much thought to such acts, and even view them "as harmless as a handshake." Full intercourse, which for the most part was reserved for serious relationships, is no longer saved for someone truly special. And that aspect has been diminishing more and more as time goes by.

Parents must get on-board and *talk to their children* about what constitutes appropriate sexual behavior. But even that, these days, is much less effective than it used to be. Socialcide has already infiltrated the beliefs and values of younger parents of today. They, too, were engaging in sexual prowess with reckless abandon as children. And their beliefs and values have already been eroded to the level where the sexual behaviors of children today are not as disturbing to them as they were to parents of older generations.

Unfortunately, though, the belief and excuse that "all teenagers are curious, and their hormones are on fire" does not save these teens from the trauma in the years of adulthood that inappropriate or coerced sexual behavior will tarnish, complicate, and confuse. We cannot simply throw condoms at our kids and hope for the best! This subject is sometimes taboo at home.

Parents are unwilling or uncaring enough to address it, or they just don't know how to tell their child not to do something everyone else is doing. Schools do not teach sex education anymore either. When kids are not being guided they will choose their own way, or let evil people choose it for them.

The information our children need regarding their sexuality and sexual behaviors is being provided by the media, violent pornography, evil, and Socialcide, instead of by healthy, realistic sources. And the information the children are getting is not information that will help them make healthy, safe decisions about sexual activity. In an era when a book like *Fifty Shades of Grey* becomes a major cultural accomplishment, is it really any wonder children are falling prey to sexual predators, or becoming one predators themselves?

As a therapist, I often see firsthand the results of current social trends that are in various ways damaging and distressing clients' lives. Issues like addiction, domestic violence, spikes of certain diagnoses, or most currently, sexual assaults, have vast and devastating effects on clients and their loved ones.

I am currently counseling five young women between the ages of seventeen and twenty-seven who have been sexually violated, and they are suffering greatly because of it. Before getting more specific, I want to point out that I am but one therapist in a pool of hundreds of thousands nationwide. That makes my firsthand experiences with clients a mere microcosm of society as a whole. In other words, if I am working with five young women presently, there are certainly many, many others seeing therapists, or not reporting the incidents at all. That is a very frightening fact.

The latest modus operandi (M.O.) of these "new" sexual predators combines three key elements of Socialcide: narcissism, evil, and technology. My clients have all described their perpetrators as having shown complete disregard for their [my clients'] feelings, demands, resistance, personal space, privacy, and lives. However, that side of the perpetrators' personalities did not appear at the beginning of the relationships, but was exposed later. Initially, these morally bankrupt and demonic individuals came across to their victims as the most flattering, genuinely concerned, and personally *attractive* men these women had ever met. The men said all the right things, all the things the women wanted, and perhaps even *needed,* to hear, effortlessly gaining the women's admiration and trust with each deceptive compliment or comment that passed their lips. Narcissists are masters of deception when it comes to fulfilling their evil needs, and good people are falling prey to them far more today than ever before.

These narcissists are true *charmers* for certain, but how socially depraved they are inside! We can only wonder where and how they learned their pathetic techniques. There are no schools for advanced degrees in narcissism, no formal training, yet narcissists are developing and surfacing in record numbers. This charming rouse is standard operating procedure for almost all narcissists, sociopaths, and psychopaths, but is especially creepy among the ones who are sexual predators, and who have their sights set on conquering their prey in the most perverse and sickening way: sexually.

These narcissistic personality traits are completely in-line with those of the *biggest* and *most evil* of them all, Satan. The method to his madness plays out exactly as does the method of today's narcissists. He also knows precisely what to say, and to whom to say it, to so he can gain trust from an innocent child of God, in order to satisfy his unquenchable thirst for human corruption. Make no mistake about it: Satan is the master planner of Socialcide's intentions, and Humankind's moral (and ultimate) demise.

The five clients I mentioned earlier eventually fell head-over-heels for their "Mr. Wonderful," and came to truly believe he would never hurt them. This is a clear example of how narcissism and evil perform in unison to gain emotional entry into victims' lives. As I share with you their experiences, I remind you they are five random women who had almost *identical* experiences with five different perpetrators, but this M.O. is sadly typical of today's narcissist perpetrators, and this scenario is being played out over and over everyday throughout America.

Once the stage is set and the victim's defenses are either way down or completely non-existent, and they feel a strong—almost desperate— desire to remain in the relationship that made them feel so good about themselves, technology is used to aid the predator in not only "sealing the deal" but ensuring that they can violate their victims over and over again. How?

First, as with my clients and many other victims, the majority of perpetrators use chemicals or *date rape* pills such as Rohypnol or "Roofies" to put victims into a state of unconsciousness. This method of rendering a person unconscious by simply dropping a pill into their drink is not only psychopathically sick, it is extremely dangerous. However, the evil narcissist cares not for anyone's else's well-being. Since he has already won over his victim, she is not on guard against any wrong doing from Mr. Right, so she falls into a comatose state, and is unable to defend herself. She will be unable to recall much of the act, if anything at all, and can be violated in any way, any number of times her attacker chooses.

The newest use of technology that furthers the success of ultimate evil comes in the form of filming an entire sexual violation or violations while the victim is out cold, and then publishing the video on social media. In the case of my clients' experiences, this aspect of their attacks has become the most difficult to get past. This is not to say that being raped and sodomized is comparatively easily forgotten, or to minimize the horrific impact of such crimes. However, understand that these women cannot recall the attacks because of the amnesic effect of the drugs they were given. To make matters even worse, now there is a video—including the horrific details—of what each of them went through with these monsters against their will.

It is impossible to fully comprehend what these women are feeling, and how drastically this experience has and will continue to negatively impact their lives after first believing they had met the "love of their life" or, at the very least, a really nice guy who genuinely *seemed* into her completely, only to learn she had fallen into a trap set by Satan himself in a crime that has no end; a trap that can now be used against her at any time, without warning, to blackmail her, humiliate her, ruin her life and reputation, or coerce her into submission to whatever the sociopath that did this to her wants until he is done with her. Not to mention that this recording of the crime will potentially be forever available for her children, her coworkers or employers, her family, or her future boyfriend or husband to find in cyberspace. In the end, the video is permanent. And when the crime goes on forever, true closure is virtually impossible.

Unfortunately, crimes like these occur frequently these days. The evil is beyond widespread, and more victims will either suffer in silent shame, or will seek professional help to regain as much of their sense of emotional wellbeing as possible.

Satan desires nothing more than to see people suffer, and such is the truth with the narcissist as well. The similarities between the devil and the narcissist are too drastic to ignore. One need not be the Pope or Sigmund Freud to see this clearly, or to understand it. I have spoken to numerous law enforcement agents and true crime authors, and am a very close friend and colleague of John Kelly, Criminal Profiler and co-star of Investigation Discovery Channel's series *Dark Minds*, who has interviewed many serial rapists and killers. All of them have said at one time or another, after having interviewed many of these psychopathic monsters, that "evil exists," and it is gaining much ground and countless souls these days—more than ever before. Victims of a narcissist's sexual, emotional, financial, or personal abuse, to whose accounts I can speak firsthand, would also say, "It was like living with, looking at, speaking to, or dealing with *the devil himself.*"

Chapter Thirteen

Destroying God

"The disturbed individual who believes himself to be Christ, or to receive messages from God, is something of a cliché in our society. Ever since Sigmund Freud, many people have associated religiosity with neurosis and mental illness."
—Robert Winston

I am always curious about why so many people—especially teenagers—are so opposed to believing in God. I have found this becoming more and more prevalent in my practice over the years, as I always ask my new clients if they have any form of religion or spirituality in their lives. I am not a Christian Counselor perse, but I am a Christian. In any case, as I attempt to assess what strengths and supports a new client may have in his or her life, I routinely ask this question, and have gotten some very interesting responses.

Many teens believe religion is a "way to control people." That's a very popular response. Another is that God and the Bible are *fairy tales* written by people to keep the crime rate down over the years. It is rare that an adolescent will express a firm belief in God. The closest I get nowadays is, "I believe there is something out there, but I don't know what it is."

There seems to be an absence of spirituality and belief in God among the majority of today's teens. What does that mean? At the very least, it means one of the biggest support pillars is missing from their lives. It also means they believe there is little, if anything, watching out for their souls and well-being in this world.

So if a person has no belief in a God or an afterlife, how does he or she find purpose in this one? It's sad—and even self-abusive in my opinion—to believe we are merely here by chance, because of some big blast, and we serve as much purpose on this earth as a fruit fly. But is that not what non- believers must think?

I also do not understand exactly why the idea of believing in a God or a benevolent higher power is so repellent to so many. What do they think it costs to *simply believe?* To believe in a purpose for being here, having the gift of life, the ability to love and laugh, to share with and help others?

Perhaps a negative experience with a certain person or religious organization planted a bad seed in a potential believer's mind. Maybe a religious institution asked too much of, or gave too little to, someone looking for comfort and support. I can also understand how some churches labeled *"Bible Thumpers,"* that base their beliefs and church culture on fear and extreme punishment for sinning, are scaring people away. Maybe one of the hard-core Fundamentalists of the 1980s, like Jimmy Swaggart or Jim Bakker left a very bad—albeit wrong impression of Christianity and religion in general—taste in their mouths. Perhaps the thought of *organized religion,* with its strict rules, regulations, expectations, and rituals, seems futile or contradictory to the Godless individual. I am not certain why people shy away from religion, spirituality, and God. But I *am* certain God Himself is getting an unjustly bad rap here in America today. And you *know who* is simply having a field day.

Sadly, there are religious leaders who have given us just cause to question their morality and trustworthiness. Look at all the cases of child abuse by clergy in the Catholic Church, and the documented cover-ups. And take, for example, the recent case of a pastor from the Pocono Mountains in Pennsylvania who was sentenced to life in prison for killing his second wife. (If that is not an extreme example of narcissism, I do not know what is.)

Arthur "A.B." Schirmer was convicted of first-degree murder of his second wife, Betty Jean Schirmer, in 1999. Pastor Schirmer had been having an affair with at least one woman from his flock when he went out for a drive with his wife. The car hit a guard rail on the passenger side at what was later determined to be fifteen to twenty miles per hour. However, when police arrived at the scene Betty Jean was badly beaten, blood all over the seat, and the Pastor was untouched, sitting in the driver's seat. He made no 911 call even though he had a cell phone, and did not move from the car when police arrived. Instead, he sat there silent and emotionless.

The police knew who he was, and because of his "Man of the Cloth" status, no investigation was initially conducted into Betty Jean's death. Her brother told police two days after her death that he believed her head had been smashed in by someone.

The husband of the woman with whom Schirmer was having an affair left a briefcase full of emails, letters, and pictures that documented the affair. The investigation was reopened, and it was determined that the extent of Betty Jean's injuries could not have been caused by the mild impact she sustained in the accident; that she was dead or dying when she was placed in the car by Schirmer. Then suspicion came his way regarding the death of his first wife. She had been found dead at the bottom of the basement stairs, her foot twisted in a vacuum cleaner cord and her head battered badly, much like Betty Jean's. Forensic reports then determined that the extent of her injuries could not have been caused by the fall down the stairs. In fact, autopsy reports showed both women had been beaten in the head with a blunt object in almost identical ways.

As it turned out, when he was done with one wife he killed her and married another, then later repeated the same crime. All the while he had been preaching to his congregation, and was beloved by them. This is pure narcissism in action. But it puts a very bad picture of *religion* and *God* into the public's minds.

And then there was Rabbi Fred Neulander of Cherry Hill, New Jersey. In 1994, this "Man of the Cloth" was convicted of paying two men to carry out a "hit" on his wife Carol, who was murdered in their family home.

Satan can disguise himself in any way he chooses, and society must be aware of that, because it's happening all too frequently today. The more we push God out of our lives, the more evil fills the void. The A.B. Schirmer and

Fred Neulander cases are very sad ones—sad for the victims, their families, their friends and the congregations who had put their spiritual trust in these men's care. But we need to understand that being a pastor, priest, rabbi, or any clergy person, is simply a job. These religious leaders are people doing a job. It is not the religion that has failed us, but the people in those positions.

Ultimate deception, manipulation, and even murder are possible from by anyone. The problem is that when a person of God becomes exposed in evil deeds, many doubts about God and religion arise and cause people to categorize anything related to God as simply a scam. We do not, nor should we, glorify any person but only other than God. We are being manipulated and scammed out of what true faith and goodness are really all about.

The media does not publicize the good most churches, synagogues, pastors, priests, or rabbis do. Instead, they expose the corruption and sickness of narcissists who dress in clerical clothing. The adulterers, the pedophiles, the thieves, and the demonically-driven individuals who truly are causing many to distrust religion or disbelieve in God are put out for the court of public opinion, and the opinion is getting bad. Socialcide proves this is done not by any accident; it's a purpose-driven force that continues to erode morality and what is right and wrong.

Evil dressed in religious robes and preaching from pulpits aside, there are also those who fear a certain religions because they do not agree with its their doctrinal bases. And there are so many who have just given up on God because they haven't found the "right fit" with a particular congregation, community religious leader,or set of religious practices, rituals, and traditions. I am not judging any religion, or how people worship, and I do recognize that God is called different things, (for example, Aten, Jehovah, Adonai, HaShem, Allah, Al-El, Brahman, Baha, Waheguru, Ahura Mazda) and is defined somewhat differently in different faiths.

Specific laws and rituals differ between religions, and even between different branches of the same religion. Different things work for different people. Not everyone loves a charismatic woman in a pulpit; not everyone is comfortable with a young rabbi; not everyone enjoys long winded sermons or "Everything is wonderful" speeches; not everyone loves "touchy-feely" congregations. But I do believe many people have a misconception that choosing God means choosing a particular church or particular religion to follow, and I think that is where they are throwing the proverbial baby out with the bath water.

Choosing God can include choosing a particular place of worship or religious doctrine (and often does), but it can also include living a life connected to God, without ever stepping foot in a religious building.

I am not sure what keeps teenagers or adults from believing we are more than just slugs on a rock here in this world. I do often tell those who ask me why this is so important, that it costs nothing to simply believe, and what if, just what if, all this "God stuff" is true? What if there is a Heaven and a Hell, and when you die your soul never believed in God? Eternity is a long time. Do you really want to take the chance that you will spend it in Hell just because you didn't believe?

Many colleges, the scientific community, and especially the media today steer people away from belief in some form of monotheistic God. We are hard pressed at best to look around the world today and recognize any evidence of a loving, protective force or God helping in the world. But as I discussed earlier, the world (according to the New Testament) is not in God's hands right now. God said He would not return to claim His believers until His Word was spread to every nation on the earth, so that they can freely choose or refuse Him and His love. He does not want anyone uninformed; He wants people to choose Him independently. It is our choice.

For my readers of different faiths and belief systems than mine, please take my words and apply them in the context and language of your belief system. The bottom line of what I am saying is this: We can choose good, or we can choose evil.

Satan has full power over the world today, including the evil, the diseases, the violence, the starvation and wars—all of it. Satan is very invested in making the world the most ungodly he possibly can through people's sick behaviors, the media, and illness. He wants people to think and believe there is no God, so when the end comes, Satan will have more demonic warriors or souls in his army than God will have in His.

The constant struggle between good and evil has been going on since the beginning of time. This struggle has no doubt been the breeding ground for many of the elements of mankind's demise, creating doubt, fear, and insecurity by leading man to ponder such things as:

"What is the meaning of life?" "Does life have meaning?"

"Where did this universe come from?"

And the most important question of all: "Is there a God?"

If we relied on faith, and accepted without doubt that God is real and there is meaning to life, there would be no choice for us to make in the matter of believing in Him or not. That may seem unfair, but who are we to question God? (I realize some religions encourage mental and emotional "God wrestling," but even that occurs only with the basic belief that there is a God to wrestle with.)

He wants us to believe in Him and His Word, to choose to do so regardless of the evil that exists today and throughout history, and despite the underlying influences of Satan in the media, technology, and the plague of Socialcide. We can choose Good, or we can choose Evil. We can choose not to choose, but if we don't choose, we are not choosing good, and evil wins. We can choose God, or we can choose ourselves. However, choosing ourselves as our own, personal god, or choosing whatever we decide to worship other than God, is all Satan in the end. Choosing God is often a blind faith, but God did not create robots programmed to love Him without choice. Humans were created to be able to choose between good and evil, to choose God or "not God."And to help us out, because life isn't always easy or cost-free, it is free and easy to choose God/Good.

Many teenagers and adults have no spiritual support in their lives. These numbers of such persons is increasing year to year, much like the rise of narcissism, and people are drifting further and further away from the dock that once held us close to God, and morality, and good.

People continually seek happiness, but in all the wrong ways and in all the wrong places. True happiness is not found in another person, an addiction, money, possessions, self-love, or status, but people put tremendous amounts of energy into making those types of things be their happiness, all the while moving themselves further and further away from true happiness and satisfaction. Each of those things can temporarily make a person feel better, which encourages the person to pursue more and more of that thing, trying to get to the "big happy." But because none of them really provides what our souls need, that point will never be reached. The effort is futile.

True, lasting happiness is always an inside job, yet people keep looking outside themselves to find it. Is this part of the Socialcide plan as well? To keep people unhappy, so they feel compelled to sample things or behaviors that may bring temporary and superficial feelings of happiness, yet ultimately destroy their lives, bodies, and souls? Or perhaps to keep us from feeling a true purpose in the world, creating a vulnerability and, sometimes, a desperation that leads us into situations where we believe we have found true purpose and belonging, but really have not? If the latter is true, that is an especially dangerous place for children and adolescents to be wandering, as fitting in and belonging are a huge part of what they are all about.

Isolation from self, (not allowing ourselves to know and love our true selves), is isolation from God, and a dangerous road to travel. When we let society and the media dictate who we really are, and when parents do not help their children to discover and respect who they really are, we end up with a society full of superficial, disconnected, confused people struggling to find their way, and not really knowing how they lost their way in the first place. When we become isolated from our true selves, and lose our connection to God and spirituality, and we live our lives as the person we have been convinced by others we are supposed to be,; we become focused on gratifying the needs of that false self. However, we can never satisfy that false self, because it is not our true self. Neither our false self nor our true self's self's needs are

129

being addressed, and our true self is not being expressed. This leaves us feeling empty and unhappy, and we think those dissatisfied feelings are because we don't have enough of this or that, but it is really because we have drifted so far away from our true selves and our connection with God. Yet we keep trying, putting effort into being better at being that false self. We keep living life as that false self, and becoming increasingly unhappy, putting more and more energy into pursuing those things that provide superficial, temporary happiness. We become very self- focused, but on the wrong self!

Completely excluding any thought of God is a typical narcissistic personality characteristic, but it is generally not typical in non-narcissists. If narcissists believed in God—truly believed—then they would not be the most important factor in their own lives, and they could demonstrate the ability to feel compassion and love. But they cannot. As I see less and less of God in people's lives, I see more and more narcissists. You do the math!

Chapter Fourteen

I Will Love You to Death

"Sometimes love can bean addiction for hurt."
—Ira N. Barin

Straight-up addictions are a mainstay in my field. Drug-, alcohol-, and sex- dependent clients are not new to me. However, more and more often, people come to me for help because they are suffering from Person Addiction or Obsessive Love Disorder. These are very new disorders that are showing up more frequently in recent years as time goes on. The increase in the presence of these disorders cannot be separated from the current rise in narcissism, as they appear to be directly related to one another.

We know there are far more male narcissists than female; the typical client who has a Person Addiction is female.

Here's how a Person develops Dependence: The male narcissist meets a female who is unhappy. The man appears (to the woman) to be the most wonderful, loving, caring soul-mate the woman has ever met. She truly believes all he tells her about how wonderful and beautiful she is, and how they will live together in a beautiful house with the white picket fence, have children and a dog, and live happily ever after.

After living some period of time with these beliefs and hopes, and even changing her life to support the picture Mr. Right has painted, reality sets in. She gets pregnant. He 's not working. Or perhaps he has had a number of jobs, but something always went wrong that he claims was not his fault, so he quit. She's working full time, and maybe more, to pay their rent, pay his debts (which often includes paying for his drugs or alcohol) and pay his utility bills, including his cell phone, which he will never let her look at.

Now the woman is miserable, but she cannot see him for who he is, because she cannot get past how he was initially so wonderful, and she cannot let go of the idea that this person saw her as wonderful and beautiful, and made all kinds of life plans with her. She attributes his new selfish behavior to his being depressed and, buys his wounded, always-getting-ripped-off-by-others stories. She feels sorry for him! She needs that wonderful man back, so she will do anything it takes to get him back.

The sad truth is, this is who he was all along; it was masked by his narcissistic con. They fight. She doesn't want to let go. When he pushes her away she begs him to take her back. She may even promise him she will change for him. He eats it up! The power and control this relationship gives him is intoxicating.

The relationship will go on and on. He will not leave it because he is in control, and he is getting everything he wants. And she cannot leave it. She doesn't want to. She just keeps putting in more and more effort to get back what is actually only the false image of himself (and of herself) he gave her at the beginning. Between the fights, some possibly physical, he will reappear as his original s1e5lf8, to regain some time and trust from her.

But ultimately, all of his problems are hers and everyone else's everyone else's—never his.

He does not see himself as the bad guy. Often, she doesn't either (see him as the bad guy). He doesn't care what he is doing to her, how he is hurting her, how he is contributing to her destruction. He just knows he keeps getting everything he wants.

If you have never known someone (or been someone) involved with this type of evil, it is very difficult to believe situations like this could last as long as they actually do. It takes the person-dependent woman a tremendous amount of self-work and courage to leave a man such as this. These men tie an emotional noose so tightly around the necks of their victims that even breathing can depend on the man's his say-so.

There is no cure for such monsters. They do not change. They may slide into and out of their role of Mr. Wonderful, but that never lasts longer than it takes to get their next desire fulfilled.

Socialcide is the "emotional noose" around America's collective neck. As a society, we have been seduced into a world of false wonder and enchantment, of how great we are, by the ultimate Mr. Wonderful in disguise: Satan. In our captivity, many of us try and try to feel happiness, but it is either short-lived, non-existent, or gets us wrapped up in dangerous situations.

In the proverbial good old days, people had much more involvement with others. They had more social stimuli around them, and experienced less despair and need for finding happiness. We lived in neighborhoods where people actually knew each other, and were not afraid to socialize. Families flourished and did things together, sometimes even with other families. Imagine that! More families also attended some form of community spiritual or religious worship, and their lives included a the presence and appreciation of God in their homes.

Depression existed back then, as did narcissism, but in nowhere near the prevalence we see today. Why? Families were more structured and in-tact. People interacted with people far more than they do now. Inappropriate behavior was actually considered inappropriate— and was addressed. The media did not glorify narcissistic criminals, or over-rated, sexually-charged celebrities. There was much more respect for worthy people who truly did good things for the world and our country. Today, such societal norms almost seem like a joke.

Depression was less present because of socialization. The best way to not be depressed is to do for others. There is no secret to this. When we work together or for others, and performing altruistic tasks, the self or spirit is fulfilled, and does not constantly need or seek things to be happy. But many people just don't socialize anymore. They stay home and connect with others only through technology.

There is no shortage of people today who could use some help, yet scores of able-bodied folks would rather take a pill to feel better than to extend themselves to others and, in turn, feel better themselves and while making the world a better place.

SECTION III

The Role of Parents

Chapter Fifteen

We Don't Think—So?

"Nothing in the world is more dangerous than sincere ignorance
and conscientious stupidity."
—Martin Luther King, Jr.

Another culprit instilled by our advanced state of technology, and one that is particularly helpful in t o the rise of evil today, is the lack of common sense and thought. Young people today probably have to actually think and problem-solve less than any other time in history. When we let machines, or others people, think for us, how do we ever learn to solve problems in life? We simply do not.

As we see in today's new college graduates attempting to join the workforce, these young professionals lack many of the skills needed to get and retain a job. These are the necessary skills that cannot be taught in a classroom, but only come from real life. But what is real life? For some, it's really hard to tell anymore.

There is a well-hidden reality going on, or should I say not going on, in American public schools: children are not being taught how to write in script or cursive anymore. The powers-that-be have determined that learning formal handwriting is a waste of time. The truth is, if you don't learn to write in script you're also not learning how to read script.

As a result, children grow up unable to read original documents such as the Constitution, the Declaration of Independence, those old postcards in their family heirlooms collections, or anything written in script.

137

Catholic and other private schools continue to teach this form of writing, but the taxpayers of the United States—who support public school education—are kept in the dark about this huge elimination of a basic skills.

Additionally, young people today text far more often than they write, and when they text, they don't d o n ' t spell out many words. There is a whole dictionary of "text speak" acronyms and "short spellings" of words that are commonly used (and usually only understood by those who write them) that are so frequently used by youth (and some adults). that they These "words" are finding their way into school writing assignments, homework, and even professional business communications. When your brain begins to process language that way, you lose the ability to write (and read) language correctly.

Is it any wonder this generation is not producing rocket scientists or intellectually superior adults? If children are not learning how to write, they will not be encouraged to read. And if they are not encouraged to read, they won't. The inability to read and write leads to ignorance. And an ignorant nation of ignorance is easily controlled.

I am not advocating for the Catholic religion, or for Catholic or private schools; I am advocating questioning why school systems that are not under governmental control and direction continue to teach basic reading, writing, and arithmetic, while 1st6a3te-supported facilities do not. This should outrage and frighten all Americans.

Is this also a force of evil creeping into the moral fiber of American lives? Evil always chooses the easy way, and while hard work and dedication are solid, time-tested, character-building traits.

Laziness, or sloth as it is named in the list of "Seven Deadly Sins," is the avoidance of physical or spiritual work. These two types of work go hand-in-hand today. If children are being taught the easy way out by not being taught the traditional way of hard work, problem- solving, winning and losing, researching, etc., do you think they will seek to work on themselves as people? Why should they?

Another set of problem-solving skills schools (elementary through college) do not teach anymore the way they used to be is research and project planning. Today, information and calculations are just a click- and- paste away. Back in the day, it took much more thinking and effort than that. Often a librarian becomes a student's best friend. I wonder how many of today's students could successfully complete a research paper if placed in a library that did not have computers with Internet access. I think they would even be reluctant to ask a librarian for assistance, and if they did, they would have trouble figuring out what to ask. How many of them have ever even seen (much less used) a card catalogue?

Without being able to type keywords into a search engine (which, by the way, will search for your information even if you spell the keyword wrong), and having that search engine provide a list of sources , most students are lost. Being able to determine w1h6a4t is a valid source of information, and then being able to use that information appropriately, are problem-solving skills that have been lost through the use (overuse and misuse) of technology, and at the expense of common sense and thinking.

Everything in life is a process. Having to learn how to manage time and tasks as part of a process isn't just beneficial in terms of producing a respectable term paper; it is beneficial to all kinds of real-life problem- solving tasks. These days, a student can wait until the night before a project is due, go online, type in keywords, cut and paste text, and email the project to their teacher—all without leaving the comfort of home. There is no problem-solving practice in that.

Some would argue that there's no need any more for thinking and problem-solving skills, but they are not looking deeply enough at the problem, or at the benefits of appropriate utilization of resources and project planning. And when we depend completely on technology, and the technology fails (gasp!), what are we then left with then? Even the most expensive computer, equipped with the latest software, highest processing speeds, and most available memory, can crash from time to time.

Let's just say that nothing good can come from a child not being taught cursive writing, correct spelling and grammar, the proper way to do research and find and use resources, how to manage time and tasks for a project, and basic problem solving in school. What is being accomplished by not teaching those skills is the training of an entire generation of people *not to think!* If we are going to "cut the fat" to save time for education, my guess is that all the time spent prepping children for standardized tests (vs. truly teaching the subject material appropriate for each grade level) might be a more useful elimination. Real life rarely requires use of the skills of successfully outsmarting the nuances of a particular standardized test. Teach writing, creative writing, how to manage money, how to balance a checkbook, how to budget income, how to get a job, and how to be a good person. *That* is a good use of class time!

There are some other very important skills that youth of youth of today are sorely lacking. Getting a job is an art, now more than ever. College graduates today expect to get a job just because they went to college and deserve a job. However, there is much more to getting hired than having a degree.

By the time a person enters college, she or he should have some familiarity and experience with having had a job of some type already. No one deserves a job; more appropriately, everyone deserves an opportunity. And the value of that opportunity is in the ability to present oneself to the best of his or her ability. The interview process is more about how a person carries himself or herself in a conversation than about what college he or she attended.

One problem today is the true lack of socialization skills young people demonstrate. Many have never worked before, and believe that going online, copying and pasting their resume into a form, and then applying by clicking "send" is how you get a job.

That may work in some cases today. But how does the *Me, Me, Me* Generation interview?

Previous generations had job application, interview, and employment experience before they went to college, which made the process of getting and keeping a job after college easier in many ways. This generation just doesn't have a clue what to do, because they have not had any employment experience or guidance.

Mark Bauerlein, in a *Bloomberg View* (May 8, 2013) op-ed report titled, "What do U.S. College Graduates Lack? Professionalism,"([which was prompted by an experience he had with a student who showed up twenty-five minutes late to a college exam, and then asked for another twenty minutes when the allotted time was up]) cites various complaints by people who work in human resources. During job interviews, "applicants check their phones for texts and calls, dress inappropriately, and overrate their talents."

Where is the *thinking?* This real scenario is one that can easily be imagined as part of a Carol Burnett comedy segment. However, this Millennial Generation grew up watching reality television shows that are primarily about narcissists, and are not presented not as comedy, but as reality; so is this behavior any real surprise? Not at all.

The importance of "paying your dues" in life is seemingly more and more scoffed at. Millennials believe they are *owed* jobs, and not just jobs, but high-paying, prestigious ones. Their sense of entitlement has been well established throughout childhood by over-doting parents, and exposure to the likes of over-night superstars bred from YouTube videos, reality shows, and even spree or thrill killers.

This generation expects success to come quickly and easily. There is less and less dependency on the real resources that once functioned to guide individuals through life, and assist them along with mutual giving and taking. Now it's all taking and no giving, which is the basic nature of the narcissist. "What can I get from him, her, them, or the world?"

They Can't Drive You Crazy. They Don't Want to Drive

Brad Tuttle's article in Time Magazine titled, "The Great Debate: Do Millennials Really Want Cars, or Not?" (August 9, 2013) reported that the answer is no. Most Millennials have no desire or intention to get a driver's license, to drive at all, or to own a car. Car manufacturers are spending millions and millions of dollars trying to entice this generation to find driving cool, but it's just not working. They blame the cost of car insurance and ownership as being "financially out of reach right now for this generation," and as they age and the economy and their income improves, so will sales to Millennials rise.

"Nonsense," says Socialcide! Adolescents today have so little motivation to drive that parents (I have seen this in many cases) practically have to beg their kids to get a driver's license.

It's not the economy. People can use family cars, or buy a "beater"car for a small price if they truly want the independence driving allows. But today, kids rarely leave their houses. In fact, adults rarely leave their houses if they do not have to. Children have become quite accustomed to being carted around by mom or dad whereever they must go. They rarely walk, for fear of the Boogey Man, or simply because they are lazy. The main cause, however, is the availability of video games at home, emails, and text messages—all allowing constant contact with whomever they are communicating with.

The back story to this, in a Socialcide frame of reference, is the erosion of true socialization and actually being with other people. What does this have to do with driving? The more self-reliant we think we are the more reliant on technology we become. And it will come to pass that technology will reveal itself as the ultimate evil destroying the two things humanity really needs to survive—other people, and God.

This information about the lack of Millennials lack of wanting to drive or own a car of their own is an extremely significant sign of what is going wrong with youth today. Think back (if you are over thirty-five) to when you counted the days until your birthday—the birthday that made you eligible to take your driver's test. Most of us simply could not wait to have that freedom and ability to drive. That was such an accomplishment and dramatic change of lifestyle, because it brought so much with it: independence, dating, friends, going places together, etc. So if the youth of today are not interested in driving and gaining freedom through the ability to drive, are all those other things not important to them? And if not, what is?

From statistics and reports from this Me, Me, Me Generation, the answer seems to be fame, their way, the easy way, adoration, instant access to anything they want, and special treatment for all their wonderful, most unique and incredible selves!

Chapter Sixteen

It's Not My Fault!

"When you blame others, you give up the power to change."
—Robert Anthony

As the Employee Assistance Program Director of a large municipality near my office, I often see police officers, fire fighters, and other municipal workers as clients. This I recall one particular case that involves involved a male police officer, approximately forty years old, married, with two children. He was sent to me because he has had a high number of "civilian demeanor complaints" against him. In other words, following a traffic stop (in most cases) the person who was given a ticket for a traffic violation or other offense filed a formal complaint against him.

To me, this option is news. I never knew a person could officially *complain about a police officer's demeanor* after receiving a summons unless that person was somehow assaulted, personally violated, or harassed. Apparently, though, that is not the case anymore. Now if someone feels the officer was even slightly disrespectful, the law allows that person to file a complaint against the officer. The cameras installed on police vehicles and the microphones officers now wear are not so much to protect the people who break the law, but to protect the department from slanderous lawsuits brought by member of the public.

This officer had a higher than average number of complaint against him than the average number, so he blipped on the department's radar. He is was an officer who took his job very seriously. He strives strove to do his job well, not allowing speeders or social disturbances to slip through the cracks. After all, stopping people, writing tickets, or arresting people requires showing diligence that many other officers are not interested in showing; especially the younger officers, but also the well-seasoned ones. So it stands to reason that these days, the more an officer does his job like he is supposed to, the more likely he is to receive complaints.

Due to his higher-than-average number of complaints, my client was sent for a "Fit for Duty" psychological evaluation, to determine if there was something wrong with him. The good doctor who completed the evaluation did not find any underlying anger, deviance, or cause for any alarm with him, but recommended he receive some psychotherapy "just to make sure." Hence the officer and I met. I, too, found nothing alarming about this police officer, except the fact that he takes his job very seriously. (Imagine that!). The man is was as *perfectly normal* as one could be. He had very effective coping skills, good judgment, and he conducted his life, family, and job with sound reasoning. Hmmm…this gets more interesting.

What I learned from him is that many of these complaints had come from people who had no current registration on their vehicle, were illegally parked with children in the car to "run into the post office," who had attempted to pass on the right over a pedestrian crossing, had been pushing shopping carts far from stores where they belonged, or had challenged his authority to issue a summons, which, in some cases, gave the recipient a huge break with a reduced charge.

In the old days, if you were pulled over you *knew why*, and any break you got was a *gift!* Today that is often not the case. That *entitlement factor* is big, bad, and furious. From whom does it come? By far, according to my client, it came from people thirty-five years old or younger, with a large portion from high school students or teenagers! No kidding!.

Here again we see the damage of Socialcide in that age group. They believe they are not accountable for their behaviors, or to authority, or to the law. They will do all they can to get out of trouble, as they have undoubtedly seen their parents do for them all their lives. They feel not a shred of remorse for the danger or potential danger to others their selfish actions produce, and they couldn't care less about causing personal, financial, or departmental problems for the officer of the law who caught them in their entitled and narcissistic behaviors.

Of course, the media is quick to show clips of officers being violent or abusive, and to put the blame on them for what appears to be a violation of someone's rights. That just may be what is happening in some cases. But the media certainly does not address the nonsensical complaints hardworking law enforcement personnel routinely receive because someone will not take responsibility for his or her actions.

It has been said that, "Seeing is believing." When children see how police officers can get into trouble for doing their jobs, or how parents intervene to bail their children out of trouble, because they are "so wonderful," they will take that message with them through life.

This is not the same country we once knew. Not even close. Yes, sometimes policemen are very out of line, or abusing abusive of their authority. But when they have to protect themselves from potential frivolous lawsuits, there is something very wrong. When did it become an option to get out of trouble or avoid paying a fine by accusing the officer of a bad attitude? When Socialcide found its way into the minds of Americans.

Chapter Seventeen

If Your Children Hate You, Congratulations

"It takes courage to raise children."
—John Steinbeck, East of Eden

I recently read that Vice President Joe Biden announced that one- hundred million dollars was going to be added to the cause of Mental Health Care in the United States. With all due respect, Mr. Vice President, are you kidding? That amount may cover the cost of construction of one decent psychiatric hospital, but it will not make a dent in the cure reduction or elimination of Socialcide. This is simply another example of Nero fiddling while Rome burns. However, that pathetic attempt to help fix things in America today is not what burns me up as much as does the public's perception that it should.

It always seems to be after the fact of a sick and evil occurrence that people, parents, the media, or society asks, "Didn't anyone see this coming? Why didn't he or she get help?" Herein, again, begins the blame game. And again I ask, "Where were the parents?" Who should know their children better than anyone else? Who should be in their children's business, for better or for worse, no matter what the child says or does to combat it? It is all too common to be presented with a new case of a teen involved in some form of deviant behavior that has brought him or her to therapy via the court system, probation, or school, only to once again uncover how unavailable or over compensating that teen's parents have been in their rearing.

What is even more disturbing than that news is that many times, once

149

the proverbial damage has been done, it cannot be undone. No amount of mental health dollars or "sense" can buy your child out of a lifetime with a personality disorder. However, parents and society would like to believe in such fairy tales, because we have become accustomed to the idea that we can just pay someone to fix it. How chilling it is to deal with people and parents such as this.

Society's Role

Personality Disorders such as narcissistic, borderline, dependent, schizoid, and histrionic are social diseases for which there is no cure. They are the result of how we were raised, and what went on, or did not go on, in our homes and families, the womb of childhood from which we gain the nutrients, and life-sustaining knowledge, and fortification to function in the world as near to normal as possible.

Socialcide is of the view that people are or should be like birds: when we are old enough to fly, we should simply take wing and do it. However, even if that were true, today's children are not even willing to use their wings.

These are a r e not psychotic disorders in the way schizophrenia, schizo-affective, or bipolar disorders can be, where voices (auditory hallucinations), visual hallucinations, or other symptoms of psychosis are present, causing the afflicted person to see things or hear things not actually there, however real they are seem to the person.

Personality disorders are more consistent with maladaptive social behaviors, especially with other people in interpersonal or social relationships, including family, friends, co-workers, or people in general.

Personality, defined psychologically, is the set of enduring behavioral and mental traits that distinguish human beings. So personality disorders are defined by experiences and behaviors that differ from society's norms and expectations, and are frequently associated with personal and social disruptions across a spectrum: from being unusually isolated to being a serial killer, and everything in between. As Socialcide has recognized the extreme rise in narcissism and sociopathic evil growing to record highs today, Psychology, especially Forensic Psychology, looks for warning signs that may indicate a child's potential to become a sadistic killer later in life.

While those attempts to distinguish evil among us are certainly hope-inspiring and needed, there are still countless people with personality disorders that w h o wreak havoc in this country by destroying the very fiber of what once made our society great; yet little, if anything, is being done to stop about them. My question to forensic psychologists is this: If you identify behaviors and characteristics in a child that indicate his or her potential to become a killer, what do you do with that child? In this scenario, the field of Psychology is backward. Instead of trying to cure or treat the criminal after the fact, they are looking at what causes the fact to begin with, and determining where we go from there to prevent the fact.

The field of Psychology is not an exact science, and the legal system takes full advantage of that fact. Highly-paid attorneys feverishly work to get their violent and murderous victims off the hook as best they can by trying to prove their client was not responsible for what they did (no matter how horrific the crime) because they were "crazy." Socialcide would agree that these criminals were crazy—crazy like a fox and guiltless as the devil.

The legal world today mirrors much of what has become family life when it comes to taking responsibility for our own actions. Can't we just blame someone or something else, or pay our way out of this problem? It is beyond reprehensible when such horrors of the world are treated this way. Is there any thought about the victims, their families, their friends, and the multitudes of others who will never live life the same because one person with a maladjusted, evil mind has destroyed another person's life? Unfortunately not, because that is how the game is played. And as usual, the devil is in the details.

Most Americans do not know what insanity really means. In brief, insanity is a legal term that indicates a defendant's ability to determine right from wrong when a crime is committed. The first line of the definition from law.com states: mental illness of such a severe nature that a person cannot distinguish fantasy from reality, cannot conduct her/his affairs due to psychosis, or is subject to uncontrollable/impulsive behavior. This becomes particularly problematic in courts of law and in media blasts that report criminal, psychopathic behavior as "insane."

The layperson sitting on a jury can be innocently and easily swayed by a highly-paid attorney with his highly-paid "expert witnesses" testifying under oath to what they find to be "insane." We cannot blame jurors who simply do not know the truth, but we can certainly blame the criminals and their Jaguar-driving attorneys for perpetrating such a farce where innocent people have been hurt, tortured, or killed because their maladaptive personality disorder distorted their understanding of what is right and what is wrong.

The prosecution, as well, may be a bit behind in knowing what truly constitutes insane behavior in cases that involve human violation, but their solution is to present their own expert witnesses to counter the defense's attempts. This is true insanity! It is nowhere close to the answer to such injustice.

So what a verdict boils down to, in many if not most cases of human torture, abuse, or killing, when the "not guilty by reason of insanity" card is drawn as a defense, is which lawyer and expert witness or witnesses the jury believes to be most credible, or perhaps the most attractive or popular, and the jury's knowledge of what insanity or mental illness is or is not. This is simply unfair.

The ideal jury for such cases would consist of qualified mental health providers. But under our laws, that would be a violation of the defendant's right to a "jury of his peers," wouldn't it? So this is how the game is played at the present time. I refer to Neil Young's quote, "The devil fools with the best laid plans." There are countless cases where insanity was determined to be the cause of the most heinous of crimes. The abundance of the sickest and most cruel crimes being committed today are, by far, committed by individuals with personality disorders—which are is a far cry from insanity.

As demented and antisocial as people with personality disorders can be, they are quite aware of what they do, and certainly can understand right from wrong. The problem with narcissists is they believe they are never wrong, whether criminally, socially, in business, in relationships, or in whatever situations humans encounter.

Void of conscience, remorse, and empathy, what sort of people are we truly looking at? Where do people gain such traits? Or perhaps more importantly, what causes people to develop without them? Again, one must return to the family of origin, the society, and God or spirituality of some sort. These are the trainers of morality in life. Without proper roots in these areas, the tree they should secure is but a prop that can be picked up and moved from here to there to suit its own needs, or it can be adapted to different situations. While appearing to be a tree, in reality, it is merely a rouse. It is not until it is kicked over that one can identify the falsehood. That is narcissism.

When people in a jury, or in regular life, come into contact with individuals with personality disorders, they are either fascinated by their ease of conversation, and complimentary style that plays to every need of attention, interest, and love the normal human has, or they are immediately taken aback by their strange sense of presence, and lack of social finesse. Either of the two can be potentially dangerous, as they are both merely masks of people who are up to something behind the scenes.

What narcissists and all personality-disordered people have grown up without is a true sense of self. A Godless or spiritually-deprived person has no soul, no moral fiber, due to neglect of parents or family, over-praise or over-compensation by parents, lack of experiencing consequences for unacceptable behavior, or sexual, emotional, or physical abuse.

Do all people who come from one of these backgrounds have personality disorders? No. What determines who becomes afflicted by them? That question is unanswerable by any science known to man. Various theories swirl around the combination of social environment, childhood predicting the potential for narcissism among other personality disorders: childhood experiences and social environment. The What the missing piece here is becomes more and more clear as the number of cases of narcissism rise in our country. Where there is smoke, we know there is fire; and where there are soulless people, we know there is something consuming them. In Socialcide, that soul-eating missing piece is the evil gaining that is gaining power and speed in our country today.

Like a tornado increasing in force, evil is strengthening itself with souls that are being consumed by lack of belief and faith in God, lack of solid family foundation, the "I'll do whatever I feel like doing. I'll do" mentality, laziness, dependence on media and technology, and everything else that allows them to disregard what we once knew and believed to be good and right in our country. We have replaced the basics of human kindness with microchip mentality. When people cease to live with a cause, their cause becomes themselves.

Chapter Eighteen
Isn't There a Book?

"If you don't teach your children to love God,
society will teach them not to."
—unknown

Evil will find its way into people's lives through any crack in the foundation. But let's take a look, specifically, at young people. Why? Because they are very vulnerable. They want and need acceptance, validation, and a sense of belonging somewhere—anywhere. If mom or dad (or whoever are the child's primary caregivers) are not around to guide, assist, nurture, instruct, discipline, or encourage, someone or something else will.

The devil delights in the vulnerable. They are easy prey! What better or easier targets are there than teenagers? Why do so many adolescents these days experiment with Satan worship, or insist that God doesn't exist these days? Mostly because many families don't support God or any form of spirituality anymore, and parents are simply not as available to their kids as they should be.

When parents ignore their children's real needs, or are simply unaware of them, the door is wide open for any form of manipulation to occur by any outside source. When parents don't parent, they are leaving the door wide open for any influence to take hold of their child's needy and fertile mind and manipulate it any way that serves that influence's purposes. The effects of Socialcide clearly show us that this manipulation is well-planned, and is already working like a well-greased machine. This is a sad reality that, if not dealt with on a social level, will only continue to gain power, and this evil will destroy anyone and anything in its path.

There are questions we should consider when trying to understand how evil makes its way so easily into the hearts of the masses. Is there a connection between personality and soul? Does one create the other, or vice versa? Do they mimic each other? Does the absence of one cause the evil in the other? These are all questions worth examining when we consider the level of pure evil we see in the world today.

By "evil" I mean bullying, manipulating spouses, abandoning family responsibilities, destroying trashing lives and reputations online or via social media sites severely enough to cause the victim to commit suicide, all the way up the spectrum to senseless mass shootings or bombings in elementary schools, movie theaters, and other public places. What type of person perpetrates this evil, and why? Does this type of person have a soul to speak of, or has it been stolen, or eroded away so badly to the point of nonexistence? And how was that able to occur?

Having a child solidifies a moral obligation and contract to assume full responsibility for that child. That obligation includes providing food, shelter, safety, protection, guidance, instruction, understanding, positive support for personality development, and instilling an awareness of and the importance for of respecting and observing the common decencies of the world, teaching right from wrong, teaching responsibility and about the importance of owning responsibility for one's bad actions or decisions, disciplining when needed, and putting nothing else before these needs you have created by taking on the responsibility of having a child.

Being a parent means you need proper balance in your own life, in order to help your child balance hers or his. Shortcuts here do not apply. Nor would they help. Parenting is a full time job. Period—period. If you don't raise your child, someone or something else will. Evil will slip in through the cracks, and influence—or even take over—your children's personalities and souls.

That is a frightening concept; too frightening, but very true. When parents do not provide for all their children's needs, the children's foundations crack (or never fully form), and all kinds of nasty things creep in to fill those empty spaces.

A huge problem we face today is that many parents miss the warning signs that serve as a call to action for that parent to get involved with their child, or to get professional help for their child. All too often the signs are recognized far too late, and then we hear, "Where were the parents?" or "Why didn't the school, the teacher, the doctor, the mental health field catch this before it happened?" Sadly, by then it does not matter. The damage is done, and families, friends, and society are left with the darkness looming over their lives forever.

Some would say, "But there is no book of rules on how to be a parent!" The truth is, there are thousands of books on parenting, but Socialcide does not look for answers, or a "How To" guide for the most important job in the world. As mentioned earlier, good parents do not need to read books on parenting, and bad parents simply won't.

Once upon a time, the art of parenting was parenting was passed down from generation to generation, much like Grandma's recipe for her delicious tomato sauce. Sadly, that unbeatable sauce is a fading memory, just like the art of raising children. The institution of the family has crumbled over the generations like a stale cookie. America has been forsaking what used to be its driving forces, and replaced them with modern conveniences and quick-fixes that, in reality, break more than they fix.

Parenting is a full time job, and requires commitment, selflessness, sacrifice, patience, strength, and love. At least, that is what past generations taught us. Those very principals are in complete contrast to today's narcissistic nation in every possible way. No, I am not referring to all parents in America today. Of course there are millions of parents doing their job and doing it well. But those parents do not make the news, or have children committing heinous crimes of selfish entitlement and disturbed pathological thinking. No indeed, and I do not blame them for being ultra-protective of their offspring in a world that is quickly deteriorating. If more of that involved parenting, occurred fewer foundation cracks would exist, and less Socialcide would be present.

Chapter Nineteen

Unspoken Addictions — Parenting and Abuse

> "Parents who are afraid to put their foot down
> usually have children who step on their toes."
> —Chinese proverb

Some form of child abuse is found to be present in every single case of criminal pathology we know. It is also a main contributor to narcissism. When we hear the phrase "child abuse," the general perception is that it is referring to violent or sexual atrocities committed against children. Those types of crimes certainly do account for some cases of child abuse. However, there are other forms of abuse that also fit this category that, until more recently, most people wouldn't identify as abuse, and they are becoming widespread, and are major contributors to Socialcide and the deterioration of Society.

These other forms of child abuse come from and include emotional neglect and abandonment of children by their parents. In other words, leaving children to their own devices, and not being a fully-involved parent, is now being more seriously recognized as a form of abuse. Most people recognize that if you don't put gas in your car, don't get the oil changed regularly, don't check the air in your tires, and don't have regular maintenance performed, you are neglecting the car. It will stop working as it is supposed to, and will eventually break down.

However, most people don't realize that same principle applies to human beings.

We all know if we don't take care of our car, there's a good chance one day we'll get in the car (probably on a day we are in a rush) and it just won't start, or it will break down on the way to wherever we are going. With that fear in mind, we are both consciously and unconsciously compelled to take care of the car, so we can to prevent that incredible inconvenience. But we don't seem to be able to apply that same logic to the raising of and caring for children, who are significantly more fragile, needy in need of our attention, and valuable than replaceable machines. Sadly, some parents actually see raising their children as the bigger inconvenience.

Again and again, we see this to be the case in the lives of teenage or young adult killers, rapists, and shooters, as well as in playground bullies and children who just can't seem to function appropriately in the classroom or in other social settings. Additionally, we rarely see a child turn pathological liar, abuser, rapist, or murderer without some form of addiction in the home. A parent addicted to anything is simply not emotionally (and sometimes physically) available to parent his or her child.

We clearly identify and understand the addictions that do not disguise themselves well: alcohol, drugs, sex, shopping, gambling, and food. These are the addictions for which there are "numbers to call" if you or a loved one are affected. But there are other addictions, that are rarely identified or discussed, that are affecting more and more people with each passing day. These other addictions also contribute (maybe even more so in some ways than the others) to the newly recognized abuses—emotional neglect and abandonment, maybe even more so in some ways than the more well-known ones. These include what Socialcide calls Self-Addiction or Me-Addiction.

People who are Self- or Me-Addicted are those who are primarily looking out for themselves. And for parents in this category, a child can quickly become burdensome, and in the way of that parent's life and true motivations. For example, when a parent becomes overly concerned about rising up the corporate ladder, or is obsessed with finding a new mate for themselves, who is available for their child to go to for love, nurturing, acceptance, and guidance?

The child in this case quickly learns that the parent—the primary source for everything needed emotionally and spiritually to develop a true sense of self—finds many things more important than him or her. The child becomes "collateral damage" of the parent's self-addiction. This directly and immediately affects the child's self-image and ability to grow up in a healthy way.

After all, the child concludes consciously or subconsciously, if the person who is supposed to love me and take care of me has a whole list of better things to do, I must not be all that important, or there must be something wrong with me! And after hurting very deeply, the child decides, I will just go out and find what I am missing somewhere else. Anywhere else.

And when the child finds it, whether it's good or bad, the parent won't even notice, and will not be able to redirect him or her from whatever negative and dangerous influences to which they've attached themselves. The gaping chasms in the child's foundation created by the self-addicted parent will be filled by all kinds of potentially soul-destroying input.

Sometimes, on the surface this devilish system may seem easy and right to both parent and child. After all, teenagers think a parent who lets them do whatever they want, or gives them whatever they ask for is "cool." But the truth is, this type of parent-child dynamic is cause for alarm, and is quite irresponsible on the parent's part. The effects of such emotional abandonment will eventually be manifested in anti-social, destructive behavior.

Again we see the devil in the details. But the truth is, no matter how teenagers appear to be content to be just left alone, unconsciously they desire rules, structure, someone to set limits, and literally care about, and love them.

As I mentioned before, this neglect is child abuse, plain and simple. This cannot be argued. Kids do not need a friend as their parent; they need a parent who can be a friend when needed. The opposite does not work. Parents must parent first and foremost. However, the Self- Addiction problem in parents is becoming more and more evident in society as it reflects the characteristics of narcissists narcissism. Narcissists are, above all, addicted to themselves. And narcissists and self-addicted parents are breeding narcissistic and self- addicted children. Satan's army grows stronger.

In my first book, Defeating Depression: The Calm and Sense Way to Find Happiness and Satisfaction, I spoke of "emotional and social maturity" as a prerequisite to healthy relationships and truly being an adult. An emotionally and socially mature adult is a person who is able to look past the nonsense around them, and focus on what is truly worth working for and dedicating energies to. To lack either emotional or social maturity does not make an individual a narcissist, but it does foster jealousy, anger issues, and selfishness, and causes failed relationships, jobs, and endeavors. These people lack simple maturity, and frequently blame others for their own shortcomings, or for things going wrong in their lives.

We see this behavior in many parents today, as well as in children, adolescents, and young adults. "It must be someone else's fault! It can't be me!" Where do children learn this? Aside from society in general, it is unfortunately learned at home, with from parents who are not parenting. And if parents are unwilling or unable to take responsibility for what they do, how in the world will their child learn to do so?

Incidentally, these types of parents are usually the first to try to get their kid out of any trouble they get into as quickly as possible, because the parents cannot be bothered dealing with it. The truth is, if the parents weren't so preoccupied with corporate ladder climbing, or chasing their next Match.com conquest (or whatever other "I have to do this for me" thing), the kid probably wouldn't be in trouble to begin with.

It is a peculiar thing children do sometimes—testing limits. It can be a cry.

When the parent buys the child out of trouble, the child's message to the parent remains unheard, and the child begins to learn and gain a sense of entitlement that eventually develops into a narcissistic personality. The child feels and believes they are entitled to special treatment from the world, because that is what they have learned. To make matters worse, some parents then feel some degree of guilt—, presumably because on some deep level they realize they have not been as responsible as they could should have been, and these futile ways of showing their kids they care are really showing them they are not fit for the job of mom or dad in its true sense.

These feelings of guilt then lead the parent to compensate for their failure by buying—or attempting to buy—love. The child may enjoy the fruits of this guilt-driven bandage, but it is just that—only a bandage on a wound that continues to deepen and fester. The old saying, "The best thing you can spend on your child is time," applies here and always. Unfortunately, this remains mostly a clever saying, and not a reminder for prompt and direct action.

I cannot tell you how often an emotionally abandoned child comes through my office door accompanied by a self-addicted parent, because it happens so often frequently. I have rarely, if ever, had a case involving a child in some form of trouble where there was a fully-engaged parent in the household. I frequently hear from parents that they are looking for appointments after 7:00-8:00 pm, or on a weekend, because of their work schedules. That is usually my first piece of the assessment process, sight unseen. A parent fitting in an appointment with a therapist to help a child through a problem is a problem in itself. This is another example of how the "You are not as important to me as other things" message is delivered to the child over and over again. "Mom and dad are too busy for me."

Every single adolescent shooter studied by the FBI has reported that they had no adult in their lives to talk to or trust. That information is not a signal that every child who has no available, trustworthy adult in their lives will become a killer. What it is, though, is a very loud warning that not having such an adult in a child's life is hugely detrimental, and can lead to other forms of self-abuse or detrimental psychological functioning and dangerous behaviors. So why take that chance?

Self-addicted adults do not and cannot adequately perform the role of parent. As a result, the child is neglected. And, as I've described, that neglect is actually abuse. No form or level of severity of child abuse is acceptable. All forms and levels of child abuse destroy individuals, families, communities, and society, and fuel the Socialcide fire.

Chapter Twenty

The Therapist as Quasi-Parent

"If we want a great future in this world, we have to take God at His
word, and God makes it really clear that society and civilization is held together by the
glue of families. This is where the next generation of human beings are is incubated and
nurtured and matured—in homes, in families."
—Kirk Cameron

It becomes more and more apparent (no pun intended) that the field of
Counseling and Psychotherapy, at least from my stand point, is taking on a new
role of "quasi-parent," at least when it comes to young clients. For the clients
who are parents the therapist's work revolves greatly around the teaching of
parenting skills and positive child development-nurturing behaviors that were
once human instinct. These skills and behaviors have historically been passed
down through generations of families, but have gotten lost in the digital mix
of the world as Socialcide has gained speed and power.

These days, many parents need to be informed about taught how to
effectively parent, and they need a tremendous amount of support putting
effective parenting skills into practice. I do not believe this has occurred by
any accident. We are becoming more and more deprogrammed as people and
human beings. Socialcidal brainwashing has been ridding us of care, concern,
and empathy for, love of, and connection with others—including their our
own children. I'm talking about real connection, not connection   through
texting, twixting, tweeting, emailing, or other electronic and impersonal
means. The art of true socializing and communicating is seemingly becoming
less necessary, and that is frightening.

Counseling can certainly be a form of nurturance for some. A good
therapist should employ genuine empathy and understanding, along with

honesty, in order to solidify trust with the client. Those things should also be provided to a child by a parent or close relative, coach, teacher, or religious figure. Throughout my career I have often noticed how the roles have shifted in many ways toward counseling as pseudo-parenting. Many parents believe much, if not all, of their child's learning is the responsibility of their his or her teachers. Many parents reach out to counselors and teachers to assist and support them in their efforts on a particular issue their child is experiencing. It truly does "take a village." Our society really does function well and thrive when we all work together for the betterment of everyone, for the greater good. However, an increasing number of parents are just leaving the responsibility of nurturing, guiding, educating, and sometimes even loving their children at the feet of therapists, doctors, and teachers.

Even when a parent expects a therapist to fill this role, it cannot be done. No monthly, weekly, or even daily interaction with a child by a doctor, therapist, or teacher can take the place of true parenting.

In addition to children being emotionally abandoned by mom and dad, is it really any wonder there are so many emotional and psychological disorders in children today? Is it any wonder children are acting out so horribly and so violently against themselves and others? Is it any wonder teachers and counselors are feeling the implied responsibility of raising today's children, instead of just providing education, guidance, and support? And to make matters worse, parents who aren't fully parenting have begun to realize teachers, doctors, and therapists aren't their stand-ins, so they are blaming the children. This twisted logic implies the that "kids should know better."

Parents (not teachers, doctors, or therapists) are supposed to be raising their children. And as for the issue of who should know better, it's the parents.

Chapter Twenty-One

Creating a Spectacle

"The spectacle is not a collection of images, but a social relation among people, mediated by images."
--Guy Debord

How much responsibility children and young adults should have, and what they should or should not "know better," is a touchy area in some instances. For example, take the twenty-year-old Newtown, Connecticut, Sandy Hook Elementary School shooter. Should he have known better? You'd think so. Actually, we would all like to believe that even a ten-year-old would know better than to go into a school with a gun, or to shoot an innocent person. In reality, part of what allows us to go out in public, send our children off to school and basically just live our lives is the basic assumption that people know better. But sometimes they don't, and we are left to ask why.

"Spectacle Killings" is the term the media has been using lately to describe such evil, horrible tragedies. Spectacle killings. "Look at me! Look at what I am capable of doing, and how I don't care who I hurt!"

The Newtown killer reportedly had been showing signs of behavior that screamed danger long before he picked up a weapon to go on his slaughtering rampage. His mother was a gun fanatic, and had even purchased the boy guns and, as soon as he was physically able to pull a trigger, had taught him how to shoot, as soon as he was physically able to pull a trigger. This kid was a narcissist with destruction on his mind, along with the lure of eternal infamy for his demonic actions.

The killer's mother had recently returned from a "test trip" away from home, to see if her son would be able to cope without her there. She returned from the two-day trip and was killed by her son just before he went to Sandy Hook Elementary School to hunt. A friend of the mother reported that the boy was resentful of time his mother spent volunteering at the school, and believed she loved those kids more than she loved him. One can easily imagine the voice of evil telling him, "Your mother doesn't love you; she hates you," and badgering, beckoning, teasing, and taunting, encouraging his anger as he fascinated over violent video games (one of which dramatized a child being shot and others depicting suicide by gunshot). Not only was he mesmerized by the 1999 Columbine High School massacre, he also created a spreadsheet of America's the worst massacres in American history. Mom knew of this fascination with Columbine, and of his obsession with violent video games.

The forces of evil apparently began eroding the soul of a boy who once played saxophone, climbed trees, rode his bicycle, and even played in the school band in fifth and sixth grades. One of his teachers noted that he had good creative writing skills, but the content of his stories about destruction, war, and battles was far too graphic to be read in class.

He was diagnosed with Asperger's syndrome, which is on the spectrum of Autistic disorders, but is not associated with violence. The police reports released stated he was diagnosed in 2006 with "profound Autism Spectrum Disorder, with rigidity, isolation, and lack of comprehension or ordinary social interaction and communication, while also displaying symptoms of obsessive-compulsive disorder." Either he or his mother refused antidepressant or anti-anxiety medication treatment for him, because of potential side effects.

He reportedly had been treated by mental health professionals, presumably with therapy only, but none of them saw any indication of the powder keg about to explode. Again we see how well Socialcide can mask itself when necessary, in order to complete what it needs to do. In this case, what it needed to do was nothing short of evil. So not only did his mother turn a blind eye to what was going on in this kid's life, but the so-called mental health professionals did not see any risk factors either. His father was reportedly estranged, and that absence certainly factored into this mix as well.

Of very interesting note however, is that the boy's psychiatrist, Dr. Paul Fox from Brookfield, Connecticut, now resides in New Zealand, having voluntarily surrendered his medical license following allegations of a sexual relationship with a female patient. The sexual encounters occurred consensually in his office for about one year until the woman pressed charges against him.

About the killer, who was fifteen when their relationship ended, Dr. Fox said he was resistant to counseling, and did not show any signs of dangerous behavior while under his care.

Now this just reeks of rotten ethics, poor character, unprofessional behavior, and narcissism on the part of Dr. Fox. But if this is the type of person who is out there practicing mental health and psychology, it is certainly reasonable to wonder if there is any real help available at all. This guy was busy planning trysts in his office with at least one patient, but was he doing his job treating the killer? We will never know.

In his defense, we are clinicians in this field of Psychology, not magicians, so it is quite easy to fool even the most seasoned therapist. However, great therapists have a sixth sense, or at least they should. Putting together the pieces of the whole clinical picture of any client involves work—and by work, I mean gathering collateral information whenever possible. In this killer's case, information was available from mom, dad, the school, other past or present treatment providers, and, of course, the boy. My belief is that this type of thoroughness is not occurring as much as it should be today, and that is a true disservice to clients. That speaks to the state of mental health care today, not to the cause or cure of Socialcide.

The point here is to look at how this type of narcissistic killer falls through the proverbial cracks, and is able to create such a horrific spectacle without anyone noticing something was going so dreadfully wrong. We have learned that, at least during the three months leading up to the slayings, the twenty-year-old never left his bedroom, refused to speak to his mother except via emails, ate only if she left food for him in a precise way on his plate, and compulsively changed his socks so frequently she was doing up to three loads of laundry a day. Then two weeks before the explosion he became totally despondent. And with all this happening in the home, his mother chose to take a "trial run" away from the house for two days to "see how he does without her?" I am not sure which of the two was most more narcissistic.

So we have a child who does not interact with others, a narcissistic mom, and a distracted (to be polite) therapist. How did this child get to the point where he became a spectacle killer? By slipping through the cracks created by the two people who were supposed to have been helping him, and caring about him, and certainly noticing when things were not right.

We cannot blame his Asperger's diagnosis either. When it comes to childhood disorders such as Autism, Asperger's syndrome, Attention Deficit Disorder, and the rest, becoming a spectacle killer is not on the menu of symptoms or associated behaviors. There is something much more sinister involved, even with the social malfunctioning of normal children. These children are looking for someone or something lacking in their primary relationships. And it is by way of these voids in their emotional lives that evil can easily step in and fill those needs, no invitation necessary.

The foundation cracks, and with no one there to care about the child and help stabilize the foundation, the angel that once sat on the right shoulder falls away, and the devil can now freely speak in both ears.

This Just In—

> "A thousand words will not leave so deep an impression as one deed."
> —Henrik Ibsen

We interrupt this broadcast to bring you breaking news…

As my editor and I were preparing *Socialcide: How America Is Loving Itself to Death* for the publisher over the 2014 Memorial Day holiday weekend, news of a very sick and stomach-twisting nature was reported that truly epitomizes what Socialcide is, how evil its grip can be, and just how elusive the devil can be in his efforts to get exactly what he wants.

Tragically, I have the answer for you already. On May 23, 2014, the devil let loose on the small town of Isla Vista, California, near the campus of University of California, Santa Barbara. Six people were killed, and thirteen others injured. The killer's self-posted YouTube videos, detailing the planned attack, and his "My Twisted World"biographical 137-page "manifesto" are available (at least at the time of this writing) on the Internet. Some of the videos had been posted much in advance of his deadly spree. Police are investigating twelve crime scenes in ten locations; thousands have attended vigils and memorial services for the victims; and one victim's father has been speaking out very loudly and angrily against the NRA, the gun lobby, politicians who refuse to reform gun laws, and our broken system that makes it possible for tragedies like this to continue destroying innocent lives.

So what happened? Twenty-two years ago (well-placed in the Millennial Generation) an evil sociopath was born to a privileged family in England. He moved to the United States at the age of five. The boy attended a fine school for a while, and eventually began attending college in California. He had looks, money, a brand new shiny black BMW sports car, and a squeaky clean criminal record. But the one thing he never had was a date with a woman. This twenty-two-year-old was disturbed and disturbing, to say the very least. He just could not seem to fit into life in his new hometown in the Santa Barbara area of California, where he wound up after a brief stint at Moorpark College. He was quoted as saying, "I have tried very hard to fit in with the social scene there, but I have ultimately been unable to do so."

But let 's let's go back a bit in time. At the age of twelve, this child became smitten with a ten-year-old girl who did not return his affections. Perhaps at the age of ten she did not understand boys, crushes or love, or have any interest in boys at all. In any case, this psychopath has held feelings of extreme hatred for this poor girl ever since then, and apparently her rejection of him was the basis for his selfish, murderous rage. He wrote, "She must have thought I was the ultimate loser. I hated her so much, and I will never forget her." This was over a girl who was just ten! He was only twelve! He referred to her as "an evil bitch" who "teased and ridiculed" him and "wounded him deeply." It is hard to imagine what kind of madman would feel such things at age twelve, and then hold onto such hatred over a ten-year-old girl throughout his entire adolescent life.

The girl has not seen or heard from this killer since the seventh grade. She recalled his being "a bit odd" but never knew he had a "secret crush" on her. Now, twenty years later, and with six people dead, this young woman is completely mortified by this madness, is terrified someone is going to hunt her down and kill her, and has unfortunately become another victim of his Satanic behavior.

The murderer wrote, "The world I grew up in thinking was bright and blissful was all over. I was living in a depraved world, and I didn't want to accept it. I didn't want to give my thought to it. That is why I immersed myself entirely into my online games like World of Warcraft. I felt safe there."

Here we find a rare testament to what goes on in an evil, narcissistic mind when something early in life does not go his way. We also find yet another "soothed" maniac who "found safety" in an extremely violent video game. Additionally, we have the over-inflated sense of entitlement, and the belief that whatever happens in his life that is not positive is unacceptable, and deserves punishablement. What is this? It is not mental illness! This is evil, and this is Socialcide, and we will be seeing more and more of it before we see less. This monster was in therapy since age eight. Someone should have seen something was wrong.

This guy had travelled the world extensively, but could not find his place in Isla Vista, California. He claimed, "There are too many obnoxious people who have ruined my whole experience at that place." He posted twenty-one selfie-type videos, pitying himself, and complaining about having no friends, no girls liking him, being a victim, and blaming everyone in the world for his sorrows, but never once asking what he may have done to cause his own misery. After all, evil and narcissism take no responsibility themselves; they blame everyone and everything else, especially when they harm, abuse, or kill others.

Why this potential suitor could not find love, specifically, is yet unknown. After watching some of his YouTube videos, one can guess part of it might be that there was just something very uncomfortable and disconcerting about him. What is known is that he was seeing a therapist, and that seething inside him was a growing hatred of women for not finding him attractive or desirable. When one thinks about "the one that got away," this young man was the one any woman would want to go away. His demeanor and actions must have sent some kind of uncomfortable creep factor through women's veins—an unpleasant feeling that probably saved their lives.

This self-proclaimed virgin was video-taping and posting his innermost evil and violent feelings toward women online. In his 107,000-word manifesto, he stated what he was going to do to "teach the blonde sorority sluts" a lesson they would never live to remember, all because they had no romantic interest in him. In this document, he stated, "Since puberty I was forced to endure an existence of loneliness, rejection and unfulfilled desires, all because girls have never been attracted to me." He also believed himself to be "the perfect guy" and said, "Girls gave their affection and sex and love to obnoxious men, but never me. But I will punish you all for it."

At some point during his video posting and blog writing, roughly three weeks before his killing spree, his family became aware of his violent and evil rants, were very concerned, and notified the police. At the time he was seeing multiple therapists. He reportedly convinced both his therapists and the law enforcement officials who paid him a visit at his parents' urging that he was stable and that, "This was all just a misunderstanding," that he was just expressing his frustration, but there was nothing to worry about. Reports from the California Sheriffs' Department said he was a "perfectly polite, kind, and wonderful human being." So, case closed. In his manifesto, however, the killer explained that had the officers who visited him that day performed a search of his apartment they would have found his arsenal.

This is exactly how evil narcissism works. The inflicted can easily turn on the charm when needed, all the while laughing at authorities and professionals for how stupid they all are. For some fortunate reason though, this demon's charm did not work with the ladies, and it was tormenting him. No demon or sociopath easily accepts being told no. And this one most likely grew up having everything and anything he ever wanted—except women.

The gut-instinct of those women he attempted to date was their ticket to life. When narcissists cannot manipulate, control, and "win" all of the time, they eventually lose their masks of sanity, and their horns protrude. This particular character was truly an anomaly in the world of evil and narcissism, because most narcissists usually can find a victim relatively easily. This one could not. The women he initially encountered should thank their lucky stars for the gift of common sense and insight they must have had to reject his attention. Who knows what he would have done to them had they let him into their lives.

It is typical narcissistic behavior that when a narcissist cannot get what he or she sets out to get, the blame for failure is placed on (and anger directed toward) the world, the police, the job, the family—anyone or anything other than him- or her-self. In this particular case, he placed the majority of the direct blame with on all the "blonde sorority sluts" at his college— and no one in law enforcement or Psychology/Psychiatry could stop that. He had no record of criminal activity, and he said all the right things to all the right people, to manipulate them into believing he was no threat to himself or others. This guy is a clear example of how this type of evil narcissism is not treatable or even diagnosable until after the damage is done. And in this case, the damage was beyond horrific and tragic.

In his manifesto, this demon described his plans to kill his two roommates, so he could turn his apartment into his "personal torture chamber" and lure people in to knock them out with a hammer and slit their throats. If any of his victims were "good looking," he planned to torture them more because he assumed they had the "best sex lives." We can only shake our heads in utter confusion trying to understand how this such rage, anger, and pure evil can manifest itself in a twenty-two-year-old, attractive, and privileged young man. Evil does not discriminate. Once its seed is planted there is no stopping its growth.

So on Friday, May 23, 2014, this killer slaughtered six people, making good on his manifesto and plan of revenge. He began by stabbing three men to death in his apartment (two of them his roommates). Then he gathered his arsenal of guns and ammunition and got in his black BMW to further release his rage of evil, leaving for the college to "punish the sluts."

His first stop was the "hottest sorority house" on campus. He was reported to be banging on the locked door like a madman, but the girls inside thought twice about opening the door. (Again, we see effective women's intuition saving lives). When he realized he was not getting in he shot three girls outside the sorority house, killing two who coincidently were members of the sorority.

He then got back into his car and drove through the campus, shooting randomly out of his car window. Reports indicate he was "smirking" and appeared to be "having a good time" in this demonic rage, while shooting and crashing into bicyclists, pedestrians, and a skateboarder, killing one and injuring thirteen others.

After two shootouts with police, the killer hit his last victim, who was on a bicycle. This victim crashed through the BMW 's windshield, causing the killer to smash into several parked cars, ending the chase. By the time the police got to his car the demon was dead, having apparently shot himself in the head.

This was senseless, wrong, horrific, unimaginable evil. Those words don't seem to convey the gravity of the tragedy. But the worst word? Unpreventable. That is what troubles me most about these demonic humans. Nothing stops them until they have slaughtered innocent people, or have in some other way destroyed other people's lives.

Socialcide is responsible for this disgusting and frightening creation of people who care for nothing or no one except themselves, and there is no end in sight. In fact, these people and demonic acts are accelerating in number and frequency, with no foolproof way of stopping them—not gun control, therapists or mental health professionals, our existing laws, or even violent video games.

Had this latest spectacle killer had a conscience, or any sense of understanding of the world outside his own, there may have been some hope for him to change, to mature, to heal from the wounds of his childhood, and to alter his eventual course of action so that six innocent people would not have had to die. Tragically, he did not, and once his evil madness pushed him over the proverbial edge to follow through on his mission to punish all of those people who "did him wrong," those random victims had no chance.

As I watch the media coverage of this event, and listen to the "talking heads" that represent the previously mentioned organizations, industries, or groups, and listen to radio talk show callers voice their opinions about how all these groups are to blame, I cannot wrap my brain around just how very blind America has become to the true culprit of the continuous violence and killings. Anger Management 's Management's new "behavior therapy" has become murder! Why?

America has kicked God out of its collective conscience on a very, very large scale. "When God is away, the devil can play," and he sure is. When will we begin to understand and accept that a Godless world will contain only Godless people, actions, and activities? And have you noticed that the media dares not mention this? Oh no! They will not—cannot—talk about God, or the lack of faith and spirituality when they report these horrific events. Why? They are facilitators of Socialcide, and benefit greatly by denying the truth. There is no monetary value in reporting or broadcasting goodness anymore. The more we become blind to the necessity of God in our lives and country, the more we will be blaming all the wrong people, things, and organizations for the continuous devastation we experience on a daily basis. And that's exactly how Satan wants it.

Speaking of an absence of God, I find it very interesting that the killer's father, a big name in Hollywood (he was an assistant director for The Hunger Games), was the director of Oh My God, a documentary starring Hugh Jackman, Seal, Ringo Starr, David Copperfield, a number of other big names, and many other people from around the world. Oh My God examines the question, *What is God?*" through interviews with people from all faiths and walks of life from in more than twenty different countries. Ironically, making this film caused the killer's father to go into debt—no doubt another item on the list of things the killer resented and allowed to fuel his demonic fire.

These acts of evil are exactly that: evil. And they are all direct results of Socialcide. These horrors are ultimately being orchestrated by Satanic influence, and the demon is having a field day!

Chapter Twenty-Two

Teach Them How to Think; Not What to Think

"The attitude you have as a parent is what your kids will learn from you more than what you tell them. They don't remember what you try to teach them, they remember what you are."
—Jim Henson

Part of the problem these days is that children are being taught what to think much faster and more often than they are being taught how to think. And since being told what to think is much easier than actually doing the thinking, most children (and many adults) are satisfied with the what, and are not disturbed that they are missing the how.

Most people have heard the proverb, "Give a man a fish and you feed him for a day; teach a man to fish and you feed him for a lifetime." This reflects the importance and value of learning how to do something instead of just having something done for you, or given to you. The information children get through music, media, social networking, and peers gets stored in their brains as the default normal; "This is how it is in the world." And without input from individuals who care enough about that child to correct the misunderstanding, or put information into a realistic perspective, what is right in a the child's head is not necessarily rightfully so in life.

Children best learn how to think from concerned parents, and by from having responsibility, consequences, and interaction in real life situations, and if they are lucky, also from teachers who teach process above memorization. Maturity develops through learning how to think, how to sort through information, and then making the best decision possible. When a child is never taught and challenged to think about the how of things, that child will grow up unable to make sound, healthy decisions, and unable to function properly as an individual.

Being able to distinguish right from wrong, fantasy from reality, and fact from fiction—all requiring independent thinking and the ability to process information within a healthy framework, instead of just accepting everything they see or hear as truth—shows true maturity, even in adults. Another key to true maturity is being able to recognize that life isn't always fair, and accepting that reality.

"There can't be a God if the world is so evil and unfair," is Satan's mantra, and he would love for everyone to buy that nonsense. And it seems people do. Many Americans today believe and act as if there is no God, so there is nothing to lose, no reason to behave, no reason to respect other humans.

I can see how narcissists and psychopaths cannot believe in anything more than themselves as God or "a god." But for others, why is it so easy to just dismiss it all, and so hard to accept, or at least consider?

Here again, it seems to be a case of people accepting what to think, instead of doing the thinking on their own. If you watch the news and see a story about a clergyman committing a crime, the reasonable response is to think, "Wow! That guy was sick," and not condemn an entire institution. However, for those who choose to not think, the easy response is to internalize the idea, "Religion is bad. God is bad." The media painted a picture, and instead of thinking about what it really means and applying it to real life, non-thinkers (those who just accept what is handed to them) take that information as a global truth. When we place our trust in a religious leader, and that trust is broken, we are required to think and to heal. We learn that sometimes people are not who they initially seem. We hurt, we grieve, and we move on. All this requires the ability to think for ourselves, and to make decisions about things based on what we know and what we feel.

Personal and intimate relationships are no different. When we fall in love with a person we believe to be Mr. or Ms. Everything-in-the-World-to-Me, and later find out that person as we perceived them never really existed at all, we are devastated. That is the difficult part for those duped to accept. When we realize they have conned us, we need to think for ourselves and look at all the information we have about that person. Even when Mr. Right goes far wrong, we hold on to what he was we thought he was tighter than to a winning mega million lottery ticket. That is not thinking.

Crafty narcissists will drop snippets here and there of who they are, in order to keep their mates or spouses hanging on.

If more people—starting with children—were taught how to think instead of what to think, these narcissists would be less able to con as many people for as long as they do, and the devil would have to work a whole lot harder.

A lack of perception, instinct, and basic common sense can be the key to making huge mistakes when it comes to relationships and going down paths of destruction. These characteristics are not available to learn online or in any books. They develop as you grow, with good guidance and experience from caring role models.

Evil minds, unable to think correctly, have a much easier chance of developing in families where emotional stability, concern, love, and role-modeling of compassion, empathy, and kindness do not exist. Promoting individuality and using our own minds is what God wants—and is the opposite of what Satan wants.

Therein lies another myth about spirituality and God, planted and promoted among the masses from the evil one. Satan desires that people follow the crowd, letting the popular perspective of the masses lead our every move and thought. Those perspectives come from the media—the movies, music, and newscasts we see every day.

Can you imagine this news report? "Tonight we have another case of evil causing the killing of seventeen innocent people at XY&Z College. Satan has stolen the soul of one more person, who carried out his will because of his lack of ability to think for himself, and understand exercise empathy." Think about it.

SECTION IV

Resulting Behaviors

Chapter Twenty-Three

No God Allowed

"The devil divides the world between atheism and superstition."
—George Herbert

Many in America get belligerent when the topic of God is brought up. Witnessing the vile horrors that are excessively occurring today, many scream, "How can there be a God when all this happens? Where is your God to stop this?" School shootings, the 9/11 tragedy tragedies, murders, rapes, and children becoming killers are all indications of a Godless world, or at the very least, a world where God is not wanted.

A huge problem existing in our country is that, for many people, God is like a bottle of aspirin that sits in the medicine cabinet. We only look for Him when we need Him. But that is not what God is. God is not a luxury or a cure to have waiting around for us to call on only in our time of need. God is available all the time to be an essential, constant part of our lives, like oxygen.

We need oxygen to survive, and it is always there for us to breathe, whether we ask for it or not. Usually we don't think about breathing unless there is a shortage of air. God is like air for the soul, and many of us do not think about needing or having God in our lives unless we are experiencing a crisis, or have a particular thing going on are in a particular situation that we need to have go well.

Like air, God is there all the time, and will be there in our times of need. But think about this: Would you run to the aid of a person who never gave you the time of day except when they needed you to help them out of a bad situation? What would the strength of your relationship be with that person? If a person calls on God only in times of need, how strong can that relationship really be? And if it's not that strong, how beneficial can God really be in those times of need?

Approximately forty-six years ago, our country began the process of telling God to take a hike and leave our schools, colleges, and public areas. Would you stick around after more than forty years of rejection? The Pilgrims and the Founding Fathers (and Mothers) of this country came here in the name of God to worship freely. Today it seems we are less free to worship. And God is a gentleman; He gets the hint. This is why He is not at our beck and call, rushing in to fix everything whenever we have a headache.

It was 1962 when the Supreme Court kicked God out of our schools and by prohibiteding prayer. The particular prayer that was prohibited (and led the way for all other prayers to be prohibited) read like this: "Almighty God, we acknowledge our dependence upon Thee, and we beg Thy blessings upon us, our parents, our teachers, and our Country."

Yes, it is clear to see how this prayer could definitely be a bad idea for America, and might damage children's minds and lives! WHAT? "Unconstitutional," they said. And behold our country now! See what it has become! Instead of God, we now have armed guards and metal detectors in schools protecting our most precious gifts—our children.

That simple prayer invited God into our lives and provided great power, because it brought with it a shield of protection from forces of evil that no science or psychology, in all their wisdom, can provide. It asked for blessings for the children, their parents, the schools, and the entire nation. How is that bad? There is not one word in the Constitution that tells us what we can teach in our schools—not one! Yet God is out.

And as if that were was not enough, and the state of our nation today were not in extreme shambles beyond its condition in 1962, movements attempts are being made to exclude the words, "One Nation Under God" from the

Pledge of Allegiance.

According to the Old Testament (Psalm 127:2), "Unless the Lord watches over the city, the watchmen stand guard in vain." So since 1962, when prayer and inclusion of God were taken away from our daily collective consciousness, we have morphed into the most self- centered, self-serving, uncaring, spiritually bankrupt society generation this country has ever seen.

When God was kicked out of school in 1962, SAT scores began to drop almost immediately and have never recovered. Premarital sex began to increase, along with epidemics of sexually transmitted diseases. Teenage pregnancies and teen births pregnancy and birth rates broke the charts beginning in 1963, as did the rate of arrests arrest rates of teens for rape, aggravated assault, and murder.

The institution of family also began to crumble beginning in 1963. Parents and families saw rates of adultery, divorce, cohabitation, and domestic abuse skyrocket; as a result the "intact family" may now be destroyed beyond repair.

Our armed forces are debilitated by functionally illiterate recruits. Teachers and our educational system have seen tremendous drops in SAT scores and other tests, as school violence and bullying are a constant problem. Demands on teachers are interfering with their ability to actually teach, as they are under constant pressure from their governing boards to crunch numbers, learn new teaching techniques, and magically make kids learn again, all while playing ringmaster of the classroom circus.

This is our country that we no longer pray for. Homicide rates are frighteningly high as innocent people are being slaughtered in cold blood by soulless sociopaths. One out of every five Americans has a lifelong, incurable sexually transmitted disease. And sexual and physical abuse of children is rampant.

Depression is expected to be the second most diagnosed medical illness by the year 2020. We already know how many millions of Americans are affected by mental illnesses of numerous types, illnesses that even pharmaceutical companies cannot keep up with. Children are being diagnosed by the thousands with both biologically-based diagnoses (like depression or panic disorder) and personality disorders (like narcissism and oppositional defiant disorder). We are eating prescription pills by the dozens, whether we need them or not, as evidenced by the rising plague of addiction to painkillers that continues to rise and cause havoc in individuals, homes, families, and society in general. Is this God's fault?

No! We can't blame God; we kicked God OUT!

We Americans, with our constitutional rights and freedoms, and with free will, have the ability to choose whether or not to include God in our lives. However, we cannot expect God to help us when we refuse to acknowledge His existence. The rates of mental illness in adults, and especially in children, should be a huge red flag to us all that something is wrong here. Something that cannot and will not go away, or be fixed by loving ourselves more and more, and while ignoring God and others around us.

Aleksandr Solzhenitsyn, an eminent Russian Nobel-prize-winning novelist and strong advocate against opponent of Soviet totalitarianism, Russian prison camps, and forced labor, may have said it best when asked how Communism and evil took over the Soviet Union. His response was simply, "We have forgotten God. That's why all this has happened." Looking at the moral fiber and what is considered "American living" today, with all the horrors and deviance we live with, read about, and see on television every day, we can say the same thing. We, too, have forgotten God.

Have We Gone Mad?

Today's crime rates are skyrocketing, and the types of crimes committed are becoming both more brazen and more senseless. They are more reflection of the evil and malice in some people's minds than ever before. When children commit murder or rape for the sake of notoriety, or to prove themselves "gang worthy," there is not one speck of love or empathy in that those person's hearts. Victims of these crimes are to the psychopathic, sociopathic, narcissist like a piece of chewing gum to a normal person. We chew it up, enjoy it, get what we need from it, then throw it away and never think about it again. This is precisely how a narcissist operates with other people.

The disintegration of America cannot be more evident than when we look at the decline of people's intelligence, along with the rising rates and types of personality disorders, crimes, and behaviors we see occurring today. Perhaps once upon a time this madness or rage came out in songs, books, clothes, or movies. But Socialcide is a hungry beast, and is rarely satisfied with safely venting its lust to be heard and recognized. Like a true narcissist, it is always wanting, needing, and taking, more and more to glorify its warped sense of self. Now it wants people—their minds, their lives, their souls. And since we fired the watchman, It's free to consume as it pleases.

A very interesting article by Suniya S. Luthar, Ph.D. was published in Psychology Today on November 5, 2013 titled, "The Problem with Rich Kids." In it, she compared youth from lower socioeconomic level families to those with parents who earned $ 150,000 a year or more. She notes that poverty is generally accepted as a major factor in the levels of crime and trouble lower-income children get into, especially if poverty is experienced by the child before the age of five. What she found out, though, is that troubled kids are not only from poor families. There are significant problems occurring in high-income, predominantly white-collar neighborhood children as well.

These are the kids attending private, expensive schools, bound for the Ivy League, to ultimately land in high-paying jobs and live affluently one day. These kids are showing high levels of maladjustment that worsen as they get closer to attending college.

A correlation existed between both socioeconomic groups in the areas of alcohol and substance abuse; however, the affluent were abusing more and harder drugs than their inner-city, non-affluent counterparts. There were also differences in the types of crimes often committed by affluent kids versus less-affluent ones. The latter were more often in trouble due to crimes that related to self-defense, such as carrying weapons, while the former broke rules relating to widespread cheating, random acts of delinquency, and stealing from parents or peers.

Additionally, affluent teens and children were found to have serious internalizing problems. In 1999, one-in-five girls experienced significant depression. Since then, in both sexes, serious levels of depression, anxiety, or somatic symptoms occur at least twice as often as in national rates. Other data reported in this article identify the more affluent youngsters as higher in the number of times intoxicated in the past month, also at a rate twice as high as national norms. Along with above average levels of depression and anxiety, this socioeconomic group showed high levels of self-injurious behavior, such as cutting, burning, and rule-breaking.

These reports are merely a microcosm of where children are today emotionally, socially, and physically. Once upon a time, there was a presumption that having the best of everything money could buy, including education, would ensure wellbeing, and the early identification of and intervention of any emotional or psychological problems. However, according to Dr. Luthar, "Something fundamental has changed: The evidence suggests that the privileged young are much more vulnerable today than in previous generations."

What was not mentioned in the article was that religion, spirituality, or God that is missing from many families today, including the affluent. It is through the practice or belief in some form of religious faith that we learn discipline, and what is right and wrong, and develop a feeling of accountability to other human beings. It has become quite apparent that religion and faith are blatantly missing in America today, and the effects of that lack are showing up in ugly ways.

In this Me, Me, Me society, rich kids and poor kids abuse drugs, cheat, steal, become depressed, kill, rape, and manipulate. Why? Because most of them do not have a clue about the real meaning of a successful life and how to achieve one it. True happiness and success are the result of caring for and helping others. And in order to care for and help others, we must be able to respect ourselves and all other humans, and have a conscience to guide us. All of this comes from religion, spirituality, and God.

If our families, schools, and country are not supportive of God's protection and presence in our lives, who or what can we expect to help end this "all about me" mindset that only causes more madness and destruction as it moves along its course?

Chapter Twenty-Four

Soul Versus Ego

"Mankind must remember that peace is not God's gift to his creatures;
it is our gift to each other."
—Elie Wiesel

Make no mistake about it: There is a vast difference between the Ego and the Soul. Where the ego wants to get and control, the soul wants to love and learn. Both need to be fed to sustain life, but there is a vast shortage of "soul food" in the country today. The ego has more than enough fodder to devour itself into obesity, while the soul struggles for its very existence unless its keeper labors hard to find what it needs for sustenance.

In the world of "drive-thru" fame and competition for superiority, power, and status, many individuals are apparently unaware of the soul's cry for nourishment, and simply do not care to hear it. Eventually, it withers away or leaves for shelter in another person or spiritual home.

Soul Search has been replaced by Star Search and, unlike the days gone by when young people often dreamed of becoming stars like James Dean, Shirley Temple, Annette Funicello, or "Cubby" on the Mickey Mouse Club, today's children have the means to broadcast themselves worldwide via YouTube and other social media sites. This possibility brings with it a feast for the ego in many ways, and leaves the soul far behind.

Souls do not seek fame, fortune, and notoriety. They do not exist to become better than anyone or anything. Instead, they try to better themselves, their host, and the world around them, fortified by the nourishment of helpfulness, goodness, kindness, love, and devotion. Are these not the very things that bring us true happiness?

Narcissists do not have souls, but they certainly have egos—egos the size of the Grand Canyon, with an equal amount of space to fill by taking and controlling others. This feat can never be achieved, of course.

Dr. Patricia Greenfield was cited in an article by Peg Streep titled, *"Are We Raising a Nation of Narcissists?"* (Tech Support: April 10, 2012) as saying, "There's been a cultural shift." What she and Yalda Uhls did was study the cultural context of fame by examining television shows from 1967 to 2007, to determine what values these shows presented by content, example, and message to ten- through twelve-year-old viewers.

In 1977, shows such as Laverne and Shirley and Happy Days promoted a sense of community, friendship, and interdependence. At that time, the concept of fame was the value rated thirteenth in importance. In 2007, shows like American Idol and Hannah Montana promoted fame as the primary value. Ironically, the value of community, friendship, and belonging dropped to number thirteen—a complete turnaround of values, at least in this study of perhaps the most powerful form of media we have ever had and continue to have: television. Again, we notice the Socialcidal thirty-year transformation in blatant terms that support how our cultural values have significantly changed.

Further studies by Greenfield and Uhls demonstrated how a celebrity- and technology-driven society has influenced the aspirations of preadolescents into believing fame, personal success, and financial success are primary life-goals. It is hard to see where soul fits into that dynamic and motivation, and easy to see how these beliefs contribute to the starvation of self as well.

Where does a self or soul go when the primary motivation of a person is fame, attention, and an audience? We can easily reference the Miley Cyrus "demonstration" at the 2012 MTV Video Music Awards show. That performance may indeed speak volumes for much of today's entitled youth, where the belief is becoming, "I can do anything because I can," especially when it draws such a magnitude of attention, be it good or bad. Feeding the sex-driven culture of America pays big, big money; talent truly seems incidental, at best. The character of celebrities today leaves much to be desired, as does their (often apparently absent) soulfulness.

Another huge role model is Justin Bieber—when he is not urinating on historical buildings, showing up stoned on marijuana for television interviews, kicking the national flag of Argentina off the stage when performing in that country, or joking about Anne Frank at the Anne Frank House in Amsterdam stating, "Truly inspiring to be able to come here. Anne was a great girl. Hopefully, she would have been a Belieber." Can you imagine why or how this guy could possibly have become as famous and rich as he is today while behaving like a stone-cold narcissistic idiot, and disrespecting some of the most sacred things in people's lives and in history? Does this demonstrate soul or ego? He has also been known to spit on his fans and urinate into a restaurant mop bucket, just because he didn't want to walk all the way to the men's room. Yet he is a role model for a huge section of today's youth, and many children believe they can or should be as famous as he is.

I could go on and on about celebrity narcissism, and how soulless the personalities of many have become; however, they need no further promotion in this book (or any other). One cannot overlook the influence these self-engrossed stars have on the youth of America today. It is blatantly obvious. It is easy to see how our children can throw caution to the wind when it comes to high-risk behaviors. Believing "this could be me" can leave many kids vulnerable to bullying and cruelty when they fail.

Egos are not indestructible, by any means. In fact, they can be quite fragile, and just as narcissistic as the narcissist who slaves for them. Souls, on the other hand, are eternal. God gave them to us to guide us, comfort us, protect us, and bring us closer to His presence while we occupy these mortal bodies of ours. However, "you know who" is doing his best to cause us to ignore them, starve them, laugh at them, and forsake their very existence.

Greenfield and Uhls stated, "Fame is an aspiration that narcissists fantasize about achieving; our results suggest that the documented historical increase in narcissistic personality in emerging adults begins in the preadolescent years with a desire for fame. A potential synergy exists between observing the fame-orientated content of TV shows and enacting the value of fame by participating in posting online videos."

Socialcide relies on these "technological tools of the trade" more than ever to get its hands tightly around the throats of today's young Americans as early as possible. It's working. Today, 10% of babies under the age of one have used a Smartphone, iPod, iPad, or other tablet, 39% of two- to four-year-olds;, and 52 % of five- to eight-year-olds. 47% of babies under the age of one watch TV or videos for nearly two hours a day, despite the American Academy of Pediatrics' recommendation of "no screens" for those under the age of two. In contrast, they are read to for about twenty-three minutes a day. 66% of children under the age of two have watched television and, as mentioned previously, television remains the most frequently-watched medium (Source: Common Sense Media Survey: Fall 2011).

Given these facts, are we not certain to have a world full of fame- seeking, narcissistic, ego-driven, soulless Americans? Socialcide is counting on it! All the while, parents are feeding their own "fame fix" by posting pictures of themselves all over the Internet, and while not paying attention to the task of parenting as much as they should be. These electronic babysitters are not helpful to anyone except absent parents, who are seemingly too busy to raise their own children anymore.

Socialcide has placed its bet on the fact that we Americans cannot emotionally outsmart technology, and right now it seems that would be a sure thing in the gambling world. I recently read something about how robots are being programmed to have empathy and feelings. Why aren't we trying to instill these soulful qualities back into people, for goodness sake?

Chapter Twenty-Five

Like It, or Not

"I think it's child abuse to have someone in the public eye too young. Society basically values wealth and fame and power at the cost of well-being. In the case of a child, it's at the cost of someone's natural development. It's already hard enough to develop."
—Alanis Morissette

As mentioned earlier, our children—as well as many adults today— are living in a world of "hook-ups" and sexual encounters that are void of any real emotional intimacy. This new lifestyle has been advertised, validated, and otherwise helped along primarily by social media and cell phone technology, not the least of which includes the now ever-present and utilized text message and instant pictures. Online tools, such as social networking sites, are virtually robbing America's youth of meaningful, loving relationships. To say today's teens are obsessed with sex is truly an understatement.

The dating ritual is a dinosaur. Today's youth don't date, they hook up. Oral sex has become the new kissing, and boys put plenty of pressure on girls to provide them with nude photos of themselves. Much of the coercion is easily accomplished, because it's not face-to-face, so it becomes impersonal, easy, and void of real socialization. This practice continues to persist simply because the supply feeds the demand; girls will do it.

Social Networking websites have become for many teens their own reality TV, and their popularity is judged by how many "likes" their posts get. As attention-starved females get many more "likes," the more provocatively they present themselves. So the popularity contest goes, and the void of human emotions, empathy, and soul continues. "It's a perfect storm of technology and hormones," Lori Andrews, attorney and director of the Institute for Science, Law, and Technology in Chicago, told Nina Burleigh in Rolling Stone ("Sexting, Shame and Suicide," September 26, 2013). "Teen sexting is just a way of magnifying girls' fantasies of being a star of their own movies, and boys locked in a room bragging about sexual conquest."

Socialcide is already reaping rewards of the conscience-less youth of today, and we have seen teen suicides because of "failure to be the most popular." Through social networking, girls have become victims of savage sexual attacks that repeatedly rape them through social networking, then followed by the texting and posting of photos, and even videos, of those attacks. "Social media is fostering a very unthinking and unfeeling culture," says Donna Freitas, who has researched hookup culture on college campuses. "We are raising our kids to be performers."

This unthinking and unfeeling culture is the intention of Socialcide, because without thinking and feeling we become slaves to the demands of evil that continuously cause us to lust for more and more. More power, more prestige, more attention, more popularity, more everything. These hungers are never full satisfied. They cannot be. And we move further away from taking responsibility for our actions, from the idea that we must honestly earn what we need and want, from acknowledging that there are consequences for every action, and from feeling responsibility or true care for ourselves and others. That is how the evil one has arranged it.

Chapter Twenty-Six

Legends in Their Own Minds

"But wait! First....let me take a Selfie."
—The Chainsmokers

Miley Cyrus may have said one thing that makes a valid point when she declared in Harper's Bazaar, "We're in a world of selfies," "Selfie" was deemed "Word of the Year" by the Oxford English Dictionary in 2013. How telling is that decision? The practice of taking pictures of one's self to post and promote one's image online is perhaps one of the most narcissistic behaviors people openly engage in today. No shame, no humility, no second thoughts, just "Here I am—again! Look at me!" Even President of the United States Barack Obama "selfied" himself with Denmark's Prime Minister Helle Thorning-Schmidt and British Prime Minister David Cameron at Nelson Mandela's funeral. All smiles! I guess the world gets the message that, no matter where I am or why I am there, a picture of ME is what is needed.

I believe selfies are called such not because they are self-taken pictures, but because they only serve to impress one's self. How full of one's self can a person get? However, when celebrities take these selfies and post them, or the media gets their hands on them, they quickly go "viral" and draw a huge amount of attention. That attention feeds that a celebrity's self-addiction for a day, perhaps, but it also influences the rest of the world to try and do the same.

On April 2, 2014, REALfarmacy.com released a very interesting report titled, "Scientists Link Selfies to Narcissism, Addiction & Mental Illness." I have been saying this (that selfies are linked to narcissism, addiction, and mental illness) for several years, but I am now able to provide proof for the naysayers. In this report, psychiatrist Dr. David Veal was quoted as saying, "Two out of three of all the patients who come to see me with Body Dysmorphic Disorder [a psychological disorder in which a person becomes obsessed with imaginary defects in their appearance] since the rise of camera phones have a compulsion to repeatedly take and post selfies on social media sites." Two out of three! How bad can this obsession become? Read on.

When he was fifteen years old, Danny Bowman began posting selfies on a certain social networking website. By the time he was nineteen, he spent up to ten hours a day, taking as many as two-hundred selfies, to capture the perfect one. In his increasingly intense need to accomplish this, he ended up dropping out of school, not leaving his home for six months, and losing thirty pounds—all in a desperate need to capture the perfect shot of himself. During this process, he lost his friends, his health, his education, and almost his life. In 2012, unable to take what he considered the perfect selfie, he overdosed. His mother, (a mental health nurse), was able to save saved him, and he has since gotten past this madness.

In describing his hospitalization following the suicide attempt, he told the Sunday Mirror, "It was excruciating to begin with, but I knew I had to do it if I wanted to go on living." Do what? Surrender his iPhone to the hospital staff for ten minutes, then thirty minutes, then an hour.

Pamela Rutledge was quoted in Psychology Today stating, "Selfies frequently trigger perceptions of self-indulgence or attention-seeking social dependence that raises the damned-if-you-do and damned-if-you-don't spectre of either narcissism or very low self-esteem."

The age of narcissism has been fueled well by digital technology. What is the goal of such self-indulgence? We cannot all be Beyoncé or Brad Pitt, yet the thirst and hunger to be increases when what should remain as fantasy morphs into an unhealthy reality. This pressure is unnecessarily enormous, and the majority of youth today do not believe in hard work to make their dreams come true. The combination of laziness and entitlement normally results in self-destruction. Let's face it, any sense of accomplishment that comes from taking the perfect selfie is pitiful at best, and ridiculous at worst. But we live in an age of Socialcide, and sure are loving ourselves to death.

The irony about selfies is that those who regularly take and post them are pretty void of having a self to speak of. These selfies are self-serving, yes, but they do not reflect a self in the true sense of the word. They are more a product, or an idea or image the person is attempting to create by saying, "Look at me here! Look at me now! Look at me, period!" The true self is the combination of soul, consciousness, values, and understanding of ourselves and the world in which we live. Selfish, on the other hand, describes one lacking care or concern for others, interested only in one's own profit or pleasure. Just who do these selfies profit or pleasure? I believe that is pretty self-explanatory. It is a great disappointment to me that The Oxford English Dicti2o3n4ary would condone and validate such a narcissistic term and award it "Word of the Year." But, then again, we are in the midst of Socialcide.

Way off on the other side of the spectrum from the selfish are the selfless. While this word is deceiving, because it implies that the person has no self, the actual meaning is the opposite of that: "having little or no concern for oneself, especially with regard to fame, position, money, etc." Selfless people are soulful, mindful, generous, caring individuals. They give of themselves for altruistic and truly loving reasons. In other words, they honor their own "self" and the "self selves" of others by putting others first. Their focus is not on their own selves; thus selfless. How far from the selfie mindset can you get?

Selfies, though, are just an innocuous tool to support the already euphemized Me, Me, Me Generation of this era of Socialcide. They seem cute and harmless, and perhaps they do fall very low on the spectrum of narcissistic tendencies in America today. However, do not be fooled by their seeming harmlessness. They foster placing self-need above others' needs, and Oxford the OED has officially entered the word into the English language. If our own president cannot refrain from selfie-snapping at a world leader's funeral, are you really going to get upset that your teenager is texting during dinner? It's Socialcide wants it.

It's all about me. That's how

Any discussion of Legends in Our Own Minds would not be complete without mentioning the absolutely most insulting, narcissistic drivel to come out of the mouth of another role model for our youth. Kanye West, a mega- millionaire rapper, was quoted as saying his stage props are "potentially dangerous" and because the staged "mountain" he uses is so tall, "If I slipped and something happened, I think about my family and I'm like, 'This is like being a police officer or war or something.' You're literally going out to do your job everyday knowing that something could happen to you verbally from the press bashing you, people not liking you anymore, or you could actually slip on that stage." Kanye, with all due respect, our troops and policemen are not concerned with such trifling things. Also, sir, you are a narcissist.

Tom Cruise is another fine example of a self-focused, entitled, conscience-lacking celebrity making millions of American dollars today. After landing a twenty-million-dollar deal for the blockbuster movie, Oblivion, which was filmed in New York City, Iceland, Louisiana, and California., Mr. Cruise was quoted as saying, "Filming this was serving in a war zone. And certainly on this last movie it was brutal. It was brutal." Mr. Cruise, with all due respect, you may be an excellent actor; in fact, most narcissists are. However, you have never and will most likely never know what true combat and battle in a war zone are is like. I do not wish you ever should. However, if you are going to make ridiculous statements such as this about something you know nothing about, perhaps you should review your net worth of $270 million, and consider contributing some to the widows of real Marine corporals who risked their lives for their $ 25,000 a year before paying taxes to your government and theirs.

Chapter Twenty-Seven

God, Narcissism, and Technology

"As individuals and as a nation, we now suffer from social narcissism.
We have fallen in love with our own image, with images of our making,
which turn out to be images of ourselves."
—Daniel Boorstin

Does a narcissist have any true religious beliefs? If you have ever been involved with one romantically, socially, or criminally, you can certainly say no. Why is that? Why can't an entitled, self-absorbed, selfish, and arrogant person, who can never admit to being wrong, be God-loving, or at least God-believing? Socialcide again returns to the concept and reality of soul. The soul is a vessel of spirituality, a connection with God and goodness, a barometer that guides our conscience and keeps us safe from the full dangers of evil.

Narcissists will get involved with religion or God only to gain something for themselves. God, religion, and spirituality become just another source of self-fulfillment, or a means to their own ends. Take, for example, Pastor Schirmer, whom I ~~talked about earlier~~ discussed above. That man had no calling to serve as a minister of God's word. Yet he was crafty enough to see that he could gain something from a congregation of selfless Christians whom he deemed to be easy targets. And he was right. They certainly were easy targets, and he certainly was able to manipulate them. However, a person with a soul would not take advantage of such easy targets (or even identify them as targets in the first place); a narcissist wouldn't ~~miss~~ pass by the opportunity.

We also discussed Jim Jones and the Guyana slaughter. Here was another prominent "Man of God" with absolutely no love of any god except himself. That is the irony. God is everything the narcissist ever wants to be: omnipotent, omnipresent, admired, much-discussed, and awe-inspiring. Ironically, or intentionally, this is also everything Satan wants to be. That is why God kicked His most beloved angel out of Heaven. Satan became narcissistic, and thought himself as good as,or even more mighty, than God! (Even angels have freedom of choice.)

David Koresh, the former leader of the Branch Davidians in Waco, Texas, is a classic example of a narcissistic, sociopathic cult leader. He used the goodness of God to gain all for himself by bleeding his flock of all they had, including their minds. He was having sex with the children of his followers, preaching that he and only he had a direct connection to God, and he created a cult of robotic individuals willing to die for him. He demanded his people listen to his words, and to his personal interpretations of the Gospel, and to do as he said—and he was quite successful.

This was large-scale narcissistic (and deadly) brainwashing, but every day, similar brain-stealing occurs with our youth and with anyone who gets involved with a narcissist. Like Satan, narcissists are very good at making us believe we are wrong and they must be right. If that is not pure evil, I am not sure what is.

God is about free will, love, openness, forgiveness, gratitude, compassion, and all that is good. I believe people who do not know that about God get confused or fearful of God, believing that He judges us, punishes us, and wants to somehow restrict us from the good things in life. Nothing could.

"Where is God?" and "This is God's punishment!" are phrases that such horrors evoke, and they fester in our minds. The media reinforces these ideas. And, unfortunately, these questions cause us to doubt, to lose faith, and to feel as if effort toward good is useless. Worse, they continue to benefit evil, Satan, and the pushing of God out of our society. The more people who believe that the ugliness in the world today is proof there is no point in pursuing goodness and God, the further Socialcide spreads.

Anyone who has been involved with a narcissist for a significant period of time will tell you that, over time, narcissists will have you eliminate all family, friends, and associates from your life. They do not want anyone near you who can reel you back to reality, or place a seed of doubt in your mind about just how sick your partner really is. Anyone who could threaten their ultimate power and control of their conquest must be removed.

As Americans, we have allowed ourselves to be convinced that a relationship with God isn't worth our energy, just like the narcissist in our hypothetical relationship convinced us our friends and family were not worth having in our lives. Yet in this real circumstance, we have consciously chosen this route ourselves.

Due to our own choices, the rise in narcissistic behaviors,and the influence and prevalence of technology, we are void more and more of family, real friends, and other people during our times of need; and when God is out of the picture, bad things are bound to happen. And bad things are happening.

"Narcissism increased just as fast as obesity did over the past twenty-five years, and a study today shows that it is twice that rate since 2002" (Dr. Jean Twenge, Psychologist; September 15, 2012). Where has all this self-love and personal entitlement gotten America? According to poll results published in "The Week" (December 31, 2013, Vol. 13; Issue 650) 59% of Americans say the Internet and social media are making Americans ruder (Weber Shandwick), and 69% think we are too distracted by our gadgets (Harris Interactive). This perception appears to be correct, because 49% of adults and 43% of teenagers admit to texting while driving, even though they are aware of the risks of doing so (AT&T/USA Today). Also, 33 % of Smartphone users say they have used their device during a dinner date, and 9 % admit to looking at their phone during sex ((Jumio/Harris Interactive).

This is simply startling news. But my belief is that the true numbers are much higher.

A new study released by High Point University in North Carolina says narcissism appears to be the "primary driver" for those who actively use Twitter. These narcissists—mostly Millennials—use that particular social media tool to attract attention. The tweets fly fast and furiously about every minute detail of the narcissist's life. According to this study, narcissists tweet more often than others, and crave followers on Twitter to satisfy their need for attention and approval.

But really, who is that important or interesting? Well, if a person grew up with parents who were constantly adoring constantly adored their every single burp, bump, and utterance, that person likely believes they are. Elliot Panek and the University of Michigan conducted a similar study in June of 2013, and found that middle-aged narcissists prefer to satisfy their approval addiction on Facebook, while their younger counterparts, the Millennials, prefer Twitter. The study surmises that this is because middle-aged narcissists have already established a social circle of some sort, and seek to gain approval from those already in it. Millennials, on the other hand, use Twitter because they "over-value their opinions" and use it like a megaphone to broaden their social circles. In either case, social media is attention- driven, and covers much ground quickly—a perfect tool for narcissists. Much like "selfies", tweeting and posting are simply another additional ways to satisfy the craving for that attention and adoration narcissists must have.

There is, however, good news for Facebook users. The study determined that, regarding narcissism, Twitter was found to be a stronger predictor of the disorder than Facebook.

Facebook is not off the hook, though. We know already how teens have used it to harass, bully, and terrorize other teens to the point of causing the victim to attempt or commit suicide. Facebook is also known to be a huge contributor to infidelity and divorce. It has become commonplace for people to look up high school sweethearts or "could-have-beens,"resulting in the destruction of many marriages and relationships. In 2012, one-third of all divorces in the United States were found to be Facebook-related. Again, we can see the devil lurking in the details.

Call me crazy, but once upon a time, people became a part of our past, and remained there, for a reason. If, by chance, we wound up running into them, it was quite the surprise, and rarely amounted to much. However, there is something very alluring today about looking up our pasts, and then somehow trying to relive them. And it gets easier everyday, especially with the power of the Internet at our fingertips. Could it be that so many people are turning to their pasts because they are living such unfulfilled lives in the present, have turned away from spirituality and God, (are of course, blaming anything and anyone in their current lives other than themselves for their lack of happiness and fulfillment), and, in a desperate attempt to find happiness, are trying to go back to a time where when they don't remember feeling so unfulfilled or unsuccessful? Could it be that the temptation presented by social media today is just too much for people to withstand?

In my practice, I have seen these sad situations too many times,where someone has left a long-standing marriage at the click of a button, because of a fantasy created by reconnecting with something that "could have been." The destruction, hurt, and questions of why are rarely resolved. I do not know how a father, for example, can explain to his child that he met up with an old girlfriend online and is now leaving that child and that child's mother for a new life. Or how, when that fantasy bubble pops and the new relationship crashes, the father can come back to the child and repair the devastation he caused.

If there are problems in a marriage, and I assume there must be in order for a person to go looking for someone else, end the marriage before moving on. To end it because one has "met someone else"—someone better, or someone from his or her youth—is ultimately narcissistic, and wholly self-serving. Yet today that should come as no real surprise, should it? It's another sad example of Satan's pulling down the fundamental pillars of society—one marriage at a time, one family at a time.

When we combine the components of narcissism and replacing spirituality or the presence of God with the power of technology, Socialcide gains an even stronger foothold in our society, and Satan rejoices.

Chapter Twenty-Eight

(Wo)Man's Best Friend

"We long for an affection altogether ignorant of our faults.
Heaven has accorded this to us in the uncritical canine attachment."
—George Eliot

The ability to exhibit cruelty to humans is most times a progression of evil. Many research studies have reported that childhood cruelty to animals may be the first serious warning sign or predictor of later problems such as conduct disorders, delinquency, and criminal behavior. Animal abuse by children occurs more frequently with children who live in homes where physical, emotional, or other forms of abuse are present—mostly from or by the parents. In these circumstances, the child may begin to abuse animals as a desperate and demented way of gaining some form of control over his or her life.

These animal-abusing children seem to gain emotional gratification or relief from the sick home environment-caused pain they feel, that is caused by the sick home environment. The ability to have power over the life and death of a living being fuels and satisfies their inability to express, in a healthy and positive way, whatever anger or fear they feel about or toward their parent(s). In cases where children live in a home where they have received or witnessed physical abuse, they will act out with an animal what their parents do to each other, to siblings, or to that child. Some children engage in this evil behavior because they do not know how to appropriately deal with anger and frustration, while other children simply do not care if they hurt or kill an animal.

This type of behavior should scream out warnings to the child's family, teachers, and anyone who is aware of the cruelty. Sometimes animal abuse—especially when coupled with remorse—is a sign that a child needs to be rescued from abuse, and once rescue and appropriate support is provided, that child will be able to heal, and will not repeat the behavior. However, it is also quite possibly the first clinical sign of a person who has no conscience, and is well on the road to sociopathic narcissism (the most dangerous type of narcissism).

Unfortunately, this behavior in a child is often either overlooked or is tragically ignored. In many other cases, it is the parents themselves who routinely abuse or neglect the family pets, and who do the same to their children. You can count on these parents to do nothing but violently punish their children if they catch them abusing animals, and they react angrily if anyone approaches them with a report that their child is doing something they ought to "look into."

To give you an idea of the correlation between animal abuse and human abuse, of more than fifty New Jersey families receiving treatment due to incidents of child abuse, sixty percent were found to have animals in their homes that were also abused (Elizabeth Deviney, et al.). In three separate studies, more than half of battered women surveyed reported that their abuser either threatened or injured the woman's animal companion(s).

Historically, most serial killers began their "careers" by mutilating, torturing, and killing animals. When their thirst for blood wasn't satiated by animals alone, they moved on to humans. Even the shooters involved in the recent rash of school killings all had either abused or killed animals, or had talked about doing it. "There is a common theme to all the shootings of recent years," according to Dr. Harold S. Koplewicz, director of the Child Study Center at New York University. "You have a child who has symptoms of aggression toward his peers, an interest in fire, cruelty to animals, social isolation, and many warning signs that the school has ignored."

It may be true that the school has ignored the potential for evil in these kids, but I do not think the blame falls solely on them. It belongs to the families, the peers, the child, and even to society. Remember that "it takes a village to raise a child,"but the neighbors have all flown from "the hood," therefore we now learn of such atrocities only when it's far too late.

This type of sadistic, cruel, and evil behavior toward animals has been present for many years, but not to the extent it is today.

Despite this increase in violence toward animals, during times of economic crisis—be it personal, national, or global—one business does not suffer. That is the business of pet care. This is reassuring news. Even more reassuring is that, in our country, laws are beginning to show positive changes when it comes to animal abuse and cruelty. Americans, more than ever, love their pets.

I do not believe there is any correlation between that fact and the existence of animal abuse, torture, or killings by children and adults. However, I do believe the surging care, love, and interest in animal welfare is a direct result of how human beings cannot depend on one another as true friends or loved ones nearly as unerringly reliably as they can depend upon their pets.

Pets satisfy people's need for unconditional love, a need we expect to find in a spouse, family, friend, or other loved one. Sadly, healthy human fulfillment of that need is simply not as present in America today as it used to be. While people are becoming more self-centered and uncaring these days, for many people, animals have stepped up to the plate to fill the growing void of love and devotion. I truly believe God has given us pets to help us understand Him more. The relationships pet owners have with their animals and the selfless love animals give in return are as close to God's presence as we can get on this earth today. In exchange for loving and taking care of them, we receive their endless love.

Is this not what God wants from us; to simply to love Him, and accept His love in return? Why has this become so difficult? Why has it become so silly to believe? The simple answer is we have been slowly programmed to deny His love, presence, and place in our lives. While it is wonderful that people who do not have healthy, loving relationships in their lives can give love to and receive love from pets, focusing love on pets instead of humans only helps widen the chasm between human beings, and allows individuals to feel good about isolating themselves from true human interaction.

The benefits of pet ownership are a true testament to many people's shifting beliefs and feelings about family life and procreation. Let me speak specifically about dogs. They give us what humans often lack the ability to provide, but every human in the world desires: unconditional love. Humans are simply unable to be void of resentments, grudges, anger, and attitudes. On a higher level, some humans are unable to be honest, faithful, and trustworthy.

As much as we all desire people in our lives who exhibit those positive attributes, and can be free of the negative ones—or at least continue to love and respect us when they are feeling the negative ones—we ourselves can most likely not deliver the same. No one is perfect, and some of us are far from it. Cheating, passive aggressiveness, disappointment, disrespect, inconsideration—the list goes on.

More and more adults are choosing not to marry or have children, because of the high potential for stress and difficulty involved, and their inability to cope with, or lack of interest in bothering themselves with, the struggles. But humans were made to couple with other humans and to reproduce. So to fill that void many people seek love and companionship elsewhere. Enter the dogs.

The Centers for Disease Control and Prevention reported a huge drop in the number of children born to American women between the ages of fifteen and twenty-nine over the past seven years. This ties in with a report in on the business news site Quartz that says the CDC's information corresponds with a tremendous increase in the number of small dogs owned by young American women. *The New York Post*, in an article titled, "More Young Women Choosing Dogs over Motherhood" (April 10, 2014; Antonio Antenucci and David K. Li), reported that New York women said they were not surprised by these findings. Most said they were more than happy to not bother with diaper changing, behavioral issues, college tuition, and all other related responsibilities that come with parenting.

This trend is both good and bothersome. It's better that women who realize they do not want to deal with the "hardest job in the world" (parenting) are choosing not to have children. After all, there are far too many negligent and disinterested parents in our country. However, are we becoming so disinterested, disgusted, or disappointed in people that we have resorted to dogs to find happiness?

The federal data behind the CDC report shows that the number of births per one thousand women between ages fifteen and twenty- nine has dropped nine percent 9%. Coinciding with this data is a report by the American Pet Products Association that says ownership of small dogs (those below twenty-five pounds) has exploded from over thirty-four million in 2008 to over forty million in 2012. Young American women have certainly made a statement.

Quartz quoted Damian Shore as saying, "Women are not only having fewer children, but they are also getting married later. There are more single and unmarried women in their late twenties and early thirties, which also happens to be the demographic that buys the mostly small dogs."

There is definitely something to dog ownership that is more alluring to young American women than having husbands and children. I believe this applies to young men as well. There are simply too many difficulties in finding true love these days, and my experience in counseling people supports that.

According to my single clients, the world of dating seems to be a never-ending cycle of difficulty and frustration. Those seeking love are most quite frequently disappointed and discouraged by their attempts. People are simply "too weird, too full of themselves, too narcissistic" or display an endless number of other negative qualities that could cause people seeking love to "go to the dogs," to find it. Antenucci and Li suggest we call them Generation Rex.

Chapter Twenty-Nine
Who Can You Trust?

"The trust of the innocent is the liars' liar's most useful tool."
—Stephen King

As much as I adore my Saint Bernard dogs, I am still saddened by the truth that these days many people cannot find unconditional love in another person much, if at all, these days. We were not created to simply have a family of animals, although they are certainly an excellent addition to any family. They are family! However, a family of animals has become the best it's going to be for millions of Americans. Why? Because in their quest to find true happiness and love they have been hurt, rejected, abused, or otherwise degraded by other people. There is a very popular bumper sticker and wall plaque out there today that says, "The more people I meet, the more I love my pets." And why not?

People have become mean, inconsiderate, uncaring, self-absorbed, selfish, unsympathetic, arrogant, and simply narcissistic. Where is a person to find their proverbial soul mate? On Match.com?

Working with as many people as I do, I hear time and time again about the horrors of online dating, and how difficult it is to meet Mr. or Ms. Miss Right. When so much is wrong in the world, I am not surprised by this. However, souls who are desperate for that soul mate, for that possibility for true, real love in this world, will take chances. And in their desperation, they are often unable to see the truth.

There are countless horror stories about how people have wound ended up dead from taking such "chances." However, there are many more who have found themselves in a sick world of lies, manipulation, frustration, bankruptcy, and neglect, because of the belief that the person they found online was their soul mate. When the search for love and happiness, or the fear of being alone forever, consumes a person's mind, that person will take tremendous risks. In taking those risks, they are vulnerable to the initial adoration, attention, interest, and excitement a narcissist will offer them—in the beginning.

The need to be needed is a narcissist's specialty, and they know exactly how to superficially fill that need for others, all the while sizing up their victim's potential to fill their own needs. It's a perfect fit for both victim and narcissist at first, as it is in most relationships. But regardless how stable or strong the victim's life before meeting the narcissist, while in the relationship, the narcissist will create situations from which they then "save" the victim. On the surface, the relationship seems symbiotic, supportive, and loving at first— especially to the victim. However, sooner or later, the victim will pay dearly for the narcissist "saving them"—over and over and over again. After all, if you doubt, challenge, or question just how wonderful a narcissist is, there will be Hell to pay. Get it? (Pun intended, with care). And in a relationship like this, truth is distorted from day one.

Jean-Paul Sartre, the infamous philosopher, once said, "Hell is other people." I cannot speak for his time in society, but today there appears to be some relevance in that statement—at least from what I observe during counseling sessions when as I speak to others about their lives. There are so many unsatisfied people in this country, and most of them are over thirty- five years old. The older generations of Americans have become fearful, frustrated, puzzled, and disgusted with what has become of society.

This is caused, in great part, by the rise of Personality Disorders, wherein humans exist without any sense of self, yet they are all about themselves. Narcissists and Borderline Personality Disordered people become who they need to be, over and over again, in countless relationships, in order to be "adored," "believed," "in charge," and to get what they want. Their victims' initial attraction to them is real and intense, because they are masters of deception, and are well-prepared to size up a person's needs and soft-spots, then to do all the right things, say the right words, and become the most perfect person for that victim that they have has ever met. There is no truth in this relationship.

Desperation is a dangerous place to be. It creates vulnerability, and blurs one's judgment. It causes good people to make bad choices and decisions, especially in the area of relationships. All the wrong people can sense the vulnerability in good people, and they are masters at taking quick advantage of it. "All that glitters is not gold," but many people seem to forget this when that wolf in sheep's clothing comes knocking at their door in clothing of sheep's wool.

It is very difficult to make sound judgments when in the emotional state of desperation. Wanting nothing more than to feel normal or right, when we look at people around us who seemingly have it all in their relationships or marriages, it becomes doubly painful if we don't. Nothing is truly perfect though. In our lowest moments it is very easy to believe other people have perfection in their lives. They appear to have all we need to bring us perfection. This "cue" is apparent to those who see a good person in need of something to make their life complete.

Like evil, narcissists initially appear so tempting, so perfect, so much the answer we have been waiting for all our lives to make everything PERFECT. They have the walk, the talk, the smile, and the lines. They know what to tell us, how to hook us, and how to feed their endless need for acceptance and adoration from us while taking each and every piece of ourselves and souls away from us.

This is a game to them. A cruel, heartless game of "bait and switch." But because they have no empathy, and they thrive on the drama they create, almost like an alcoholic thrives on drink, they do not care how they get what they need, nor whether if it is at another person's emotional, financial, physical, or social expense. Their manipulation is so often so precise, so often, that their victims frequently believe it to be their own fault when the abuse— the lies, the broken promises, the failures— rears its ugly head.

This is how Satan works his magic as well. What is very interesting is that many years ago mental illness was believed to be demonic possession. People hearing voices, acting bizarrely, talking to things or people not really there, believing someone or something was out to get them, were seen as nothing less than the victims of evil spirits possessing a person's their minds and souls. Murderers, rapists, and other types of "sane"criminals were said to have had "the devil in them"to cause them to do something so evil.

It's the latter that we see so much of today. These people wear what is known as a "Mask of Sanity," because they do not appear crazy, evil, or insane. I agree they are not insane; they are evil,. They are morally and emotionally bankrupt people, who are void of soul and conscience. Their "mask" is better called a "Mask of Goodness," because that is exactly what they present themselves to be—initially. These people are the devil incarnate. Deceptive, alluring, attractive, believable, flattering, and helpful, until their mask comes off to reveal the demon you have chosen to dance with. Now the truth appears, and it is ugly.

Psychiatry and Psychology have all but dismissed these so- called Personality Disorders entirely from their scope of research and treatment, because there is next to nothing a Psychiatrist or Psychologist can do to cure them. There is no treatment for them at all. But that doesn't matter much, because to be treated, the afflicted would have to admit they have a problem, and choose to seek treatment for that problem. They don't ever do. To them, everyone else is the problem.

In reality, to the rest of the world, these people are a huge problem, yet nothing is done, or can be done, to stop it or control it through medicine, instead of humans to keep them feeling loved. There is so little truth in human relationships it's almost impossible to trust anyone. And when you cannot trust, you cannot have a healthy relationship. On the other hand, animals cannot lie.

SECTION V

What Can Be Done?

Chapter Thirty

Diagnosing Demons

"Knowing when to exorcise and when to refer for psychiatric
treatment is a nagging problem for priests."
—John L. Allen Jr.

I mentioned earlier that Satan has found the perfect cover for infesting this country with the virus that is his Seven Deadly Sins: the Personality Disorders (Paranoid PD, Schizoid PD, Narcissistic PD, Obsessive- Compulsive PD, Antisocial PD, Histrionic PD, etc.). Here's here's what I mean: People commit sins and crimes, and disrespect other people in all sorts of ways. When they are caught and charged with a crime, they claim, "I have a disorder.; I am not responsible for my actions!"

For a while we took that at face value. "He did that because he has a disorder." And while buying into that conclusion, we had no need to look for another, no need to look deeper for an explanation of why that person behaved in such a horrific way. We were satisfied. And Satan laughed, having pulled another one over on us.

Today, however, Personality Disorders have become so commonplace that the field of Mental Health Care has been phasing them out as true diagnoses. In other words, behaviors and characteristics that were once defined as notably "abnormal" and "out of the ordinary"are now so common they are thought of as"just how it is,"and more chilling, "just how people are now." There is nothing crazy or insane about it.

You see, the more of us who we live to serve ourselves, and the more of

223

us who do so, the more the virus spreads. And the more the virus spreads, the more people consciously or unconsciously succumb to it. Most importantly, the more we live to serve ourselves, the less we seek and believe in God. And the more ground Satan gains.

There has always been a relationship of sorts between evil and mental illness/behavioral abnormalities (if I can call them such for now). These days it seems this relationship has come full circle. Let me explain. There was a time when our ancestors believed deviant and bizarre behaviors were the work of the devil. When our country was founded, people believed that many of those who behaved significantly differently from the general population, or who held beliefs that did not conform with their own religious beliefs, or who committed crimes that involved the desecration of a human body or an animal, were "possessed by the devil." We were a nation that believed in God and in goodness, and we were very strong in our faith. As such, it was easy to believe that a person who behaved in a wicked manner, or committed acts that were against God and goodness— acts of "madness"—must certainly be manipulated or "possessed" by an evil force. Exorcisms were a legitimate rite in the Catholic Church beginning as far back as the fifteenth century.

Since then, the fields of science and medicine have evolved and taken their turns at trying to understand what makes some people mad or insane. In time, science and medicine began to define and categorize some of those behaviors, and created names for them. This, of course, called into question the validity of "possession" and exorcisms. In short measure, "mental health disorders" became available as explanations for unusual or irrational behavior, and as diagnosis options, and the fields of psychology and psychiatry developed to help those afflicted with such disorders.

During this time, the frequency of exorcisms in America declined. By the late 1960s, exorcisms in the US were seldom performed. It is interesting that the criteria for personality disorders were more clearly defined in the 1968 revision of the *Diagnostic and Statistical Manual of Mental Disorders (DSM)*, and narcissistic and borderline personality disorders were added to the document in 1980. It seemed the devil had disappeared into the population, disguised as a personality disorder!

Despite being able to define and diagnose mental health conditions, there were (and still are) no definitive medical certainties as to the causes of psychosis or personality disorders, and there are no cures. Of course, plenty of medications have been developed and sold to treat certain conditions, such as depression, bi-polar disorder, and even schizophrenia, but none of them are foolproof, and no medications treats the personality disorders themselves.

The number of people who "meet the criteria" for the disorders is disorders is growing exponentially. So much so that professionals in the field of mental health care are slowly removing the diagnoses for these disorders from their professional diagnostic guides (specifically the DSM). The professionals say, "Let's leave personality disorders out of the mix. That's just how people are now."

The biggest problem with that solution is that those types of disorders are the most damaging, dangerous, and destructive to society. Schizophrenics are hardly the dangerous, hard-core criminals that narcissists can be, yet there is no treatment, no concrete diagnosis for narcissism. The solution is to "send them back to society, and let society deal with them." However, unlike the old days, our society is far more Godless than it used to be. Therefore, narcissists are free to roam and destroy what good is left in the world.

Families are creating them, the media adores them, and people want to be more like them. With support like that it's no wonder narcissists are increasing in such alarming numbers. And their influence on our youth is devastating. They create monsters that cannot stop taking selfies, because they are so marvelously beautiful to in their own demented minds; minds that silently plan and execute the murders of innocent preschoolers for no reason anyone else can understand.

If this "disorder" (narcissism) is not the product of pure evil, then what can it be? And why, may I ask, did the Vatican feel the need to update its exorcism guidelines in 1999? (This update includes the text, "the person who claims to be possessed must be evaluated by doctors to rule out a mental or physical illness.") And is it just coincidence that since the 1990s, exorcisms are being more frequently performed in America again than they were in previous decades?

Maybe we need to address what insanity really is. The term "mental illness" conjures up fear. Most people really do not know what true mental illness is, or even realize that "lunatic," "psycho," and "insane" are not labels that reasonably apply to most people who currently suffer with legitimately diagnosed mental illnesses.

When we think of someone who is "mentally ill,"many of us picture people bound in straight jackets, with disheveled hair and wild eyes in straitjackets, moaning, suffering locked in padded rooms, or tied down to gurneys, fiercely struggling to get loose. These images come from the way movies and media have portrayed insanity over the course of history. The true cause of society's misunderstanding of what mental illness actually is, however, is factual ignorance. We simply do not know what the term means. And most of us, unless we have either been treated in a psychiatric hospital, or had a friend or family member who has, have no real information at all about what is going on within the walls of psychiatric hospitals such institutions, or what the people who live there actually look like unless we have been there or visited one. True insanity can be defined as "the inability to distinguish reality from fantasy, or truth from delusion." According to law, a person who is truly insane suffers from a mental illness so severe in nature that the person, due to psychosis, cannot conduct his or her affairs due to psychosis, or is subject to uncontrollable, impulsive behavior. This definition is used in court to help determine a defendant 's defendant's guilt or innocence. And while the definition is certainly informed by mental health professionals, it is not a psychological definition (there is no "insane" diagnosis in the DSM); it is solely a legal one.

I spent five years, from 1992 to 1997, employed in one of New Jersey's most prominent state psychiatric hospitals. Greystone Psychiatric Hospital opened its ominous doors to patients in 1877 under its original name, The State Lunatic Asylum of Morris Plains. Although the new name, Greystone, does not sound much more welcoming, The State Lunatic Asylum of Morris Plains certainly does did little to help the public understand mental illness.

Greystone was a huge, prison-looking building constructed because of the demand for hospitalization of the insane of New Jersey. Around the time Greystone was built, existing jails and almshouses could no longer house or treat the growing number of alcoholics, drug addicts, and vagrants (homeless). To solve the problem, many of these people, as well as personality-disordered people, were given "lunatic" status, so they could be sent to the new asylums being constructed. There, bizarre therapies and experimental treatments were experimented with employed: hydrotherapy, consisting of water of varying temperatures applied to patients for varying periods of time; and electro therapeutic treatments, utilized with "state-of- the-art" equipment.

I cannot speak for the specific population of Greystone at that time, but we can assume that if narcissists, drug addicts, rapists, and murderers were all housed together with the truly insane (schizophrenics or bipolar- disordered people) in institutions all across the country, it must not have been a pretty picture within the walls of these buildings. Over time, more and more people were "thrown into the mix," because it was just easier— and maybe even felt safer to the general public—to handle a problem by confining it within a secure building. Then, as with the jails and almshouses, overcrowding became an issue, as did sanitation, nutrition, and finding and employing qualified staff. Hence, stories of the "horrors of insanity" were told and, over time, gained color and momentum, as they continue to do today.

One interesting point about Greystone is that in the main building, a beautiful chapel, complete with stained glass windows and a true pipe organ, was built with the initial construction. Patients were expected to attend services of their faith as part of their treatment. At that time there still existed a belief in the combination of spirituality and modern medicine to cure the afflicted, as it was presumed either there was evil in their hearts, or at least a lack of God's love and power in their lives.

Back to the history. However, as time went on and institutional overcrowding became more and more of an issue, both financially and health-wise, the legal world stepped in to determine what exactly qualified a person as "insane." Community-based care became the new method of treatment for those not deemed a "danger to themselves or others," and the availability of medications made releasing (or not institutionalizing) most of the patients a viable option, provided they continued taking their medication. (That is a topic for another book.)

I present this brief history of Greystone to give you a bit of insight into how society's problematic people were treated, and where some of the distorted images and beliefs of what true insanity looks like came from. In fact, the insane were not frightening, creepy, threatening, or dangerous people at all. Many were committed because of doing bizarre or dangerous things, but the great majority of them were dangerous only to themselves.

There is a huge difference between a psychotic mind committing a crime and a narcissistic mind committing one. In fact, most heinous-minded criminals are well aware of what they are doing, and simply do not care what damage they cause. Schizophrenics in a delusional psychotic state are truly not in control of their thoughts, actions, or behaviors when they have "decompensated" or had a "breakdown,"normally due to the onset of their illness, or discontinuing their prescribed medications.

The narcissist's audacity to commit a crime, get caught, and plead "temporary insanity" is simply a self-engrossed attempt to get away with their actions, and hopefully "do their time" in a psychiatric facility instead of a jail, because a psychiatric facility is much more comfortable and safe, and is usually for a significantly shorter sentence.

Let's go back to my point that the relationship between evil and mental illness/behavioral abnormalities has come full circle. First, it was the devil. We did exorcisms; we cast people out of their colonies our communities, or ended their lives, to remove the devil from our presence. Then we defined mental illnesses and behavioral disorders because we decided it wasn't the devil making people do horrible things to other people. But then we decided too many people were behaving in ways we originally thought should be categorized as disorders, so we removed that category of mental illness from our diagnostic menu. That has left us with a society plagued by rapidly increasing numbers of narcissists with the numbers rapidly increasing, and we have no explanation for the prevalence of evil behavior in our country.

In a society where so many people fall into the "un-Godlike, but not insane" category, we are still left with the question, "What causes people to behave like this, and why are is the numbers of people behaving like this increasing so rapidly?" And my answer to you is Socialcide and its sponsor: Satan. We have come full circle.

Chapter Thirty-One

Seeing Through the Mask of Sanity

"Narcissists are great con-artists. After all, they succeed in deluding themselves!
As a result, very few professionals see through them."
—unknown

On a smaller scale, but one much more common familiar to many people, are the everyday narcissists with whom they are involved. They may not be criminal in legal terms, but they are certainly criminal in the court of human morality and kindness. When they are not getting their way in a relationship, they may plead depression, or a terrible childhood, always being picked-on by others, or any other lie they can conjure up to win the sympathy of their victims. It's a fascinating irony that they crave empathy, sympathy, and attention, yet are incapable of feeling any of those things for others. It is the need for those things that drives their behavior.

Another chilling irony is that, although they initially present themselves to a potential "target" as too good to be true, they eventually become too bad to be human. This is especially important for people in the dating world to understand. What you see is not always what you get, especially with so many narcissists on the loose today.

Speaking as a psychologist, there are important factors to look for when seeking a new love interest, and while avoiding a narcissist. The most important aspect relates to the previous paragraph. If anyone comes across as "all you ever dreamed of," be cautious. The narcissist's expertise in becoming your soul mate is superb! All their lives they've been honing this technique for their own benefit, and they are gifted in the art of manipulation, in to fooling people and gaining control of people in their lives. It is important to never rush into a situation with someone who appears "too good to be true." Let time help you see if this is truly the case.

Another identifying characteristic of narcissists is their lack of long- term friendships. Do they have close friends? Have you met them? How long have they been friends? How do they interact? Most narcissists come up dry when it comes to long-term, stable friendships, because they don't have any. They either "use up" their friends for what they need, and then end the relationships, or they became so intolerable to their friends that others those friends end the relationships. Keep this in mind when Mr. Personality seems just so lovable but has no friends. This should be a huge red flag.

What about their families? This is a tricky situation, because for most narcissists, their sense of god-like status has come directly from the over-protection, coddling, adoring, and excuse-making behavior of their parents. In many cases, the family is truly proud of their narcissistic family member (and have no idea what a manipulating, using, devious, dangerous person they he really are is), and frequently and overtly express how wonderful this person is. On the other hand, some families are so desperate to get their family-member-narcissist out of their own lives that they will tell a potential love-interest all kinds of wonderful things, in hopes the new relationship will flourish and the narcissist will no longer focus his or her attention on the family. So if the family seems even a little too "in love"with the relative, there may be a problem.

Consider the case of Scott Peterson, who was convicted of killing his pregnant wife, Lacey, on Christmas Eve, 2002. With a wife at home who was eight months pregnant, he claims he went fishing on Christmas Eve. Later that night he reported her missing. She was never seen alive again. The circumstantial evidence against him was overwhelming. His behavior during the search for Lacey was beyond suspicious. In fact, while his wife was missing, he was having an affair with a woman named Amber Frey. He went on television shows, speaking with no true emotion whatever—that is, besides the crying that was so obviously phony to viewers.

This true narcissist's mother was convinced of his innocence to the day she died, in October of 2013. Peterson remains in San Quentin State Prison, on death row. He was raised to believe he could do what he wanted, when he wanted, and not have to feel guilty about it. So he did!

Peterson's mother is an extreme example of a narcissist's family's over-indulgence in their relative's member's wonderfulness. But the same can be found in the families of everyday narcissists as well; that is, if the family is involved with the narcissist at all. The narcissist will either have a family that treats him or her as a god, or will have cut him or her out of their lives altogether. The narcissist has no real or true ability to truly emotionally connect with others. What appears to be understanding and interest in you or anyone else is merely the narcissist's way of breaking you down emotionally until you believe that fairy tales can come true—and we all know they cannot and don't.

It's important to understand that some people who do not have a good relationships with their families are not necessarily narcissists. Many people have no contact with their families for valid reasons. With that said, the important thing is to get the facts about that situation before proceeding in a relationship. Does the person tell a story of how badly the family has treated him or her, to the point of qualifying for a Lifetime movie? Does the person seem to absorb your sorrow and empathy like a sponge in the Mojave Desert? Listen and watch this person carefully when they relate to their family and other people, like a parent would do upon meeting a daughter's new boyfriend. (That is, if that still happens today.) A family situation where there seems to be far too much, or far too little, connection should set off warning bells. The thing to look for here is balance. The emotions we feel in the beginning of any new love relationship—which are influenced by many factors, including a very real change in body chemistry—easily overpower our common sense. We are listening with ears that want to hear, want to believe, and want to appear acceptable to the other's heart. Being in this state leaves us quite vulnerable, and that is exactly what narcissists wants us to be: vulnerable. They play their tune perfectly to every emotion we have and every compliment we need, perfectly filling in the spaces we feel in our hearts and lives. They push all the right buttons every single time in order to gain entrance to our very souls. This is the narcissistic grooming process in action, the process used to set you up to fulfill their every need.

No one believes this can happen to them—to be ensnared by such a manipulator, to believe they have their soul mate, and but to eventually find out they have a soul abuser—especially because he or she "knows everything about me" and "we have so much in common." Friends and family may express skepticism or even alarm, but that usually falls on the deaf ears of what feels like true love.

That is clue number three. Do your friends and or family have reservations, concerns, or strong negative feelings about this new love interest of yours? Remember, they can see a bit more clearly, because they are not under the spell of the narcissist, or the influence of the chemistry of new love. When friends and family react negatively to this new partner, they are not jealous of your happiness. It's not that they "just don't know him or her," though that's what victims often believe. In reality, they are viewing the person and the relationship through eyes that see past the blinding light of "true love," and quite often are most times spot-on in detecting that this new person is up to no good.

Keep in mind that once the narcissist has your heart and soul, it will not be long before he or she methodically has you eliminate your support system, in order to have total control of your life, emotions, and world. Any threat to this plan must and will be dealt with, to keep you trapped in the world of lies, manipulation, and gain. No method for achieving this, no matter how cruel, is beyond the capability of a narcissist.

One more point to note is that most narcissists move from job to job frequently, or do not work at all. They always seem to be "waiting for a friend to set them up" with a new job, have had nothing but problems with "bad bosses," or somehow have been "victimized" by their past places of employment. Like teenagers today who say, "It's not fair," on an average of eight times a day, the narcissist will use that excuse for every encountered problem. It is simply never, ever their fault. Red flag alert!

So before you get on that long road to nowhere, a road that may leave you more devastated than you can imagine, use your common sense. Listen to those closest to you. Explore this new person's social and family life. Take a good look at their work history.

Now take a moment and think about these warning signs and the narcissistic characteristics I just described. Consider the state of our society right now, and how void of true happiness, real socialization, community, love, and morality it is. Life is far different than it used to be, and it is only getting more and more self-serving, manipulative, evil, and bizarre. A tremendous number of people are seeking fulfillment from falling in love with themselves and their toys, or are seeking some sort of demented revenge against innocent people, because they are of the belief that life is not fair and owes them something.

Life itself owes us nothing at all. Our parents owe us their true best attempt at parenting to the best of their ability, but so many parents are failing at that. Our partner in marriage owes us respect and a lifetime commitment in good times and bad, through sickness and health, 'till death do us part. That is failing. The Law owes us protection and justice in our lives. This, too, is failing. Our government owes us respect, protection, freedoms, and rights, and our elected officials consistently fail us. With failure running rampant throughout, society feels powerless and discarded, much like individuals in relationships with narcissists.

Chapter Thirty-Two
Where Have All the God Times Gone?

"Be good. Do good. The devil wields no power over a good man."
—Harry Segall

The media intentionally and constantly attempts to distract people with celebrity nonsense and antics, new technologies, and any other diversions that keep people entertained and pacified, so they will overlook or not even notice the ultimate narcissistic powers influencing society. When we removed God from our schools and government, or stood idly by and allowed it to happen, we signed a deal with the devil, for which we are bound to pay in full. Payment is now being extracted by and through the deterioration and destruction of our morals,our moral-supporting institutions (community, family, and marriage), our personal and business relationships, and our care for and about others.

There can be no other explanation for the pervasiveness of childhood emotional and social disorders seen today other than the breakdown of community and family, and with it the rise of "video parenting." The frequent and widespread bullying, and child and teenage suicides and killings that happen every day are impacting our nation's collective sense of wellness to the point where these things have just become expected, and we are giving up on being upset about the fact that there are no answers, no plans, and no cures. Some of shake their heads and ask, "Where will it end?"

We have allowed our nation to be looted of life, love, caring, empathy, values, and morality, all the elements necessary to feel human, balanced, and to maintain emotional and social equilibrium to survive with true purpose and progression. Living in a world where anything goes has created a world where everything goes—away, leaving a barren land where true love and the potential for personal growth and success are becoming more and more elusive; indeed, are on their way to becoming extinct.

Ours is a country determined to practice "political correctness," seemingly wanting to keep from insulting anyone's heritage, culture, beliefs, or religion. But this expectation of respect does not seem to include the feelings of believers in God. Do not misunderstand me, please. I wholly support being politically correct and respecting people's beliefs and backgrounds. I just want to point out that while we "talk that talk"and "walk that walk" of inclusiveness and political correctness, we seem to be a bit exclusive in who and what we respect. So I ask, how does the removal of God from classrooms and public areas fit into the picture? Why are believers and God's faithful met with negative reactions from so many other people, as if they are from a different planet, or are to be feared? This did not just happen.

In our society, the resistance to God that has been cultivated throughout the past thirty-five years is part of a plan; part of a spiritual contract in which many people are unwittingly signing over any and all their rights to true happiness and everlasting life with God in the next world. And the are doing it with the false belief that it 's it's perfectly normal to want, take, do, and use whoever they want, whenever they want now, because there is no significant presence or understanding of God or goodness, and what it means to include them in our lives. The common denominator of all the social and personal evil and rudeness in today's world has to be the result of the absence of God and the results thereof.

Before naysayers dismiss this idea, at least consider the reason our forefathers came to this land in the first place. Our ancestors were not running from God, they were seeking the ability to worship Him freely, without the demands of the monarchies or political rulers of the Old World, which were telling people how or if they wanted God worshiped, and then forcing the population to comply.

People came here for freedom of religion as well as to seek opportunities to better their lives. Yes, freedom of religion also means the freedom to have no religion at all, but that was not the main factor that inspired so many to pick up their lives and families and cross the Atlantic. Their inspiration, by far, was their determination to have God in their lives, based on their particular doctrines of faith.

Native Americans were also an extremely spiritual people. Their gods' presence was apparent in all they did, and it their faith kept that spiritual equilibrium among them, so they could prosper, survive, and peacefully coexist. As far back as history can trace, most—if not all— cultures have had a spiritual component, with a God or gods they worshiped and relied upon for life and survival. This American generation of Millennials is perhaps the first generation that just doesn't seem to care about spirituality at all. It is the furthest further removed from spirituality than as compared to any other generation in American history, and the effects are apparent.

Goodness is not being taught to our children anymore. Kindness, respect, courtesy, and regard for others are propagated and reinforced by the same in ourselves. They are learned by observation and experience. One would think that, with the plague of grandiosity and self-love in America, everyone would be loving each other love one another. That is what truly happy people do.

However, the self-love we see so much of today is not real love It's false, and induced by artificial and evil means. It does not come from accomplishment, achievement, hard work, good deeds, and determination to be a good person. Today people expect to be loved and glorified just because they exist. Youth and young adults, by far, expect to be adored and rewarded for little or no effort, because that is what they have learned to do.

This raises the question, "Is goodness possible without God, or without an awareness and inclusion of spirituality in our lives?" If we are not living here on earth to spread some form of goodness and significance to the world and others around us, what exactly are we doing here? Are we here to take what we need and, in our quest for that, forsake the lives and needs of others around us? There's only one spiritual force that supports that thinking, and it's evil.

Chapter Thirty-Three

Are People Evolving or Dissolving?

"Non-violence leads to the highest ethics,which is the goal of all evolution.
Until we stop harming all other living beings, we are still savages."
—Thomas A. Edison

What are we here for then? That question is as old as time. But remember, so is faith and belief in some form of god or spirituality. Did we truly come from a snail in the ocean, or from a "Big Bang?" Personally, I would like to believe mankind was not once a slug or the result of any explosion. To me, both ideas are rather repulsive, and truly discredit humans and God's abilities. If the theory of evolution were true, wouldn't we be getting smarter and more peaceful? In reality, the opposite holds true. We are dumbing down, and becoming more mean and evil. Animals do not show such evil and ugliness, but humans do.

Some say the dumbing down of America is due to the foods we eat and pesticides used on the nation's food supplies. Dr. Gerald Crabtree, a Stanford University researcher and geneticist, has much to say about adverse genetic mutations that cause suffering in human intelligence. According to Crabtree, "our cognitive and emotional capabilities are fueled and determined by the combined effort of thousands of genes. If a mutation occurred in any of these genes, which is quite likely, then intelligence or emotional stability can be negatively impacted" (Undergroundhealth.com).

Dr. Crabtree described how an average person from 1000 BCE Athens would appear to us if he suddenly arrived here today. He described a "bright, quite intellectually alive man with good memory, a broad range of ideas, and a clear-sighted view of important issues." He also went on to say he would certainly stand out in mental ability far above our colleagues or social friends.

These are both theories and, as with all theories, there is always room for speculation and debate. However, over the course of history, we do seem to be losing men and women of great intelligence and benefit to mankind, and we are seeing rapidly decreasing levels of intelligence in our school children and college graduates. Can this loss in intelligence, compassion, creativity, empathy, and greatness be evolution?

With the disappearance of goodness, and the declining levels of intellectual, emotional, social, and spiritual intelligence, it is seemingly futile to believe that mankind is evolving. If we are evolving, what are we evolving into? Statistics show we are evolving into a nation of narcissists on varying levels, and statistics do not lie. So again, why are we here?

Whether or not we acknowledge God in our lives, we are not here to satisfy ourselves by indulging in the Seven Deadly Sins,. which are: And if you who are not aware exactly what they are:

Pride: the excessive belief in one's own abilities that interferes with one's recognition of the Grace of God. Pride has also been called the sin from which all others arise.

Envy: the desire for others' traits, status, abilities, or situations. Gluttony: an inordinate desire to consume more than that which one requires.

Lust: an inordinate craving for the pleasures of the body.

Anger: manifested in the individual who spurns love, and opts opting instead for fury.

Greed: the desire for material wealth or gain, ignoring the realm of the spiritual.

Sloth: the avoidance of physical or spiritual work.

The true origin of this list is not known. These sins do not appear in this form in the Bible. However, they read as the story of any narcissist's life, and sound eerily like what is wrong with America and many of its people today. It seems they are reflective of what many people believe we are here for.

I am hard-pressed to believe that insecticides or genes can create this type of human being, and I can certainly say these are not the characteristics of anyone who is grounded in spirituality or God. These characteristics personify pure evilness and narcissism. That should scare anyone to the point of immediate reckoning. With In a narcissistic nation with narcissism on the rise, we God- and others-centered people are soon to be hugely outnumbered by a society of purely evil people. When we kicked God out of our country, we opened the door wide for evil or Satan to step right in.

Chapter Thirty-Four

Empathy Lost

"Education without values, as useful as it is,
seems rather to make a man a more clever devil."
—C. S. Lewis

There is no cure for narcissism. There is no known scientific explanation for it either. The fields of Psychology and Psychiatry were about to eliminate the term "narcissistic personality disorder"from the official 2013 *Diagnostic and Statistical Manual of Mental Disorders,* because it is becoming so commonplace and untreatable. At the moment, Satan is winning the American lottery of souls.

Most psychotic individuals suffer internally and rarely cause harm to others. Their inner torment is sad and tragic, and it would not surprise me if it is somehow caused by demonic forces. Narcissists, on the other hand, are not psychotic, and they live to cause harm and wreak havoc on and in other people's lives, solely to feel good about themselves, and fulfill their sense of entitlement. They do so without no remorse, or and without empathy for those whom they hurt, terrorize, abuse, or kill. Call them psychopathic, sociopathic, or narcissistic, but know them as evil personified.

Why can't narcissism be cured? For the same reason demons cannot be cured: they no longer have the ability to repent. They truly feel no remorse, and they have no conscience. When we hear or read news about horrors and tragedy inflicted upon innocent people, no matter what the specific crime was, we ask ourselves, *"What kind of monster could do such a thing?"* Many people are

245

fascinated by serial killers and other criminally-minded psychopaths, because we simply cannot fathom having no conscience or empathy whatsoever.

And, speaking of fascination, the Investigation Discovery channel airs true crime stories twenty-four hours a day, seven days a week, and their its number of viewers continues to grow. Watching these stories becomes an obsession, much like watching the high-profile criminal trials that are televised from start to finish. Millions of Americans become fixated with hearing what human beings are capable of doing to each other, and they follow every detail from gavel to gavel.

Is it entertainment or education? Perhaps it's a little of both. Perhaps it's a warning. In America today crime is not going away anytime soon, and the types of crimes we watch and read about are becoming more and more evil than anything we have ever seen. Watching the offerings on Investigation Discovery, any viewer can receive a thorough education in pure, demonic narcissism.

I am not sure if such exposure to evil is beneficial or detrimental. We do know that, beginning with the Columbine High School massacre in 1999, copycat crimes have been committed, because demented psychopaths have made these murderers their heroes, and carried on their evil legacies in some form of twisted allegiance to them. If that is not demonic influence, I am not sure what is. However, we cannot stop even the well-minded individual's fascination with evil, let alone the psychopath's.

Besides, the broadcast coverage is not the cause of the problem. Even so, we can reduce or eliminate the names of these killers from the news, to reduce or prevent any sick glorification of them and their crimes.

I do not believe watching true crime television, or following high profile criminal cases through trial can turn a person into a psychopathic narcissist. I do believe if a person already is a narcissist these cases either mean nothing to him or her, because they aren't him or her, or they inspire a basement-bound evil mind to create her its own evil.

The volume of media coverage about stalkers, murderers, kidnappers, pedophiles, and other evil-minded people does serve to scare many people to such a degree that they will keep their children at home and indoors most of the time; and many parents have opted to homeschool their children. This new locked-up lifestyle is certainly understandable. No good parent wants to put their child in any harm's way. But it is also quite unfair, and may very well be causing the rise in this younger generation's sense of entitlement. Homeschooling must be balanced with some forms of real social involvement with peers. When children don't learn to work together with other children and other people they lose many of the skills necessary to communicate, empathize, and realize that fairness is not always an option.

The current overexposure to and fascination with true crime is a double-edged sword of sorts. On the one hand, it creates a vivid awareness for the public as to how many boogeymen are out there, and what they are capable of doing so steps can taken to in crease awareness and safety. On the other hand, it causes a rise in isolated living situations, which in themselves can breed emotional, social, and psychological problems for the under-exposed child.

A recent study conducted by Sara H. Konrath of the University of Michigan at Ann Arbor was published online in August, 2010, in Personality and Social Psychology Review. This study found that in college students, empathy is not the innate cornerstone of human behavior many have believed it to be. Her research challenges that assumption by showing that empathy levels have been declining over the past thirty years.

She found, through direct questioning of college students, their self-reported empathy had declined since 1980, with the highest drop occurring during the last ten years. A staggering seventy-five percent of the tens of thousands of students surveyed now rate themselves as less empathetic than the average student did thirty years ago. This is no coincidence, and is truly concerning. Socialcide is very real, and it 's it's getting "realer" as time goes on. What does this research say is behind such a change in Americans?

It is fascinating to me that there continues to be no known medical or biological blame reason for people's lack of care and empathy today. Some say it's the water we drink, the air we breathe, even the high levels of high fructose corn syrup in our food. But this does not sound plausible. This is a social disease, not a creation of any biologically-based toxin. Socialcide is the plague of evil in our world. Again, we must look at any common denominators over the past thirty to thirty-five years,. to see where some thing or things have changed. Konrath's study did just that.

Humans—or even primates, for that matter—are not the only living beings that can feel and exhibit empathy. Mice have been studied and observed to feel the pain of their cage mates when they were subjected to stressful or painful stimuli. Six-month-old babies have been observed demonstrating a desire for empathetic behavior as evidenced by choosing the doll perceived as helping others over visually similar ones that were not.

What this research suggests, and Socialcide agrees, is that we most definitely are born with empathetic abilities, but we can lose them somehow, somewhere along life's path. Konrath cited our country's increase in social isolation as a common denominator along the continuum of declining empathy. More Americans are choosing to live alone, and they do not join organizations as frequently as they used to. She noted that some studies hint to this aspect of Americans' lifestyles taking a toll on their levels of empathy. Other studies have shown that socially isolated individuals, after interacting with others over a period of time, evaluate them less generously than socially integrated individuals.

It has been suggested that another possible factor affecting society's empathy levels is a 50% decrease in the reading of literature for pleasure over the past ten years, mostly among college students. Some studies have suggested that reading is directly related to increased empathy, inspiring people to feel other's trials and triumphs through written words.

Chapter Thirty-Five

The Elephant in the Room

"I fear the day that technology will surpass our human interaction.
The world will have a generation of idiots."
—Albert Einstein

Where all of the research and scientific information appears to end is at the true root of what is causing America to become a society of self-serving lovers of themselves: we have become encouraged toward and accustomed to "virtual living" through social media and home entertainment for every aspect of our lives, including schooling, shopping, and communicating.

There is a huge problem in our society when a sixteen-year-old boy does not know how to make a phone call and actually speak to his friend's parents and ask if the friend is at home. There is a huge problem in our society when men and women can get bored with their marriages and have no problem or guilty feelings going to a website to connect with other married individuals who are also bored and looking for sex. There is a huge problem when young girls are being drugged and raped by their teenage peers, and the abuse is videotaped and broadcast to the world via computers or cell phones to the point that, because of the resulting bullying and torment , the victims take their own lives because of the resulting bullying and torment, (and meanwhile the boys who attacked them don't suffer any consequences, or feel any remorse).

There is a huge problem when our kids go off to school and never come home because some psychopathic monster decides today is his day to shoot as many kids and adults as he wants can, because he is "mentally ill," or no one saw it coming.

Honestly, if a kid is spending his life in a dark room, playing violently graphic video games twenty-four hours a day, never coming out for air or food, living a creepy and isolated life, and then goes and commits some violent atrocity, no one saw this coming?

All these examples of the varying degrees of tragedies occurring on a daily basis that are only the tip of the proverbial iceberg of just how destructive and real Socialcide is in America. We live through means that are simply not human. We do not know how to communicate, care, love, get involved, or give a damn anymore. Our youth are lazy, entitled, and can be very dangerous. Our marriages and relationships fail continuously when people become involved with narcissistic demons, who strip them of their self-esteem, emotional wellness, dignity, trust, and even their safety, because of being bored, or simply wanting someone or something to feed the never-ending appetite for power, sex, drugs, status, or money.

We have to be constantly on guard wherever we go today, because we can be injured, maimed, or slain while watching a movie, shopping at a mall, ordering a cheeseburger, going to class, working on a military base, or even walking down the street where some child is playing Knockout. It's your lucky day to get pummeled into unconsciousness or worse, just because you decided to walk down that street on your lunch break.

Our heroes have become the people who are the epitome of self- indulgence and conceit. These celebrities and sports stars earn millions upon millions of dollars and yet show absolutely no grace, gratitude, or couth in their raging antics that serve only to make fools of themselves to some, and inspire like-behaviors in others. The media cannot seem get their behaviors broadcast frequently or quickly enough to meet the voracious demand of the public for more and more.

There is a tremendous problem when school children do not know who Neil Armstrong is, but who know what Snooki had for lunch yesterday.

Speaking of Neil Armstrong, he was a true hero. As the first man to step on the moon, this man should have all the bragging rights in the world. And rightfully so! However, the man did his job and kept a very private, low profile for the rest of his life. He was looked up to by the youth of his time as a real hero, yet today children don't even know his name, or why he is famous. However, they do know Honey Boo Boo passed gas on last night's show. Do you see the change in the times? More importantly, do you see the change in our society?

We are addicted to technology to the point of losing our ability to live, love, and learn. When a person lives in a virtual world, that person is a virtual person: fake, not real, fantasy, made-up. Those traits are the very essence of a narcissist's life. Nothing is real about them, except the damage they do to other people. And with all the science, research, medicine, and, yes, technology we have today, no one can say what causes narcissism, or why it is plaguing America? No one sees the cause of the lack of empathy, self-entitlement, deviance, bullying, infidelity, divorce, neglect of children, lack of taking responsibility, laziness, social isolation, or evil we face every single day?

There is a huge elephant in America's living rooms, and no one wants to acknowledge it. It is *Satan,* and the evil one has his proverbial split-hooved foot up on our collective coffee table, picking at his horns with that pointed tail of his, enjoying every minute of his plan coming to fruition at the expense of American's souls.

Chapter Thirty-Six
The Message of Guilt

"My guiding principle is this: Guilt is never to be doubted."
—Franz Kafka

The fields of Psychology and Psychiatry are never going to admit that the narcissism, entitlement, crimes, and evil deeds running rampant in society today are the result of any ongoing spiritual warfare. Even with all their very valuable knowledge and theories about the human mind and psyche, they cannot establish a valid, provable, scientific reason for the decline of goodness and empathy in this country. In fact, as we have discussed, they are all but done even acknowledging narcissism as a true personality disorder.

There is not one single, definitive, scientific fact that explains why the most evil, hurtful, selfish, self-centered, uncaring portion of the population is *flourishing* in our country, or where these traits come from. So, they say, "Let's eliminate it from our responsibility." There is no blame to be placed on these fields, because there really is no cure or treatment for narcissistic personality disorder. So there it sits, pure, self-indulgent evil, left to grow, and spread, and destroy.

If you think about it, this situation is a huge win-win for Satan. Make no mistake about it, dear readers. Narcissism is demonic possession. Narcissists are hell on earth to those around them, and living hell indeed. Do they know it? They may know they are hurting people, but they have no capacity to care. Do they know they are possessed? Probably not. After all, they are their own god, and they believe no one is more powerful or important than themselves.

So why does Satan want to take over humans? Remember why he was kicked out of Heaven by God. Satan fancied himself more powerful and more important than God. And indeed, he was a very powerful angel— perhaps God's most beloved angel. However, God tells us we can worship no other God but Him, and Satan wasn't digging that plan. So God gave him his walking papers.

Off goes Satan into the world to prove himself more powerful than God, because *that's what narcissists do*. His spectacular entrance into the world began the moment he conned Eve (and indirectly, Adam) into taking a bite of that forbidden fruit. God warned Adam and Eve about that tree, just that one tree out of probably thousands of others, but Satan knew how to manipulate his the first narcissistic victims of his narcissism by promising all kinds of great and wonderful things, and telling them their "parent" had lied to them. All they had to do was take a bite of that fruit, and the world would be theirs. That's another thing narcissists are so good at: convincing their victims of how wonderful and right they are, at least initially.

Understand, Adam and Eve already had all they wanted and needed in Eden: plenty to eat, no unpleasant work, no sweat, no pain, no shame, no need of any kind. They also had free will, as all of us still do. God wants souls to choose Him, not be forced to worship Him. I would say that's a fair deal. So as Adam and Eve allowed the talking serpent (Satan in disguise, and by the way, animals could speak in the Garden of Eden) to convince them to take a that bite, they forsook God's one request, and all bets, in the world as they knew it, were off. Now Satan had introduced "original sin" for all the rest of mankind to bear.

This is the rationale behind Satan's Socialcide plan: the more souls he can win over or take from God, the more powerful he believes he and his spiritual army of demons will be. Temptation is his ruse, along with millions of disguises, beginning with the serpent suit of long ago. Satan does not care if people are worshiping him directly or not, at least not yet. But if they are worshiping any god other than the true God, they are worshiping him.

For narcissists, their one god is themselves. Sex, drugs, alcohol, money, fame, power, and other self-indulgences can be considered gods to some people (both narcissists and non-narcissists), but to narcissists, these are secondary at best, compared to him- or herself.

I am not in any way attempting to challenge anyone's spirituality or religion, or the validity and value of a belief system that is not the one to which I personally subscribe. I believe if you have an awareness and acceptance of spirituality, in whatever form it takes, as long as it supports the "Golden Rule" and kindness to others, you have a conscience and can feel remorse and empathy. I am not suggesting individuals must or should subscribe to any specific religion, or belong to any certain faith, to have God and spirituality in their lives.

The reality is that if a person can do wrong and then feel bad or remorseful about it (which most of us have on countless occasions), we either apologize for it, or otherwise fix it as best we can. The feeling of guilt is not pleasant, and it 's it's much like the check-engine light in our cars. It bothers us, and serves as a constant reminder that we need to correct something. Guilt and remorse normally come "standard" in humans, and they are there for a reason.

SECTION VI

Cause and Effect

Chapter Thirty-Seven

Narcissistic Parenting and the Carnage Left Behind

"Half the harm that is done in this world is due to people who want to feel important. They don't d o n ' t mean to do harm, but the harm [that they cause] does not interest them. Or they do not see it, or they justify it because they are absorbed in the endless struggle to think well of themselves."

—T. S. Eliot

Narcissists do not feel guilt or remorse. We know this well. They also have no capacity to empathize with others. What people are to them is merely a means to some end or need they have, and in the case of the children of a narcissist, they serve merely as an extension of themselves—a way to make the narcissist look better to others. This, again, explains why most relationships narcissists engage in eventually fall apart. Healthy-minded adults soon catch on to a person who is all and only about themselves, and will frequently end the relationship (or at least try to). Children, unfortunately, do not always have an opportunity to break away from their narcissistic parent, at least not during the most emotionally and psychologically important years of their lives.

Because children of narcissists are unable to recognize the danger they are in, and do not have the power to leave the relationship, they become brainwashed by the soulless parent to the point of never believing in themselves, and always believing everything wrong that happens in their lives is their own fault. These children may constantly hear people outside the family talk about just how "wonderful your father is," or that "your mom should be Mom of the Year." But the narcissistic parent 's parent's "mask of sanity" comes off when they are behind closed doors, and their children are the most susceptible to their rage, monstrous outbreaks, and stabbing tongues.

These children, tragically, think to themselves, "He must be right! Everyone loves him. What am I doing wrong?"

There is never an answer to that if you are questioning your relevance to a narcissist. Some adult children spend their entire lifetimes trying to figure it out. They may become romantically involved with someone like their parent as they unconsciously try to "finally make mommy or daddy happy"through this new relationship. Most children of narcissists doubt every move they make through life. They may always have the feeling that, at any point in time, especially at their jobs, they are somehow going to be caught doing something wrong, or exposed for who they really are. None of this is true, or accurate; however, it's very true in their thinking, and is at the core of their self-esteem.

Today, the growth of narcissism is being fostered by the shortage or absence of effective parenting. What is happening is that when children show more and more narcissistic behaviors at home, school, or elsewhere, parents are not doing enough to snuff that tendency before it becomes too late. It certainly does not help that kids today increasingly have increasingly less responsible, less available parents. Another trend I encounter in my work, which is getting more and more widespread, is that when a parent does try to enforce consequences, the child or teen simply does not care. I have seen situations where a child is suspended from school for bad behavior, and not only does the child not care, he or she actually enjoys it. A day off to do whatever he or she wants! Two days off? Even better! No embarrassment, no regret, no lesson learned. Just "What's in it for me?" And that seems to be plenty!

For an increasing number of children, consequences such as "grounding," taking away cell phones, video games, computers and the like, really do not have much impact. This seems to be because either their parents are very inconsistent in following through and enforcing the consequences, or the child makes the parents' lives so unbearable with nonstop badgering, they simply give in to make their own lives easier. What lesson does this teach? "Be a bother and get what I want," and "I'll get over it somehow. Who cares?" Apparently, there is truth in that question: Who does care?

Self-love and remorseless living are the cornerstones of narcissistic behavior. Be it a serial killer, a serial cad, or any other ego-inflated individual who goes about their lives using others for their own gain, while giving absolutely nothing back but heartache, emotional destruction, death, and despair, they such persons can only be inspired by a true separation from goodness, God, and any sense of love except for pride in themselves. This is quickly becoming the new American way, and something must be done to stop it.

Chapter Thirty-Eight

Evil Exists. Does God?

"The people answered and said, 'Far be it from us that we
should for sake the Lord to serve other gods!'"
—Joshua 24:16

Why are we less inclined to include God or spirituality in our lives today than in times past? Years ago people believed the world was in fact inhabited by demons being governed by Satan himself. The God-fearing sought out His protection and the protection of His angels to battle the evil forces.

This is not a fairy tale; this is history. Now, speaking of demonic influences in the world must begin with the disclaimer, "I 'm I'm not crazy or anything, but—" When did belief in God become crazy or insane, and narcissism become so normal it is being put on the chopping block of Mental Disorder classifications? History, with respect to these issues, has completely reversed itself.

Lily Tomlin once asked, "Why is it when we talk to God we are praying, but when God talks to us we are schizophrenic?" This question points out the widespread, common, damaging, negative judgments society very comfortably places on personal relationships with God, judgments that make us think we should avoid having that kind of relationship, or at least avoid telling people that we do. Many people wonder, "If there is a God, how and why can He allow so much horror and suffering in the world?" This is another statement that accurately reflects what much of society believes today—that God has abandoned us, or that He never really existed.

When we began to forsake our spiritual God for technological gods, we also must have been watering and tending to that seed of doubt so deviously planted in our society by none other than Satan himself. Why must we declare our sanity before we acknowledge our belief in God? In other words, society looks at those of us who do believe as somehow "not quite right" or perhaps "just a little gullible." Really?

Many people want proof of God's existence. That is exactly what Satan expects his followers to do. Ironically, many of those who seek some proof that God exists wouldn't recognize it if they were to get it.

There is plenty of proof in this world today that evil exists. It is, unfortunately, everywhere. Can this be denied or questioned? Even in my world of Psychology, the evil some people inflict on their families or spouses is horrifying, and that is small-scale evil compared to the real evil in America today. It is evil that people do when they believe they are God. No matter what they do, they have no shred of remorse or regret for how they use other people for their own personal gain. This behavior can only be demonic.

If such evil is so widespread, so visible, so tangible, and so blatantly present in our world, why is goodness not just as real to non-believers? It becomes too easy to simply deny that God exists because we are not looking for Him. We have kicked Him out. Some have put Him in their medicine cabinets. Others somehow think they are deserving of Him stopping by their house with flowers to say, "Hello! I heard you wanted proof I am real? Well, here I am! Can I perform a miracle or two for you? You might want to video this for your YouTube account. Show your friends!" Honestly, how narcissistic can one be? "Prove it to me, God."

It is as if some believe this epidemic of evil that is occurring is God's fault. However, when God gave Moses the first of the Ten Commandments, "Thou shall have no other gods before me," the phrase "no other gods" certainly included the self, as well as things like golden calves. When people worship themselves before God, they have broken commandment number one, and immediately disconnect from goodness and Him. The more evil we see, experience, and continuously hear about, the more inclined we are to deny God's existence. Evil rises as more and more people worship themselves, money, power, celebrity, sex, and control. This is a complete win-win for Satan, at least for now, and a huge lose-lose for society.

Chapter Thirty-Nine

Lost Family, Lost Love, Lost Souls

"The narcissist has no conscience and no feelings for others, especially
their own children. The only thing that matters is their own selfish ego—coercing,
manipulating, causing chaos, and damaging lives everywhere they go. "
—unknown

Psychiatrists and Psychologists are flooded with clients today, more than
ever before. The most commonly reported complaints with which people
come for help are depression, anxiety, panic, and relationship problems. In
other words, millions of Americans are unhappy, scared, nervous, and facing
some sort of communication or trust issues with their significant others. Those
who seek help are normally not narcissists because, as we know, narcissists
never believe they have a problem.

There are so many people suffering with depression because we live in
a world where we feel no connection to people or activities. They see what
love should look like on television, in movies and commercials, and do not
believe they can obtain such lifestyles. Of course, these images are not real,
but they do influence many people's moods, especially around holidays such
as Christmas/winter celebrations and Valentine's Day. They feel alone in their
world.

Families function quite differently than they used to. This reality has been
linked to depression.

Many people grow up in some form of family, but at the same time,
very much on their own. Communication is often through notes, texts, or
emails. Dinners are "every man for himself." Proper nurturing, and modeling

of marriage and adult behavior just doesn't happen enough. These are the essential tools for parenting and establishing an emotionally-well child, but they too many parents are falling by the wayside, leaving children much to their own devices. If the child does not wind up narcissistic, he or she can easily become very depressed.

The depressed population, suffers silently more and more, and in greater numbers now because society has been disappearing, and there is no one to notice, to care, or to whom they may gently, quietly reach out. Gone are the organizations, clubs, or extended family members and friends once very present, giving us purpose, and meeting our human need to feel involved and relevant. The decline in socialization over the years is a direct result of Socialcide, and thus a likely cause of depression. Conversely, the narcissist does not get depressed, but meets his or her own need to feel involved and relevant at the expense of others. Depression does not work that way.

Feeling alone in a world of millions is a sad reality for many. How does one meet new people or find a love interest? One would think with all the people in the world this should be easy, and perhaps it was when society was more—well—social. Because we have become a nation of isolation, now we look for love online. My discussions with clients that have tried this tell me this dating format made them even more depressed. I am not saying that many people have not had success with online dating, but I have yet to counsel one in my practice.

The main point here is that when we as a the members of society cease to act as a society, and spend more time alone than not, there are repercussions that extend deep into our sense of wellbeing. We were not created to be isolated creatures, and yet we have pushed and pushed the proverbial square peg into the round hole to force it to work. The huge lie here is that it seemed to be working for a while, but now we are beginning to see just how much damage going against nature can cause psychologically, socially, spiritually, and personally. The level and frequency of sadness, evil, arrogance, ignorance, rudeness, and self-love among us today is, by far, higher than society has ever seen. It is more than is needed to cause a person to be depressed, anxious, nervous, and scared to death enough to want to run and hide in isolation from it all. However, that 's that's exactly what evil wants us to do.

Chapter Forty

There's One Born Every Minute

"You can fool all the people some of the time, and some of the people all the time, but you cannot fool all the people all the time."
—Abraham Lincoln

What is very, very important for people to understand is that, when we are sad, lonely, or depressed, we are also quite vulnerable. If we were raised doubting much or most of our abilities, we grow into adults who seek more reassurance than do other adults do. If we grew up isolated, we most likely entertained fantasy-like images of how life should be or will be someday, by watching images in movies, on television, or online more than in real life. There may have been a true lack of real life altogether. This can be a recipe for disaster.

Those who are depressed, or self-doubters, in their search for happiness or companionship, can easily and quickly be swept up by the attention, attraction, and enticement of a that wolf in sheep's clothing—the narcissist. Mr. or Ms. Wonderful will seem to be the answer to every single need and dream imaginable, all in one prize package. The narcissist can convince them, while showering them with adoration, attention, presents, time, and promises, that they will never need anyone else.

The Hallmark card has come to life. We are just not in any way prepared to suspect or imagine the horrific reality that truly lies ahead when we dance with the devil. In fact, many victims of narcissists have said they felt as if they were dating Satan himself.

The truth is, Satan and narcissists use the very same scam on their victims. Here's the formula: Find the weak and lonely, give them all they want and tell them all they need to hear, promise them how much better their lives will be now, and do everything they could wish and more to thoroughly manipulate and brainwash them to the point where they cannot live without you. Once they are completely under your spell, treat them like they are the worst, stupidest, ugliest, and cruelest person in the world, and take from them whatever you want while you cheat, lie, and tell them they are crazy. Torture, torture, and torture some more. Criticize them constantly. Beat them if you feel like it. Show no care for anything they try to do for you to win back your love. If they challenge you at all, scream every wicked word you can think of in their faces. Throw in a moment or two of niceness, the way it used to be, to screw up their thinking a little bit and give them a little false hope, then disregard it once they seem to be more agreeable. Lastly, be sure they have no contact with friends or family, because those people just might try to talk some sense into them regarding you.

Those are the sad realities of life (or any relationship) with a narcissist. If you are strong enough to get out of the relationship, healing is possible, but it can take a very long time. The lesson or warning here is this: If you are in a sad or lonely situation, do not make the mistake of thinking anyone or anything can change it except you, with some help, support, and guidance, of course! Get your thinking and emotions in check order well before you fall prey to one of these monsters. They prey on the vulnerable, and can spot them from miles away. Nothing that wonderful ever comes without work, and that work begins and ends with you.

The number of victims of narcissists in our society today is rising, because the number of narcissists is rising, and because many innocent people are under-socialized, and want to be loved. The lure of evil is well hidden in mystery, and lonely people want to believe in magic and the possibility that magic will happen in their lives. But every magician knows that behind every magic trick lies a gimmick. There is no such thing as magic. However, the devil and the narcissist are both excellent magicians and masters of deception.

The good news is that you can be aware and avoid the terror of both, with knowledge. How ironic that knowledge—and, specifically, the knowledge of good and evil, the thing Adam and Eve did not initially know—was only given to them after the serpent tricked them into eating the fruit of the forbidden tree. They disobeyed God and lost paradise forever, but walked away from it with the ability to see that some things are good and some things are bad. Satan, while trying only to do evil to humankind, ended up ensuring we have the one thing that allows us to recognize the difference between good and evil. It is only because of the trickery of Satan that we have the ability to identify and understand evil. And now it's it's time to use this gift against him! Knowledge and self-understanding are powerful weapons, and will serve as our best defenses against evil people and forces, both of which are becoming more and more present in America today.

SECTION VII

God Is The Answer

Chapter Forty-One

"Getting" God in Today's World

"God can show Himself as He really is only to real men. And that means
not simply to men who are individually good, but to men who are united together in a
body, loving one another, helping one another, showing Him to one another. For that is
what God meant humanity to be like; like players in one band, or organs in one body."
—C. S. Lewis, Mere Christianity

We are quickly becoming a nation vastly desensitized to the evil and
horror occurring all around us, and because narcissism is fueled by having
no empathy or care of others, many people simply shake their heads and
say, "This is terrible," and then go on about their lives until the next tragedy
crosses their screens on the nightly news. Despite this, there are millions of
Americans today who have God or some form of spirituality in their lives.
They are praying, they have been praying, and they will continue to pray, in
whatever way they see fit. Unfortunately, many of them have been forced into
hiding, so to speak. Not literally, but socially. Talking about God has become
politically incorrect, or even likened to speaking about extra-terrestrial aliens.
(I think many Americans are more prone to believe in aliens than in God
these days. Personally, I have my own theories about extraterrestrials, but
that's also for another time.) It is truly unfortunate that who believe in
God's love and presence have become looked upon as predators of some
sort, or as if they have the plague. Phobias evolve from fears. Those who, for
whatever reason, fear the truth of a Higher Power in the universe will ridicule
believers as crazy. This is typical behavior for someone who is afraid of, or
feels threatened by, some person or group of people. They mask their fear in
jokes and harassment, and sometimes directly express their discomfort. This
shift in thinking, that today's believers are crazy, is the exact opposite of how

society used to be, back when it was believers who were the majority and the respected. Very interesting turn of events! However, par for the course of Socialcide.

Televangelists of the 1980s and 1990s did little to help society's trust in God, with their Bible-thumping rants, their fire-and-brimstone warnings of coming destruction, and their damnation messages for all who rejected God (and did not send in donations to their causes "ministries"). Many of these video preachers were found to be nothing but liars, adulterers, and actors. However, even though they have been exposed, and in some cases even imprisoned for what they have done, they left a lasting—and inaccurate—image in many people's minds as to what believing in God or religion looks like. Who wouldn't run from that madness? What they did was to capitalize on people's fears, and turn God's Word into scary warnings and threats, leaving out the true love of God, and how we should be spreading that love in all we do, and to all we meet.

Sadly, our epidemic of self-love and isolation, along with the sick and evil activities and crimes we see every day, has transformed society into a world where we are just not nice anymore. We do little, if anything, for our neighbors, friends, co-workers, or fellow humans, to simply help them or make their lives a little better in small ways.

Such "random acts of kindness" are how we can spread God's goodness and love. And actions are far more important than words. When we do these things, others feel better, and so do we! That's a win-win situation. And when we see others "spreading the love," we are inspired to do it too also! That's the win-win-win!

Unfortunately, many people find these small kindnesses just "too weird" to do these days, and many others just don't care. That is because we are detached from God and goodness. It's a vicious cycle—a downward spiral, and it all ends in a place where we are tempted to believe God doesn't exist, or if He exists, He is on vacation. Ultimately, I believe most Americans deny God's existence because they do not know how to see Him or celebrate Him.

It is not rocket science, scary, or weird at all. It is how we were wired, but we've been fooled into believing otherwise.

Putting the psychopaths, sociopaths, and narcissists aside for a moment, let 's let's consider the rest of us. Overall, we are a fairly unhappy, unsatisfied, lonely, and under-achieving bunch. It is a rare individual who fully embraces God or spirituality in their lives. Even some of those who are living lives of tremendous despair or misery still fear to do so.

As Socialcide progresses, we are running out of options for finding true happiness in this life. How many "Apps," video games, cars, dollars, love interests, shopping sprees, smart phones, tablets, play dates, social media sites, friends, selfies, hook-ups, pain pills, or pounds lost will it take to finally feel happy? None! None of it will ever make anyone truly happy. We have been led so far off of the path to happy, and now we are either afraid to get back on it, or simply don't know how. Perhaps it's both.

Chapter Forty-Two

Sharing Goodness for Goodness Sakes

"This is my simple religion. There is no need for temples;
no need for complicated philosophy. Our own brain,
our own heart is our temple; the philosophy is kindness."
—Dalai Lama

There is an enormous difference between loving ourselves and self-love. The current and destructive trend today is self-love, the one reflected in the First Commandment, where God said to worship no other gods but Him. When we have self-love we put our own needs and pleasures above all else. This is not, in itself, evil or wrong; however, when those needs and pleasures come at the expense of other people's feelings or possessions, that is when it becomes a big problem, and the conscience or soul dissipates. Once that is gone, there is no turning back, and narcissistic traits begin to grow.

We never feel we have enough. And like an addict, we do all the scamming, stealing, and conning necessary to keep getting our fix of self. Again, like any addiction, there is never an end to the need, and the process or chase toward the fix becomes as big a part of the addiction as the drug itself.

Extreme examples of such a self-love addiction would be serial killers. Out-smarting the police, wanting and having to capture and torture victims before killing them, then dumping their bodies, are all part of what they want and what they need to feel satisfied and to feel *alive*. All this is done repeatedly, with not a shred of remorse or guilt.

Loving ourselves is a very, very different concept. God wants us to love ourselves. He wants us to take care of our emotions, our time, our needs, our health, and our overall well-being. However, He also wants us to take care of one another, our families, our friends, our neighbors, strangers we meet, whoever we may come in contact with as we roam this world.

This does not mean over-extending ourselves to the point of emotional or physical exhaustion. That is not healthy. What it does mean is perhaps holding the grocery store door open for the person coming behind us. It may mean using directional signals when driving, so others know which way we are going. Perhaps it means smiling at people and saying hello. It may mean calling(yes telephoning) an elderly friend or relative just to "check- in" more often, and asking if they need anything like some food or a visit. Being mindful and simply nice to others is a dying trend today, and doing so may make the recipient puzzled or suspicious. But, so what?

I watched a YouTube video recently of a young man named Jusef, who conducted an experiment on a college campus. He spoke of how we as a society have lost the art of reaching out to others just to say, "Hello! You look beautiful!" or "I love your smile! Have a wonderful day!" because the vast majority of our communications today are via text messaging, social media, or email.

So off went this college-aged man with a bunch of flowers to distribute to random women on campus with a smile and a compliment followed by, "Have a wonderful day!" Most of the recipients were somewhat astonished by this random act of kindness, and some thought he was trying to sell them something.

Watching this experiment was bittersweet. Let's face it; these days one would be suspicious of such strange behavior. "What do you want from me? What's the catch?" That is the bitter part—wondering how and why we have evolved into a nation of suspicious individuals when someone simply says something nice to us, then walks away, no questions asked.

I realize this is probably not the ideal way to demonstrate loving ourselves, but it did make a point. We can be happier simply because someone says something nice to us for no good apparent reason, and we can feel happier when we are the ones who extend ourselves "just because." This does not get taught in our schools, though, and when we lock our children up at home with a computer, iPad, and video games, we are not teaching them this. In fact, we are most likely teaching them to be suspicious, untrusting, and avoidant of such things.

Now, of course, there is some value to that too also. However, keeping our children that close does deprive them of at least some amount of trust and caring. The whole world is not out to kidnap our children and do terrible things to them, but if kids grow up with the belief that the world is not ever a safe place, we have done them an injustice, and have contributed to the growth of Socialcide. Loving ourselves, and experiencing true happiness, cannot normally be performed as a solo act. We need others, and others need us. Is it any wonder our youth today are so uncomfortable in social situations, have extreme difficulty following rules or taking directions, and seemingly have been to have no respecting for or fear of adults and authority figures? less and fearing nothing?

Perhaps they seem to have no fear because they are afraid of the wrong things. Much of society is afraid of the wrong things, such as God and human kindness, for no good reason, except that such fear is what has been taught over the past thirty-five years. We are teaching our children they do not need others, and certainly do not need God.

Chapter Forty-Three
Why Should I Care?

"Selfishness is not living as one wishes to live,
it is asking others to live as one wishes to live."
—Oscar Wilde

Why do we fear? Does it serve any benefit to us? My belief is that the word fear is not the best way to explain what we need to keep us out of harm's way. Concern is a more positive way to explain exactly what keeps us out of trouble. The problem today is that many people are fearing less, and concerning themselves more, and perhaps only, with getting what they want, when they want it.

Historically, people feared starvation, so they hunted and planted. When areas grew barren, fear pushed communities to move on to more bountiful lands and areas. They did not want to starve to death, and had they simply waited around for miracles or handouts, they surely would have.

Today we fear not being able to eat and pay our bills to maintain our standard of living, be it what it may, so we concern ourselves with making money by working, to keep us (and our families) afloat. So one could say we work out of fear of poverty. We pay our bills and taxes out of fear of losing what we have.

We try to obey the law and not hurt or kill people, hurt people, steal, or purposely violate traffic regulations, because we fear we will lose our freedom, and we fear going to jail or paying huge fines. We try to stay out of trouble, because we fear the consequences.

Fear, then, constitutes the presence of conscience or a soul in a person. That little voice that guides us to do the right thing and remain safe is our guard and common sense. Most of the times we listen to it; sometimes we don't d o n' t. But more and more, people are not hearing it today. This is a dangerous trend, and is a major contributor to Socialcide.

As a this current generation is being raised with little to no fear of anything, what does that mean to the future of America, or of the world for that matter? Children raised with no fear of their parents or other authorities will never have fear of much at all. This is a recipe for disaster and narcissism.

Human kindness and compassion are becoming as obsolete as the belief in God, and we are in trouble, America. This is occurring because we are raising a generation of individuals who believe they are their own gods, and can do what they want, when they want, to whom they want—because they deserve it.

As far as I know, the workforce has not quite yet given in to the self-indulgent college graduate's graduates' insistence that they "rise to the top" quickly, without earning their wings or paying their dues to prove themselves.

The things that count as a success in the workplace are reliability, dedication, openness to direction, respect for bosses and co-workers, honesty, and hard work. These qualities serve to earn us merit, and the confidence of those with whom and for whom we work.

Many college graduates today do not exhibit these traits and qualities. They have no need to fear. Much comes far too easily for them, and less emphasis is placed on earning what is necessary to succeed both as a person and as a worker. For goodness sake, young people today don't even know how to have a real conversation anymore!

It is safe to say the same about gaining God's love and acceptance. It must be earned. If we want to live an eternity of happiness and extreme peace with God in Heaven after we die, we need to be doing our best to create such a world in our own lives today. Imagine for a moment the day you leave this temporary thing we call "life" in your human body. The next thing you experience is a surge of overpowering peace and joy. Then God appears to you. You say, "Oh, WOW! You're real? I knew it!" However, you never actually knew it; in fact, you never lived anything near a life close to God's presence. What do you expect Him to do with you? What happens then? There is no reset button in life!

That extreme feeling of peace and belonging will not last long, because God wants His believers to be rewarded for all their hard work, and for the goodness they tried their best to spread throughout their lives. Heaven is not for narcissists, or evil, self-indulgent people. They have not earned it by simply believing and trying to live by standards of dignity and goodness. Oh well. Those who are not concerned with God in this life will not be a concern of God's in the next one. Are you ready to take that chance?

Chapter Forty-Four

I'm Here for the Party

"Also that everyone should eat and drink and take pleasure in all his toil
—this is God's gift to man."
—Ecclesiastes 3:13

I do not understand the rationale of non-believers in harboring a huge fear of having to compromise too much to include God in their lives. There's too much change required, and no one wants to live the life of a saint.

I do believe God wants us to be saints, but He also knows we are sinners by nature. Now that does not mean we can go about our lives intentionally sinning our way to Heaven because we know God is forgiving. It does mean we need to be much more concerned and conscientious in our work and relationships in this world. That little voice that speaks to us is trying to keep us in check. If we listen to it and follow it more than not, we are on the right path to pleasing God and acknowledging His love and presence in our lives. It's really quite simple. It is about being kind, honest, compassionate, present, and loving, and making the effort. This also benefits us in our own lives and relationships.

However, Satan wants us to believe that living this life with God in mind and heart is far too hard, pointless, and simply not fun. How true is it today that life is supposed to be all about the party? Do you really think God doesn't want us to have fun? Why do you think He gave us the gift of laughter? As far as I know, we humans are the only creatures on God's earth that has have this ability. That is not a gift from Hell, my friends. Believe me, there is no laughing down there.

The reality is, however, that sometimes life involves things that are not fun and games, but must be done to survive and to help others survive. You can call it sacrifice, or you can call it "taking care of business."Work, school, parenting, extending ourselves, planning, praying, and learning lessons are some of the things most people have difficulty enjoying, but they create goodness in us, for those around us, and most importantly perhaps, for our children.

Role-modeling is extremely important to children. They will lose or gain positive character traits depending on what they see and experience being modeled in their lives. Nowadays the pool of positive influences for our kids is running pretty dry and, in fact, it's being replaced filled up with terrible influences. As parents, we need to step up to the plate ourselves and do our very best to steer our children toward other positive role-models. God makes a pretty good one, by the way.

There will always be time to have fun, but even that is most enjoyed when It's been earned by our own hard work and good deeds. This is what God wants, but we have been brainwashed to believe otherwise,; and brainwashed right into committing Socialcide. Seeing all the evil and self-love going on in our country today, it has become too easy to give up on God, and believe He can't c a n ' t exist "if this is how it is!"The truth is, "this is how it is" because we have given up on Him, not the other way around.

What are we to do to remedy this plague of Socialcide? How do we keep America from loving itself to death spiritually, socially, emotionally, and mentally? Essentially, how do we put the "fun" back into the "fundamentals" of living, and not simply live for having to have "fun"?

Chapter Forty-Five

Who Am I?

"Caring about others, running the risk of feeling,
and leaving an impact on people, brings happiness."
—Harold Kushner

As a licensed therapist, publicly sharing this concept of Socialcide I have developed is a huge risk for me., Actually, both professionally and personally. I can hear the critics now, asking how I could encourage advocate God and religion as an answer to what is going wrong with America and Americans today. I can hear others asking what right or credentials I have that allow me to speak on (any) religion's behalf. Am I a Biblical scholar of some sort? The answer is no, I am not. I know some Biblical facts, but I am no expert or authority in that area.

I am not attempting to preach anything other than a very heartfelt, highly- concerned alert warning about the intense rise in narcissism on all levels that is alive and well in America today. At some point or another, in some capacity, we will all be involved with a narcissist. We are already being influenced by them, through the news we hear and watch, the movies we see, the music we listen to, the social media we participate in, and the politicians we vote for. Nationally, they are unavoidable. Personally, we will raise them, work with them, date them, marry them, or otherwise be angered by them in supermarkets or on our highways.

The damage they can inflict can vary, from being carelessly cut off while driving to having a loved one senselessly killed. In marriages or relationships, they can lead us to believe they are the most appealing, important, and love-worthy persons we have ever met, while simultaneously they degrade our emotions, drain our bank accounts, bankrupt our self- esteem, and use our children against us. Narcissists have no scientific or medically-based reason to be as evil as they are, yet they are growing in numbers.

In a society that was born with high morality and a deep love and belief in God, no matter what religion, there must be a reason that society has evolved into one with a "Me, Me, Me" mentality.

There is no medical or psychological cure or treatment for narcissism. No cure medically or psychologically. Those who have it will neither believe they need help, nor seek it. We know the fields of psychology and psychiatry have all but washed their hands of this annoyance, and, seemingly, so has America. This will be our ultimate downfall, unless we take action.

So I am not a preacher, a Biblical scholar, or authority on God. However, I do know a little about human nature, and I can read the statistics and reports. I can also speak for myself and for the clients I have worked with over the past twenty years. I can say with clinical confidence that there is absolutely something good about this "God thing." I can also say that the decline in belief in Him, and the rise in narcissism are, without a doubt, related. Our children are not being taught goodness and compassion today as much as they used to be, and we are suffering as a nation because of that. We have drifted so far from the days when religion, God, spirituality, faith, or just a belief in a higher power or presence, were more prevalent in American homes.

However, it is not solely the absence of God or spiritual presence in the American home today that is causing such dramatic rises in personality disorders, crime, infidelity, under-achievement, and entitlement. The decline in actual *family life* and *community* also plays a large role. As the fundamental family structure we used to know morphs into "bits and pieces of a group," at best, and we live more isolated and solitary lifestyles, have less opportunity of gaining those socialization skills that encourage kindness, cooperation, fairness, and healthy respect for other people. We also don't learn how to interact appropriately or successfully with people of different types, and in different positions. As computers replace people and the "gift of gab" more and more, the less each new generation even knows how society is supposed to work together, simply because they have never seen it, or had to participate in it.

Our youth today do not see much of a point in real communication, and in following traditional rules of life, because they never knew them and are not learning them. Is this a problem? What do you think? Where do all the profound problems with children today come from, compared to thirty-five or more years ago? Why are so many psychopathic, narcissistic crimes and behaviors being committed and reported daily, many of which are committed by children?

For a nation as young as we are, our society is not progressing in any positive direction. In fact, we *should* be *regressing* to a simpler, more meaningful way of living. This is America's only chance of salvation—socially, emotionally, and spiritually.

And this, to me, is worth talking about.

Chapter Forty-Six
Where Do We Go From Here?

"America's future will be determined by the home and the school. The child becomes largely what he is taught; hence we must watch what we teach, and how we live."
—Jane Addams

There is true evil in America today. The forces of such are not only potentially fatal;, they are already devastating our youth, our emotional equilibrium, and our belief and care of others. And they have subjugated our spiritual liberties right under our noses. We have welcomed the darkness in, somehow believing it would bring us light, only to find out— too late—that we've been fooled. Now for those of us who still remember "how it used to be," and for those who cannot but feel as if there is something wrong with the world today, *we are the ones who have to stop the slaughter.*

We are right in believing this is not how we were meant to live. We are right to believe there is no reason for the evil some people do, except pure evil itself. We are right to care, and we are right to believe that spiritual warfare is very real, and that right now, evil is winning.

The power of prayer to help us align our souls with God and His goodness is tremendously effective in fighting the darkness with all that is bright. What many Americans already know is just how powerful God's love is, and what peace, balance, and quality of life can be found by asking Him into our lives, and thanking Him for what He gives us.

That old saying, "There are no atheists in a foxholes," is true. But why should it take imminent danger or the real choice between life and death for

295

us to seek God? It shouldn't. But folks, we all have to wake up and take a good look around us. We *are in the foxhole!*

How much goodness are we spreading to others? How often do we spend time in quiet thought, giving thanks for what we have, and asking that others have the same? How often do we encourage our children to do the same? What, exactly, would be the harm if we did? We already know what the harm is in *not* doing it.

America, to cure the many social diseases strangling us today, our very way of living and believing must change. Am I implying we all must find God or some form of religious belief to conquer the demonic influences in America today? Well, to me, that would be ideal. The devil hates those who walk in the light with the Lord. However, the choice to accept God is an individual matter. People do not have to accept God to be good people—to be kind, loving, respectful, and compassionate. On the other hand, to continue on our current path will only bring more social malice, and foster the development of more soulless people capable of doing terrible things to others.

What I am suggesting is that you look closely at the problems in America today—in crime, in relationships, in children, in the workplace, in public, on the roads, and everywhere else.

The changes in America began in the late 1970s. Prior to that, America was not perfect, but it was functioning more like a society should. The world of technology has caused a detrimental shift in human relationships, and continues to do so. Television shows have changed; the ways children learn, interact, and play have changed. The ways we shop, do business, and communicate as adults have changed. The less frequently people have to see other people, the less important they become to each other. Choosing technology over personal contact has become the norm, yet we are aching for love and cannot find it—and are wondering why.

One of the roots of Socialcide is detachment. We are detached from each other. We are detached from our families; we are detached from our communities, from our values, our traditions and, yes, from God. This detachment is no accident. Many of us have even brought it on ourselves.

Evil wants us to be detached from all that is good, just as narcissists wants us to be detached from people who love and care about us. Why? Because in either case, that "voice of reason" can influence us to make sound decisions, instead of being manipulated and used—by him, by her, or by evil. Complete control over us is the goal, under the guise of "you are entitled to do whatever you want." It is deception by adoration. It is bait and switch.

If we can return our lifestyles to include more real communication, devotion to our families (especially our children), social involvement of some type, a commitment to helping someone else feel better at least once a day, teaching that to our children, shutting off the video games and computers more often, making phone calls to relatives, and including our children in those contacts, we may be onto something big. History needs to repeat itself with respect to many social aspects. Reconnecting with each other for the sake of being human again is what God wants. Social detachment is not of God, nor will it ever be of God.

Think for a moment about Hitler, Kim Jong-un, Jim Jones, Charles Manson, David Koresh, and every other evil cult leader throughout history. They demanded complete detachment from society, family, and friends so they could hold their followers physically and psychologically captive. No voice of reason was going to expose them. Although some of these psychopaths used God to glorify themselves, and convince their victims of their goodness, God will never exact such detachment from others, and He will never attempt to brainwash anyone. The decision to believe in Him is always up to us. No tricks, no gimmicks. What you see is what you get, and what you put into Him is what you will get back. The choice is yours. What is your voice of reason telling you?

Chapter Forty-Seven
We Are Getting It All Wrong!

"The best remedy for those who are afraid, lonely or unhappy is to go
outside, somewhere where they can be quiet, alone with the heavens, nature and God.
Because only then does one feel that all is as it should be."
—Anne Frank

To feel good, we must *do* good; not only for ourselves, but for others. To
be *cared* about, we must care *about.* I am not certain why many atheists have
such disgust for organized religion or belief in God. I do understand that
some churches and religious sects emanate ugliness, and what appears to be
downright *hatred* for certain lifestyles and choices people make. I do not, DO
NOT, agree with such disdain, nor do I think God is that unforgiving.

Organized religion can be a very powerful force. It has caused wars, and
killings, and makes a great deal of money in some cases, but that was never the
intention of God, and is not found in any Scripture. Where can one say the
Bible demands we must ascribe to an organized religion of any denomination?
It's not in the Ten Commandments, and it's not ever specified. Organized
religion is a *man made creation,* and as with anything man made, it is subject
to flaws. However, because one detests organized religion does not mean the
fact that some organized religion is detestable is not evidence that God does
not exist. If that is some people's perception of God, that 's that's what they
will run from. Understood, but unfair.

If we have been led by the media, organized religion of any sect, or Satan to
believe that God is going to chase us around and shove His demands down
our throats, and command we live a life of misery, abstinence, and twenty-

299

four-hour-a-day prayer, I don't think we "got the memo." What exactly is with the hell-bent (pun *extremely* intended!) feud between atheists and the extreme right-wing conservatives?

This *is* a war of spirituality. There will be no winner until the end of time. What camp you choose to pitch your tent in is your choice, but we must be extremely careful where we get the information that guides our choice.

Today, there are more books concurrently on the *New York Times* Best-Sellers List about atheism than there are about God. According to CNN. com, there is a *New Atheist movement* growing. *The God Delusion* by Richard Dawkins, *Letter to a Christian Nation* by Sam Harris, and *God: The Failed Hypothesis; How Science Shows That God Does Not Exist* by Victor J. Stenger, are all generating revenues and impressions from people today.

It makes sense that society is looking toward or considering the absence or non-existence of God in the world that we live in today. "How could there be a God?" is a question I am sure has crossed millions of people's minds from time to time. No one can blame the hurting and afflicted, the angry and the lost. And unfortunately, there are millions of Americans who fit those categories. Nothing is getting better, and surely *we must be wrong* about a *God of goodness in a world so horribly evil and terrible.* But there, again, is the ruse!

Satan himself told God to "prove Himself "by jumping off a cliff, as He would surely be caught by His angels. God told the devil, "No way! I do not have to *prove* Myself to you!" Today, we have countless people *demanding some sort of PROOF from GOD that He exists!* Really? How narcissistic can we get, America, to think God should have to *prove His existence* while our hearts beat and our lungs breathe? *No one is THAT important,* compared to our Creator. That denial and doubt is all about anger and rage. Who exactly do some people think they are?

We will never have *proof* of His existence without *faith.* To those people of "belief " in God who have been setting an erroneous example of what love and compassion are truly all about in God's will, shame on you! For those who have based their non-belief and atheism on the aforementioned "Holy

Rollers," and on an all-inclusive condemnation of organized religion, shame on you, too! There *is a God* of goodness, compassion, and forgiveness, who asks only that we believe in Him and do our very best to emulate those same things. Why do good, and show love, if you do not believe? What keeps you from breaking laws, hurting others, stealing, cheating, and lying, if there are no consequences? What causes you to spread kindness to others if you truly believe there is no reward for such a life of sacrifice? Why would atheists bother? Why do the attitudes of extreme right-wing conservatives cause people to *hate* the God-loving? Evil forces at work are to blame on both sides.

Misguided devotion to what no one truly knows about has infected our country's well-being, and until we get back on track and cease the glorification of our own needs and desires, things will only get worse. We have let go of all that was truly important to our society's stability, and have adopted a new belief that *nothing but me matters.* Well America, it's time to reconnect, and take back what matters! Family, love, friends, decency, kindness, care, respect, responsibility, sympathy, relationships, goodness, meaningfulness, and empathy are just the beginning. From them we grow as people; from them we will be inspired to nourish our souls, rather than starve them and ignore their cries for help.

The connection between spirituality and well-balanced emotional health cannot be doubted. The rise in America of the *New Atheist* (and even of "anti-theism") is a ploy to make us believe we can live a life void of God, but none of the leaders of this movement seem to know how to do such a thing

To deny God's existence gives a person the social permission they may be seeking to worship themselves, do harm, manipulate others, and not feel a bit of remorse about it. If there is no God, or no force of goodness overlooking our souls, then what is the point of helping, following rules, caring, loving, or being a part of society? The disconnection from belief in some form of spirituality causes great discord in our social and emotional wellness. If this life is all there is for us, then what exactly are we doing here? That question can be answered if we ask the right source. Non- believers are *not* that source.

Emotional wellness *is* spiritual wellness. The unrest many people feel that causes them to suffer internally is caused, in most cases, by unanswered questions. This can bring a person to seek therapy, or cause them to make very destructive decisions.

Returning to basics in the home is absolutely necessary to restore America to wellness, both socially and psychologically. We have to begin teaching our children that the world *could* be theirs, with hard work, dedication, following rules, respect, kindness, and taking responsibility. The fundamentals of some form of religion or spirituality can be our guide in doing this. I believe as families have been leaving God and goodness out of the mix, due to media, technology, easy parenting, non-involvement, and overcompensation, they have lost all sense of direction as to what is right and what is wrong. If parents do not know this, and live by some form of morality, they can never expect their children to know, exhibit, or aspire to it either.

We once trusted in, respected, thanked, praised, and rejoiced in God through whatever religion, faith, or belief we had in Him. We celebrated spirituality daily in some way, even when we were not in life-or- death situations, or in need of some sort of immediate relief. Unfortunately, God has become very much like a bottle of aspirin, only to be sought out when we experience pain.

How selfish can we be? One moment God doesn't exist, and the next He must take away our pain. We cannot have it both ways. But when we try, and God doesn't deliver that immediate miracle, we say, "See? He doesn't exist."

Twelve-Step Fellowships such as Alcoholics Anonymous and Narcotics Anonymous rely on a "Higher Power" as the basis for members' recovery from addiction. Since Bill W. began in AA in 1935, that principle has not changed. Why? As they say in their meetings, "It works if you work it, so work it; you're worth it!" The success rate of Twelve-Step groups is extremely high, and has consistently been the addict's strongest support system. The "Higher Power" makes that difference, and can make a difference for *anyone,* whether they are in crisis or not.

Chapter Forty-Eight

Choose Wisely and Prosper

"It is in your moments of decision that your destiny is shaped."
—Anthony Robbins

America must begin to intensify its awareness of the rise of evil, self- love, entitlement, isolation, and separation from meaning and goodness. Narcissism in all its various forms and levels of danger is spreading rapidly, and it is *targeting our youth* like a buzzard circling its prey. If we are not teaching our children meaning, morals, values, and respect, someone or something else will teach them otherwise, and we will eventually live in a world void of them all. As of right now, we are almost there.

So you may ask, "Where do I start?" If you have faith in God already, you are there. Simply ramp up that faith and spread it in whatever you do with whomever you interact with, especially your children. Teach them what you know, and learn more *together*. I know parents who play video games with their kids. Why not spend time volunteering together, visiting family together, reading a book together (or separately but then talking about it together), or talking about God? (Hey, there's an idea!)

If you fall into the category of "soon to be former doubter," one of the first things you should do, as I have suggested already, is disregard the media's portrayal of religion and God. They, of ALL sources, are not to be trusted! Seek that best friend you have always wanted and needed by taking a look at the Bible or by doing some reading about God and His promises to mankind. These three Scriptural promises are a good place to begin:

"Ask and it will be given to you, seek and you will find; knock and it will be opened to you. For everyone who seeks finds, and to him who knocks it will be opened" (Matthew 7:7-8).

"I sought the Lord and He answered me; He delivered me from my fears" (Psalm 34:4).

"Take delight in the Lord and He will give you the desires of your heart" (Psalm 37:4).

That is all it takes to begin to change both your personal world and the world around you. Do not complicate loving God with false beliefs. He made you, He knows you, and He wants you to be happy. He does not want you to suffer, be punished, or live in misery or despair. That lie is coming from the "other guy." Rise above it!

Unlike narcissists who "love themselves to death," God "loves us to death." We all have a clock ticking here on earth. We do not know when it will stop. When that day comes—and it will come—what if all this "God stuff" wasn't real after all? What if the Bible really is just a bunch of fairy tales created by men to keep peace in the world? Well, if that is true, we will never know it, will we? We will simply be gone. But before we are gone, the world we lived in will have been so much better for our having believed.

Conversely, what if it *is* true? What if your time comes and you find out it was all true, but you never bothered to include God in your life? What if you laughed about Him, denied Him, and lived as if some "Big Bang" happened and there you are, so you just did whatever you wanted to do? What if? Do you want to take that chance? The chance that there was really something to living a life with God's love in it— but you chose not to? If that was the choice you made, I would imagine God might say something such as, "I have loved you from birth to death. I have watched you have chances to choose or reject Me. Oh, how I wanted your soul to enter into my Kingdom of Heaven more than anything on earth you have ever wanted or needed. I have loved you to death, but now that you are gone, so also is gone that chance of our eternity together. I'm sorry." And that will be that.

Eternity is *forever.* The issues, losses, pains, and problems we face and suffer in this life will have no bearing on us in the next. We will be in the form we began in. All suffering and physical pains or deformities we may have endured on earth will be wiped away. Any striving we ever did to please ourselves and to outdo others will mean nothing. The scoreboard will be reset to all zeroes. No amount of money, things, or triumphs you had on earth will make one shred of difference to God. All He will want to know about is whether you believed in Him, whether you lived by the Golden Rule, whether you spread His love to others, whether you sought Him in good times and in bad.

If you have, you will be welcomed into Heaven to spend all eternity in extreme bliss with God, far happier than anything or anyone on earth could ever make you. That is the *Good News!*

If you have not had a relationship with God for whatever reason, never knew Him or cared to know Him, perhaps only sought Him as a last resort in times of crisis, laughed about His existence, condemned His Word (the Bible), or worshiped gods other than Him, He is likely to say to you, "I have known you and loved you all your life. I waited for you to seek my love and get to know Me, but you never did." Would you let someone who treated you like that into your home? That is the bad news, because that person's soul will live in eternity too, but not in the Kingdom of God. If Hell exists, are you willing to find out that way? With no chance of getting out, no chance for a pardon or parole, no escape *ever?* Do you believe the devil cares? Do you believe the devil exists? If you don't, he's winning already!

Socialcide is happening. It's been happening for a long time, and the sickness is spreading and worsening, faster, and more intensely with each passing day that passes. We all still have the opportunity to do something about it. Whose team are you on?

Chapter Forty-Nine

Sleeping With "Slenderman"

*"Those who play with the devil's toys will be brought by degrees
to wield his sword."*
—Buckminster Fuller

The writing of *Socialcide: How America Is Loving Itself to Death* has been a terrifying yet intriguing journey for me. In researching and reporting on the indications of madness in our country, so as to expose Socialcide, seldom did a day go by where even *more* proof of its existence did not appear in the media, as more precious lives were either lost or destroyed forever by the hands of someone infected with evil.

When asked, "When will your book be out?"I would typically think to myself, *"When information to support it ceases to occur."* However that has not been the case, and that is frightening. It seems that every single day in America something horrific happens, and people are being killed or hurt because others are uncaring, under-parented, self-engrossed, entitled, mislead, or just simply evil personified.

News reports by so-called "experts" in their respective fields of psychology, psychiatry, law, or medicine keep blaming all the wrong possibilities culprits as they try to explain to why evil people exist. What keeps the media from including the clergy in their reports? Many believe doing that would be crazy.

They want us to believe the world of God and spirituality is all "make believe."

But in reality, they are denying the reality of evil forces, and encouraging everyone to live on their *Fantasy Island* of ignorance. And in doing so, they only assist people in dismissing the *TRUTH* and fostering more and more evil.

Until America wakes up to the reality that evil exists, and there is no other hope than to bring REALITY back, and REALITY involves some form of spiritual belief in something of GOODNESS, we will only see and experience more and more senseless atrocities and evil. Our children *must be taught kindness, compassion, tolerance, responsibility, and humility* NOW to turn our country around. Instead of allowing who-knows-who to shape their little minds online, on television, in music, and in all other forms of entertainment, parents need to assure that their children are not getting into things they cannot handle emotionally, period.

Children do not have the brain capacity to decipher fact from fiction. What better subjects to brainwash? Children today are becoming more commonly guilty of horrible, heinous acts of violence, torture, and even murder. The last example of Socialcide I am compelled to address in this work involves two twelve-year-old girls from Wisconsin who attempted to stab to death their twelve-year-old friend, with the belief believing that in so doing they would prove the existence of a fictional, yet very evil, character who has become very popular in the darkest of depths of cyberspace, *Slenderman.*

Slenderman was born out of a Photoshop contest in 2009 to fool or lure other web users by submitting him to various paranormal websites. Since then, his notoriety has grown by leaps and bounds as countless Web users have taken his image and created their own twisted stories, tales, urban legends, and lore about the faceless creature in a dark suit who lures children and haunts those who seek to expose him.

Anyone with even a morsel of advertising know-how understands how companies lure young customers: with characters, such as Ronald McDonald, Tony the Tiger, the Burger King, Lucky the Leprechaun, the Scrubbing Bubbles, Joe Camel, Mickey Mouse, etc. Now there is Slenderman. What is he selling? In many reports, he's promoting serial killing, murder, and demonic influences. *"To prove I exist, you must murder someone."* That's a far cry from a

Big Mac, and seems ridiculous, but it has nearly happened.

The site that compiles such fiction, as in the Wisconsin case, is called *Creepy pasta Wiki*. They issued a statement following this attempted murder that read:

"This is an isolated incident, and does (not) represent...the Creepypasta community as a whole. This Wiki does not endorse or advocate for killing, worship and otherwise replication of rituals of fictional works. There is a line between fiction and reality, and it is up to you to realize where that line is. We are a literature site, not a satanic cult."

I find it quite compelling that this Creepypasta representative specified that they are *not a satanic cult*, when there are quite possibly thousands of other things he or she could have said. Is there a consciousness of guilt in that statement, or perhaps a Freudian slip? We cannot say for sure, but Slenderman has been called "demonic"in many other reports. Now take a child who starts getting involved in this dark and evil fictional site. Do you think a twelve-year-old is going to "know the line between reality and fiction?" We have already discussed how video games can blur that line so much that children are committing murders, so it is not hard to see the same type of mental manipulation here. Now I certainly do not believe Creepypasta Wiki is attempting to destroy children's minds and souls; however, I do believe there is a much more powerful, evil entity working through such sites, and we know who that is.

In a report from the *Huffington Post* dated June 4, 2014, one of the twelve-year-old girls told the police, "Many people do not believe Slenderman is real, [and we] wanted to prove the skeptics wrong."Their attempted murder was months in the planning, and quite calculated for children their age.

In this same report, James McCann, co-founder of A Paranormal Group, was quoted as saying, "Slenderman appears in crowd-sourced fiction as a demonic character who stalks, traumatizes, and abducts children. It's believed that, to reach his realm level, you have to kill somebody." One of the girls agreed with that statement, and planned on killing to "become a proxy of

Slender."

Many questions come to mind about this near killing. Why would these girls want to be nearer to "Slender?" What was the attraction? At what point in time did they decide to *murder* their friend to meet an evil, dark, and creepy cartoon character? Where were their parents while they were worshiping a fictional demonic force?

Herein lies a further reminder that parents absolutely **must be monitoring all their children's online activities!** This creepy thing is a cartoon character. How tricky Satan can be! I am certain many parents paid it no mind any more than they would Alvin and the Chipmunks. But, alas, *that is exactly what Satan was banking on!*

Since this news came out, I have heard from numerous parents on my social media sites who have watched Slenderman for themselves, and were horrified by its contents. Some even knew their kids were watching it, but thought nothing of it until they actually watched and listened. At this point in our society, with Socialcide running rampant through humanity, we should assume that *nothing is harmless* to our children until we have checked it for ourselves, and know for sure.

After these two girls stabbed their friend nineteen times in a park restroom (where they knew there was a drain in the floor) and left her for dead, they began a walk—or more like a pilgrimage—to the far off woods where they believed Slenderman lived in a castle, and would now appear to them for their sacrifice. Thank goodness, the victim lived and was able to get help and identify her attackers, who were quickly apprehended by police.

Under interrogation, neither girl expressed a shred of remorse for their actions. Both are being tried as adults, and the nightly talking heads on court television rant on about their simply "being kids," or being "insane," and every other excuse in their professional books, while not one single professional will simply state that *this is another example of the epidemic of evil we are living with in America today! **This is Socialcide.***

Epilogue

Epilogue

The fields of Psychology and Theology are separated by a very thin line. They are almost like neighbors who would like to get to know each other better, but for some unknown reason never do. They pass each other every day, share pleasantries every so often, want basically the same things (happiness and emotional balance in life) for their families, friends, and other people, but rarely engage in joint efforts.

Neither field is an exact science, or is based on any tangible proofs. One deals with the brain while the other deals with the soul, both of which are very hard to know with any certainty. The brain is a physical object that can be seen and touched, of course, but how it works and what it stores in it are hardly able to be seen. Unlike the brain, we cannot see or touch a soul, at least not in our mortal form. But some studies have shown that at the moment of death the body *does* actually become lighter, leading to a belief that something measurable *leaves* the mortal remains when human life ceases. That is fascinating! Science cannot explain it.

Experts in the fields of both Psychology and Theology readily agree that healthy spirituality supports happier living. This has been proven true time and again. The point of both Psychology and Theology is to eliminate suffering by helping us to understand our purposes here on earth. Our hearts and souls are directly connected to our minds. If we understand why we suffer when we suffer, we can find meaning in our being, and live happier lives. Unfortunately, the trend to seek an active and healthy spirituality and an emotionally happier life through self-exploration and understanding seems to be dying out. People are seeking answers and reasons in all the wrong places— places which are usually *outside* themselves.

Once upon a time, the hierarchy or chain of human development was this: mother, father, preacher, teacher. This structure, and the people who filled these roles, were the foundation for creating a healthy, well-balanced person. They provided the guidance, empathy, nurturing, lessons, information, and education our ancestors used to make this nation great. Today, that chain has been rusted, rotted, broken, and forgotten. If parents are not teaching morality and basic life skills, who is? If our parents are not teaching children about God or a religion, who is? If teachers are not teaching students how to learn, is it their fault, or has the damage already been done?

That team of mother, father, preacher, teacher was a solid, interdependent social device that covered all bases in child development—an invaluable, fail-safe way to help children become good, solid people. Today that system has clearly fallen by the wayside, as much more deviant, defiant, and destructive behaviors have been coming from today's youth. If we cannot make a change in exactly how we raise our children, the fields of Psychology and Theology will become pointless.

Eventually, all of society will not *think* it needs any help, and it certainly will not think it needs any God. We are already well on our way there now. Before Socialcide finally wins the souls of the masses, we Americans need to take action and save our society before it literally does *love itself to death*. We have "dropped the ball" far too many times already.

Now it is time to "play ball" again, and reinvent the wheel by returning to what is right, and to what we know has worked in the past to build a nation, not to destroy it.

"Some believe it is only GREAT POWER that can hold evil in check. But that is not what I have found. I have found that it is the small everyday deeds of ordinary folk that keep the darkness at bay. Small acts of kindness and love."

—Gandalf